PERSONAL COMPUTING

with the

UCSD p-SYSTEM

p—System Personal Computing Series

CLARK AND KOEHLER,
The UCSD Pascal Handbook

OVERGAARD AND STRINGFELLOW,
Personal Computing with the UCSD p—System

WILLNER AND DEMCHAK,
Advanced UCSD Pascal Programming Techniques

PERSONAL COMPUTING

with the

UCSD p-SYSTEM

Second Edition

Mark Overgaard
Stan Stringfellow

Prentice–Hall, Inc., Englewood Cliffs, New Jersey 07632

Library of Congress Cataloging in Publication Data

Overgaard, Mark. (date)
Personal computing with the UCSD p-System

Includes index.
1. UCSD p-System (Computer operating system)
2. Microcomputers—Programming. 3. UCSD Pascal
(Computer program language) I. Stringfellow,
Stan, 1953– . II. Title.
QA76.76.063084 1984 001.64'2 85-3502
ISBN 0-13-658030-0

Printed in the United States of America

10 9 8 7 6 5 4 3 2 1

ISBN 0-13-658030-0 01

Prentice-Hall International, U.K., *London*
Prentice-Hall of Australia Pty. Limited, *Sydney*
Editora Prentice-Hall do Brasil, Ltda., *Rio de Janeiro*
Prentice-Hall Canada Inc., *Toronto*
Prentice-Hall Hispanoamericana, S.A., *Mexico*
Prentice-Hall of India Private Limited, *New Delhi*
Prentice-Hall of Japan, Inc., *Tokyo*
Prentice-Hall of Southeast Asia Pte. Ltd., *Singapore*
Whitehall Books Limited, *Wellington, New Zealand*

CONTENTS

PREFACE

The p–System is one of the most widely used operating systems for personal computers. This book is an introduction to the system for novice users and a reference tool for experienced users.

This second edition can be used with any of the Version IV p–Systems produced since 1981, including the latest: Version IV.2. Like the p–System, this book is designed for convenient use on most personal computers. A special appendix provides specific details for the using the p–System on IBM PCs and compatible equipment.

The p–System provides a pleasant and productive environment for developing programs, particularly in the popular UCSD Pascal and p–System FORTRAN–77 languages. We don't try to teach you programming or the details of either of these languages since many excellent programming texts are available for that purpose. Instead, we address a topic that most of those books do not cover: the specific details of entering a program into the computer and preparing it for use.

After you've used the p–System for programming, you will probably come to realize how useful its editing and printing facilities are for simple text processing as well (e.g., writing memos and small papers). In addition, a variety of p–System–based **application programs**, developed by others, are available to help you with your specific personal computing needs. We introduce all these topics and show you, for instance, how to edit and print a memo and how to acquire p–System applications.

Part 1 of the book, called "Getting Started," provides a hands–on, step–by–step introduction to the p–System's facilities in each of these areas.

For the more experienced p–System user, we provide concise reference descriptions of the major p–System facilities in Part 2 of the book, called "Getting Interested." Several useful appendices list p–System error messages and provide explanations and possible recovery actions for many of them. Much of this error explanation cannot be found in any other source (even the official user manuals published by p–System vendors!). A handy quick index inside the back cover helps you to quickly find the reference descriptions or error explanations when you need them.

"Getting Serious," Part 3, provides a "larger view" of the p–System. One chapter describes aspects of the p–System's design that may influence how you use the system in the long term. A second chapter introduces the wide range of additional tools and program building blocks that are available for the p–System. We don't teach you how to use these facilities; we just want you to know about them and how they might be useful to you.

We hope that these three parts provide a useful mix of step–by–step tutorial guidance, easily–understood reference material, and valuable background information.

We are pleased to thank a number of people who helped us in the preparation of this second edition of the book. SofTech Microsystems, through Gary Pritchett, graciously allowed the use of its laser printing facilities for preparation of the master copy of the book. Bill Milburn and Shawn Fanning helped in facilitating that use. Geoff Clow did a thorough technical review and saved us and you from many a slip.

As with the first edition, the ScenicWriter text formatter program did its usual splendid job of producing camera–ready masters. We particularly thank Erik Smith and Bob Fenichel for that.

One of us (Mark) took principal responsibility for producing this second edition. He particularly acknowledges the loving support of his wife Bonnie throughout the project.

We are grateful for each of these contributions and hope that the final result is as pleasing for these contributors as it is for us.

Mark Overgaard
Stan Stringfellow

San Diego, California

PERSONAL COMPUTING

with the

UCSD p-SYSTEM

INTRODUCTION

1 THE PERSONAL COMPUTING PHENOMENON

The first electronic computers were "personal" in the sense that they served one person at a time just like today's personal computers. Those early computers were impersonal in the sense that they required huge amounts of floor space, power, and air conditioning. By comparison, today's personal computer can sit on a desk in an ordinary office or travel to Afghanistan as an aid to a traveling reporter. And yet these tiny packages of electronics are more powerful than their giant predecessors!

Those early machines were also very difficult to use. Today's personal computers, in contrast, can be used by almost anyone.

Even with the drawbacks of these early computers, it is still a big surprise to learn that back in the early 1950's the **total** market for computers in the United States was projected as less than one hundred machines. Today, the industry rallying cry is: "A personal computer on every desk!"

One of the reasons why these small computers are popular is that they are very versatile. A reporter did, in fact, take his computer to Afghanistan (during a war!) and used it in preparing and editing his story. Personal computers were used to write this book. Farmers in Nebraska use personal computers to manage their dairy herds. Mental health professionals use small computers to help their clients develop an appreciation for their "bio–rhythms."

Two principal factors account in large part for the dramatic difference in the way computers are used today, compared to three decades ago. The first factor is stunning advances in the physical technologies used. The circuits that used to fill rooms have been shrunk to patterns on pieces of silicon the size of your fingernail. At the same time, these circuits have become much more powerful.

The fundamental operations performed by today's computers are not nearly as different from those of their predecessors as you might expect, given the enormous differences in physical construction. Today's computers still use operations such as adding two numbers together, moving a number from one place to another, or comparing two numbers.

Why then are today's computers accessible to millions while the early machines could only be used by the scientific elite? The explanation is the dramatic differences in the **software** built from those fundamental operations. Software turns an assembly of wires and tiny silicon chips into a useful tool that can help you make plans for a new business or control a model train.

Another name for software is **programs**. Computer programs are detailed directions for a computer that guide it in the performance of some task. **Application programs** are those programs which address specific needs such as keeping track of the accounts of a business. These programs are ultimately composed of the simple primitive operations mentioned above (like adding two numbers together). But they combine tens of thousands of these instructions to achieve great internal complexity and power. The challenge in developing one of these programs is in harnessing this power in such a way that everyday use is pleasant and productive, even for people who are not computer experts.

There are two principal ways in which you can use your computer. This book is intended for people with either of these two kinds of interests in personal computer software. First, you can use programs that others have developed. These programs may provide entertainment (such as a video action game), or they may serve a serious business purpose (like getting out a payroll). To use existing application programs, you usually don't need much technical background. Mostly, you need knowledge of the application area in which you want computer assistance.

Second, you can develop your own programs. Developing programs takes considerably more technical skill than using programs that others have written. Program development is still much easier, however, on today's personal computers than it was "back in the old days."

This book does not have much to say about personal computer hardware, since relatively little hardware knowledge is needed for productive personal computing. Instead, we concentrate on software. To provide a foundation for that discussion, however, it is necessary to briefly sketch the hardware components of a personal computer.

2 COMPONENTS OF A PERSONAL COMPUTER

A typical personal computer (an IBM Personal Computer) is pictured in Figure 1. Even if your computer is not the same as the one pictured, its major components are probably similar.

Figure 1

The first thing to notice is the keyboard, which is similar to that of an ordinary typewriter. The alphabetic keys ("A" through "Z") are laid out just like on a typewriter. A large variety of special keys are available (only some of which have corresponding versions on a typewriter).

Another necessary component of a personal computer is the **display**, which looks like a television screen (and may even be one!). The display is capable of showing characters and in some cases graphic pictures.

Underneath the display of this computer (and out of sight inside the unit) are its principal electronic components, including the **microprocessor**, which directs its operation, and the **main memory**, where computer instructions and data are stored when they are being actively used. On the right side of the unit is the main power switch.

This particular kind of computer also has room in the base unit for two **disk drives**. When a **diskette** (or **disk**) is inserted in one of these drives, the computer can store information on it and retrieve information from it. This information is stored (relatively) permanently, even when the diskette is not in use.

Another important (though optional) part of a personal computer is a **printer**, which can be used to make permanent printed copies of textual (and possibly graphic) information stored in the computer.

Some computers have all of these components packaged together. Others allow you to mix and match functional components just as you can with a component stereo system. For instance, the display and keyboard may be packaged separately from the rest of the computer and called the **terminal**.

Your personal computing can be very productive even if you know very little about the inner workings of the electronic and mechanical parts of your personal computer. You do need, however, to know something about how diskettes work so that you can handle them properly. When diskettes are well cared for, they can last through years of frequent use. When they are mistreated, however, valuable data and instructions stored on them can be lost.

A diskette is pictured in Figure 2. There are several kinds of diskettes, primarily distinguished by their sizes. A particular computer usually uses only one of these sizes. The most popular sizes are 8 inch, 5–1/4 inch, and 3–1/2 inch.

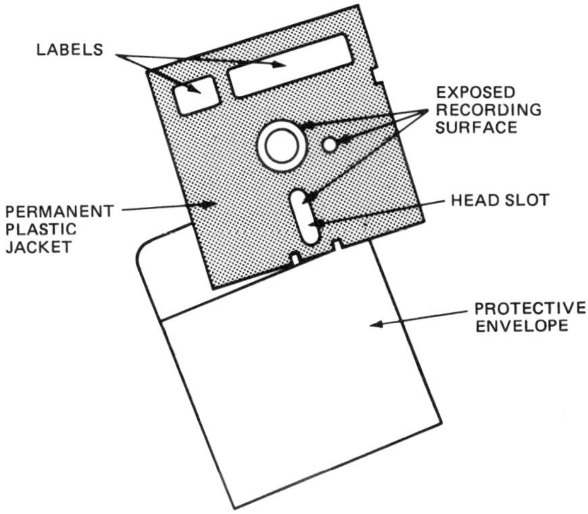

Figure 2

All of these types of diskettes work in fundamentally the same way. Their essential component is a circular piece of magnetic material similar to recording tape. This material is flexible and rather delicate, so it is protected by a square plastic jacket. When the diskette is in use, the recording material spins inside the jacket. A read/write head comes in contact with the diskette through a "head slot" in the protective jacket. This allows a computer to play (read) or record (write) computer information on the diskette just as a tape recorder plays or records music.

You should keep a diskette inside the protective envelope when not in use, so that dust (and your fingers!) do not come in contact with the magnetic material through the head slot. Also, you should treat diskettes in a friendly fashion——no folding, spindling, or mutilating! Writing on the label with a ball–point pen or laying heavy objects on the diskette can also be damaging.

Some personal computers use another kind of disk——called a **hard disk**——usually in addition to diskettes (which are also know as "floppy" or "flexible" disks). As the name suggests, the principal distinguishing feature of a hard disk is that the recording surface is rigid rather than flexible. Hard disks usually have many more times the storage capacity of a diskette (along with substantially greater access speed). Often the hard disks are not removable. That is, there is no way to take the disk out of the drive and put in another disk with different information on it.

Hard disks are not treated differently by the p–System than flexible disks. If you use a hard disk on your computer, however, you may have to adapt some of your procedures. For instance, you may use different methods for keeping **back up** copies of your important information. Since hard disk handling procedures can vary widely among brands of computers and brands of hard disks, we have chosen not to cover them in this book. We concentrate, instead, on the flexible disk environment.

On some personal computers, you can use part of the main memory area to simulate a disk. (Because RAM––for "Random Access Memory"––is a popular name for main memory, a disk simulated in main memory is often called a **RAM disk**.) The main advantage of a RAM disk is that it is extremely fast, since access to it occurs at electronic speeds, rather than mechanical speeds. One disadvantage of a RAM disk is that the information on it is generally lost when the personal computer is turned off. (Mechanical disks, on the other hand, can store information indefinitely.) We don't deal in detail with RAM disks in this book, but we do mention them in a few places where their differences might be a source of confusion for you.

One principal use of disks (whether flexible, rigid, or RAM) is for storage of the software that makes your personal computer a truly useful tool. The next section discusses this software in general, and the p–System in particular.

3 PLACING THE p–SYSTEM IN CONTEXT

A personal computer system can be viewed as an inverted triangle like that in Figure 3. The widest part of the triangle represents the application programs that meet specific needs of personal computer users like yourself. Since there are so many users, each with a different collection of needs, an astonishing quantity and variety of application programs have been developed.

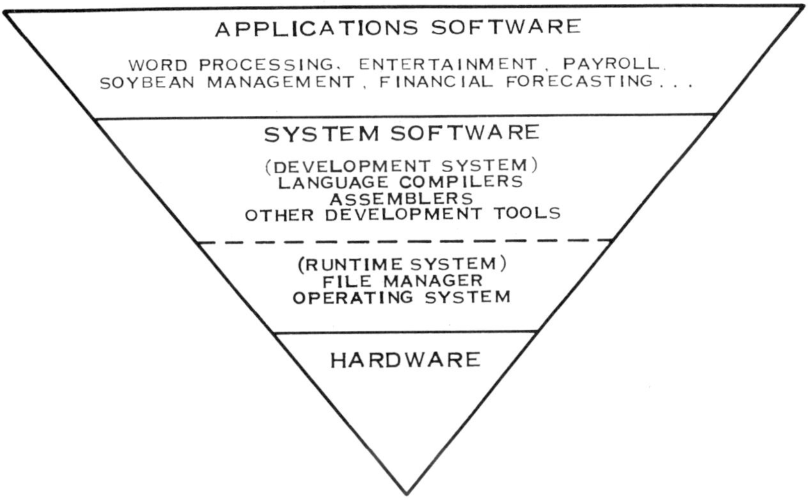

Figure 3

One reason why application developers are so prolific is that they can depend on **system software** to handle the fundamental interactions with the hardware, and to provide the tools necessary for building application programs.

The p–System is one of the most widely used types of system software for personal computers. It has several major components. The most fundamental one is the **operating system**, which is basically in charge of the personal computer hardware (subject to your direction, of course). One important thing you can do with the operating system is start and stop programs. Even after these programs are started, however, the operating system is crucial to their continued operation. It handles the details of reading information from disks and writing information to them. It also manages the other peripherals on your personal computer, including the keyboard, display, and printer.

In the p–System, there are other system software components such as a file manager that allows you to check and rearrange stored information ("files") on disks, and text editors, with which you can create, read, or modify stored textual information.

If you are interested in developing your own programs, the p–System includes a variety of facilities to assist you. Most important are the computer language translators, which take the programs you write and convert them to the coded form that the computer understands. In Chapter 3, you will use one of these translators to write some short programs. There are also various other program development tools. We leave further discussion of them to Chapter 8.

Figure 3 shows two categories of system software: **runtime** software and **development** software. As the names suggest, the first category is the software needed to run existing programs, while the second category of software is the tools you can use to build your own programs. When the p–System is packaged in a runtime configuration, the operating system and (usually) the file manager and text editor are included. The development configuration includes the runtime components, along with a number of program development tools and other tools.

At the base of the structure in Figure 3 is the personal computer hardware. A hallmark of the p–System is its ability to run on almost all kinds of personal computers. We have paid specific attention to several of these in the appendices of this book. In Chapter 7, we describe how this **portability** is achieved.

In some p–System configurations, the foundation on which the p–System rests is not the personal computer hardware, but another operating system, instead. The p–System is said to be **hosted** by the other operating system, which itself rests on the personal computer hardware. For instance, the other operating system could be MS–DOS, which is widely used on IBM PC computers and compatible equipment from other manufacturers.

When p–System applications are installed in a "hosted" p–System, users of those applications may not even be aware that the p–System is involved in supporting their applications. Such applications can be made to look just like applications designed specifically for the host operating system. Development configurations of a hosted p–System are invoked from the host operating system, but provide all the programming tools and convenience features of a standard p–System, while offering convenient access to peripherals, such as hard disks, supported by the host operating system.

4 THE BACKGROUND OF THE p–SYSTEM

Development of the p–System was begun at the University of California, San Diego (UCSD) in late 1974. This early work was directed by Professor Kenneth Bowles. The principal objective was to provide programming tools for a large introductory course in computer science.

The course had previously used the central campus computer and the Algol programming language, but Bowles thought that small computers handling one student at a time could provide a more responsive learning experience. Furthermore, it seemed that the language Pascal was more suited to teaching novice programmers than Algol (a predecessor to Pascal). Finally, Pascal appeared to be suitable as the implementation language for building the necessary software tools.

Two principal objectives guided the early evolution of what was initially known as the **UCSD Pascal System**:

- The System had to be easy for first—time computer users to learn. It also had to be usable by experienced programmers (such as those modifying or enhancing the System, itself).
- The software had to run on small, inexpensive computers comparable in capability to many personal computers in use today. (For instance, those computers had about 56,000 bytes of main memory and about 500,000 bytes of diskette storage. Each byte can store one character.) This objective was quite a challenge, since no one at the time had succeeded in installing the Pascal language on machines that small.

The UCSD Pascal System was initially intended for use inside the University, but as word of the software spread, copies were distributed to other campuses and to people in industry starting in the summer of 1977. Then in May, 1978, an article describing the System appeared in *Byte* magazine. The surprising result: the University received over a thousand inquiries about the software from all over the world!

It was soon clear that this level of demand could not be met by the small University project, and a search began for ways in which support for the growing community of UCSD Pascal users could be moved off—campus. This search ended in June, 1979, when the University awarded full responsibility for support and continued evolution of the UCSD Pascal System to SofTech Microsystems (SMS).

At the same time, the University reached agreements with Apple Computer and Western Digital Corporation which allowed those companies to market the UCSD Pascal System on their computers. Apple's version, dubbed Apple Pascal, is now widely used on Apple II and Apple III computers.

One of the first moves of SMS was to add the programming language FORTRAN as an alternative to UCSD Pascal, originally the only programming language available in the p—System. When the time came to name this new product, several unappealing possibilities were considered:

- UCSD Pascal FORTRAN?
- UCSD Pascal System FORTRAN?
- FORTRAN for the UCSD Pascal System?

All these names sounded rather like "vanilla chocolate ice cream." Clearly the name "UCSD Pascal System" was not very compatible with the addition of FORTRAN to the product line. That's when the name of the main product was changed to the **UCSD p—System**. Recently, the name has been further shortened to **p—System**.

The burning question, of course, is "What does the 'p' in 'p–System' stand for?" No one knows for sure, but there has been plenty of speculation. One pair of enthusiastic users wrote an article about the p–System that they called "P for Perfect?".

One possibility is that the "p" stands for "Pascal," since even today, it is the principal language supported by the p–System. Another possibility is that the "p" stands for "personal," since the p–System is a relatively friendly software environment to work in. Better yet, the "p" may stand for "portable," since the p–System is widely regarded as the most portable system software for microcomputers.

The best solution is not to worry about that "p." If for some reason you can't do that, the ultimate solution is to make the "p" silent when you say "p–System." p–Sychologists have been doing that for years!

Before discussing the p–System itself, we close this introduction with some recommendations on how you might proceed through the rest of this book.

5 HOW TO USE THIS BOOK

Here are the three parts of this book:

- Getting Started: A "Hands–on" Tutorial
- Getting Interested: A Systematic Reference
- Getting Serious: A Larger View

If you are new to personal computing, Part 1 is designed for you. In it, we assume that you are sitting in front of your personal computer and are able to follow along and participate as we provide a tour through the p–System. We strongly recommend that you don't try to skip randomly around in Part 1, because you could easily stumble into a part of the p–System that you aren't prepared to deal with. You wouldn't do any harm to the p–System or to your computer, but you might get confused or frustrated.

We have organized this "Getting Started" part so that you only need to read the chapter or chapters that deal with the kind of use you want to make of the p–System. If you simply want to use available application programs, you can stop after Chapter 1. If you also want to use the text editor (say, for some simple word processing), go on through Chapter 2. Finally, if you want to develop your own programs, you should work through all three chapters.

To follow along in Part 1, you need a computer and a p–System that runs on it. The computer needs a display and a keyboard of some sort and one or more disk drives. You can use a printer, also, but that is not required.

Part 2 ("Getting Interested") is organized for easy reference, though you may want to read straight through it. In fact, if you are already an experienced computer user, you may want to skim through Part 1, and concentrate on Part 2, which contains most of the information presented in Part 1, but with a more systematic organization. What's missing in Part 2 is the step–by–step directions intended to keep a first–time computer user on the right track.

Part 2 concentrates on the basic facilities of the p–System. For sophisticated work with the System, you still need to use the standard reference manuals that come with it.

Part 3 can be read at your leisure, but we recommend that you take time for it as soon as you can. It should improve your understanding of the p–System and how it can be useful to you in the long term.

There are several versions of the p–System in wide use. These tend to be similar in the overall way you use them, but different in details. This book is oriented toward Version IV of the p–System and emphasizes the release of the version (called "IV.1") that is most widely used at the time of this writing. If you're not using a variant of Version IV, you can get general help from this book, but you should be prepared for the possibility that the keystroke by keystroke descriptions in Part 1 may not be applicable on your computer. Similarly, some of the p–System facilities discussed in the other two Parts may not be available on your system.

If you're using Version IV.0 (the release prior to IV.1) or IV.2 (the subsequent release) there are some statements (including a few specific keypress sequences) that don't apply to you. We use footnotes to highlight these. Each such footnote indicates the classes of users it concerns. Don't assume that the footnote marker used (e.g., "*") indicates the class.*†

Liaison is a variant of Version IV.2 that is configured for use in collections of computers connected by a **local area network**. Liaison can also be used to connect multiple instances of the p–System running on a single computer (what you might call a *very* local network). At the time of this writing, Liaison availability is limited to a small number of p–System vendors. If you're using Liaison, consider yourself a user of Version IV.2 for the purposes of this book.

One of the big challenges in writing this book was finding a way to deal with the inevitable differences that exist between implementations of the p–System on different types of personal computers. A major thrust of the p–System is to minimize those differences, but they still exist. This can be a source of confusion, particularly if you are a beginner following the step–by–step instructions of Part 1.

We have addressed this problem by providing an appendix that describes the specifics of the p–System on one of the more popular families

---

* *IV.0 users, note:* Pay special attention to a footnote like this.

† *IV.2 users, note:* Pay special attention to a footnote like this.

of personal computers: the IBM Personal Computers. If your computer is a member of this family (or a close compatible), you will be in good shape. If you have some other kind of computer, another appendix provides general guidance on the kind of computer–specific information you need, and where it might be found in the p–System documentation provided by your supplier.

Even for the computers that we specifically cover, these appendices are no substitute for the p–System manuals provided with the software. We just provide enough computer–specific information to get you going.

We have provided a place on the front inside cover of this book for you to record the most important details about the p–System on your computer. We suggest that, early in Chapter 1, you "fill in the blanks" there. Once you get that information recorded, the differences among personal computer types should cause you few problems as you proceed through the rest of this book.

We've also put the back inside cover to good use. On one side, a quick index to the major facilities of the p–System is provided. On the other side, the p–System's "File Conventions" are summarized. (Chapter 1 discusses what "files" and "file conventions" are.)

Just in case you try to do an operation with the p–System that is not allowed, you will be happy to know that, in Appendix A, we have listed the error messages that can be produced by several of the major components of the p–System, along with brief diagnoses of what might be wrong in each case, and possible recovery actions.

In Appendix B, we provide similar advice on general errors that can occur while you're running an application program.

Our overall goal has been to make your introduction to the p–System, and your continued use of it, as pleasant and productive as possible. We welcome you to the world of personal computing with the p–System.

1

MANAGING FILES AND RUNNING PROGRAMS

1.1 INTRODUCTION

This chapter shows you how to begin using p–System programs that others have developed. If your principal interest is in developing your own programs, this chapter gives you the necessary foundation.

Hundreds of p–System programs are offered commercially, covering a very broad range of application areas. Here is a small sample, just to give you some notion of the breadth of the possibilities:

- One application area that is well covered is known in the trade as "GLAPAR," which stands for General Ledger, Accounts Payable, and Accounts Receivable. These fundamental areas of accounting are often the first aspects of a small business to benefit from computer assistance. Almost any business has needs in this area, and a variety of p–System programs address these needs.
- There are also industry–specific application packages in such diverse areas as corn and soybean crop management and resort rental properties handling.
- Various management productivity aids are available, including several electronic spreadsheet simulators, project planning tools, and tax planning systems.
- There is even entertainment software based on the p–System, such as "Wizardry," an adventure and fantasy game. This game simulates the

adventures of a group of explorers (including men, dwarfs, "mages" and "berserkers") in a dangerous land.

How can you find out about p–System programs that address specific needs that you have? One way is to acquire the *p–System Applications Catalog,* which is published periodically by SofTech Microsystems, and lists commercially offered p–System applications. For each of several hundred applications, a brief description, price range, and ordering information are provided.

Another source of application leads (and lots of other p–System information as well) is the UCSD p–System User's Society (USUS–– pronounced "Use Us"). This group publishes a periodic newsletter. This newsletter includes a *Software Source Directory* that lists vendors of p–System applications and other p–System–related products.

You can get the newsletter by becoming a member of USUS. If you do that, you'll be able to take advantage of other USUS services as well, such as a low–cost library of contributed software, bi–annual meetings, and various special interest groups. Appendix H provides some more details on USUS member benefits and a membership application.

Once you've located some application programs that look useful, you need to know how to acquire them. Application software that runs in the p–System is very likely to be usable on your computer, but you still need to be careful in making acquisitions. The last sections of this chapter discuss this topic.

What do you need to know about the p–System to use these tools? It depends on the program.

For example, you often need facilities for making "back up" copies of information created by an application program on disk. Sometimes these facilities are built into the application program, but often the program depends on general p–System tools to meet this need. If every application you use provides these housekeeping functions, then you have little immediate need to know the material presented in this chapter. In most cases, however, this chapter will be useful, and perhaps even crucial, to your productive personal computing with the p–System.

Before we get into specific details on p–System facilities, some background on the concepts of programs and files is necessary.

Files in the p–System environment are collections of (usually related) information. They are similar to the everyday file folders that are used to keep information organized in an office. In the office, files are stored in file drawers. When p–System files are stored, disks play the role of file drawers. Each p–System file has a name. Two files on the same disk cannot have the same name. You can think of diskettes as small file drawers that you can remove and replace as you want to use the files on them with the p–System.

Most application programs use files, either to store information for later reference or to reference previously stored information. Some programs, such as the "Wizardry" adventure game mentioned above, have no need for file storage, since each use of this program is a self–contained experience. However, this type of program is the exception.

Files on p–System disks are permanently stored (at least as long as you don't damage the disks or explicitly discard the files). The more personal computing you do with the p–System, the more you will come to depend on your stored files, and the more careful you will need to be in preserving them.

Each file is made up of an integral number of **blocks**, each of which can hold 512 **bytes** or characters. The size of a file and the size of the disk on which it resides are usually reckoned in blocks.

What are programs? The noun "program" usually refers to a detailed schedule of events and participants in an activity (say, a graduation ceremony, or a picnic). In the computer context, program has a similar meaning, except that a program for a computer must be very detailed and explicit, since computers have none of the judgement and common sense that we take for granted in human beings. In fact, one of the research frontiers in computer science is the creation of programs that would allow a computer–controlled robot to navigate among the rooms of a house without demolishing the furniture!

Programs are stored as files on p–System disks. A program file contains the coded computer instructions that direct the operation of a computer when that program is in control. Many programs contain thousands (or even tens of thousands!) of coded instructions.

When a computer follows the instructions of a program, it is said to **execute** the program. The same word can be used when you start up a program: You "execute" it. "Running" a program means the same thing.

Now it's time for you to see files and programs in action by using the p–System yourself. If you already have a p–System that is ready to run on your computer, your next step is to start using it. To do that, skip the following section and go on to the section called "Starting Up the p–System."

If you don't already have a p–System that runs on your computer, read the following section to learn what's involved in acquiring a p–System.

1.2 ACQUIRING AND INSTALLING A p–SYSTEM

We mentioned in the introductory chapter that one of the hallmarks of the p–System is its ability to run on most kinds of personal computers. For each type of computer on which the p–System runs, there is a portion of the system that is specific to that computer. This computer–specific portion of the p–System caters to the particular type of microprocessor used in the computer, and to the details of the input/output devices that are attached. In order to run the p–System on your computer, you need a p–System with the right computer–specific portions installed. (Chapter 7 provides additional details on these computer–specific p–System components.)

One attractive source of a p–System for your computer is the vendor that provided your hardware. If that vendor or other local dealers can't provide a p–System for your use, you may be able to get a list of p–System implementations from SofTech Microsystems. The USUS *Software Source Directory* (mentioned above) is another source of this kind of information. See Chapter 9 for details.

If no one provides a pre–configured p–System for your type of computer, you may be able to acquire an **Adaptable System** from SofTech Microsystems and do the installation yourself. Be forewarned, however, that this installation process is likely to involve sophisticated low–level programming (probably several weeks of it, at least). You probably shouldn't attempt the job unless you are an experienced programmer and have detailed knowledge of the internal operation of your computer.

Even if you can acquire a p–System that runs on your computer, there may still be one (relatively simple) configuration step that you have to handle. On some computers, the terminal component (made up of the screen and keyboard) is not integrated with the rest of the computer. On this kind of computer, different types of terminals can be connected, each with its own peculiar conventions about communication with your computer. If your computer is like this, you may need to adapt the p–System to your terminal. This adaptation can probably be done in a few hours. You may need to do a small amount of Pascal programming.

If you need to do any adaptation work in order to install the p–System on your computer, we recommend that you read over a good part of this chapter (at least through Section 1.7) before you begin the adaptation. Even though you can't see the p–System operating during this dry run, you should still get a very useful introduction to the use of the p–System. That introduction should make your adaptation project easier.

1.3 STARTING UP THE p–SYSTEM

Once you have an appropriate p–System, you need to load it into your computer so you can use it. The process is really quite simple, though the details vary with computer types. Usually you start with the main power switch for your computer in the off position. Then you insert the diskette containing the p–System into the primary disk drive and turn the main power switch on. (On some computers, it's important that you turn on the main power *before* inserting a disk in a disk drive, since the disk could be damaged otherwise.)

The start–up process is also called **bootstrapping**, by analogy with the phrase "pulling yourself up by your bootstraps."

One of the first concepts you'll need as you begin to use the p–System is the notion of **special keys** on your keyboard. These keys are called "special" because they do not represent standard letters, numbers, or symbols. Instead, they have special meanings, such as "erase the last character typed." For instance, the special key ⟦bs⟧ (pronounced "backspace") allows you to erase and correct typing errors. Keep in mind that many of the special key names we use may not appear on any keys on your keyboard. We will help you build a table that indicates what keys on *your* keyboard you should type to activate the p–System's special keys. Throughout this book, we use the double bracket symbols "⟦ ⟧" to enclose the names of special keys.

Now you need to start up the p–System on your own computer so that you can follow along as we explore the capabilities of the p–System. The details of that start–up process depend on what kind of computer you have. The way in which you type p–System special keys also depends on the kind of computer you have. Therefore we address both of these topics in the computer–specific appendices to this book that were mentioned earlier.

Locate the appendix that deals with your computer and read the introduction and the first section: "Starting Up the p–System for the First Time." If you have an IBM Personal Computer, a member of the IBM PC family, or a close compatible, read Appendix E. Otherwise, read Appendix F.

After you follow the instructions in the appropriate appendix, you should have filled in your inside cover (describing the details of the p–System on your computer), your p–System should be running, and your display screen should look something like this:

```
Command: E(dit, R(un, F(ile, C(omp, L(ink, X(ecute, A(ssem, D(ebug,? [ ]




Welcome  SYSTEM, to

U.C.S.D. p-System  [version]

Current date is January 1, 1985
```

What if the top line of your screen shows only part of the top line in the screen image above? Don't panic! The likely reason is that your computer's display is not set up to show the entire width of an 80–character line. If this appears to be your situation, check the documentation for your p–System (or the appropriate computer–specific appendix to this book). It is possible, for instance, that all 80 columns of the screen above are stored in your computer, and that there are special keys you can type to choose which portion of the 80 columns you want to see.

In the remainder of this book, we assume that you have an 80–column screen. All sample screen images have this width. It should be easy for you to follow along, even if the lines on your screen are not as wide as those shown here.

One other note: on some computers, the greeting lines (starting with "Welcome") shown in the sample above are replaced by some other kind of welcome message, such as a company logo. The display in Figure 1 (in the introductory chapter) shows an example of such a logo. In Chapter 4, we describe how this is accomplished via a special file on your disk called SYSTEM.STARTUP, and how you can modify your disk so that the standard p–System greeting lines appear, instead of the logo.

1.4 INTERACTING WITH THE p–SYSTEM

In the center of the screen image in the previous section are three "greeting" lines that the p–System displays when it has just been started. We discuss this greeting in detail later in this book. For now, let's concentrate on the line at the top of your screen. It is called a **menu** because it shows you the p–System actions that you may select.

The p–System makes wide use of this menu concept. The main reason for this approach is to make the System easy to use. These menus help you use the system, especially those parts of the system that you don't use very often.

Menus in the p–System are usually displayed on the top line of your console screen. They list a set of **activities** that are available to you. Each menu has a name (like "appetizers" or "desserts"), that appears as its first word. Succeeding words indicate the activities that can be selected from that menu.

If you look at the screen, you can see the Command menu. This is the main menu of the p–System, and the activities listed here are the major ones available. You can select an activity from a menu by typing the first letter of the activity name. The "(" after the first letter tells you that you only need to type that first letter. Even though a capital letter is shown (for example, "E" for "E(dit"), lower case letters can also be used to select menu items.

The first part of this book (through Chapter 3) is designed for you to "follow along" on a step–by–step basis. Underlining emphasizes characters or keys that you are expected to type immediately on your personal computer keyboard. Even though you can use either capital letters or lower case letters to select from menus, we always show those selection keys as capital letters.

When a "?" appears on a menu, that is a sign that there are more activities in that menu than can be listed on the screen. You can see the rest by typing ?. (Remember that you should type underlined characters directly on your keyboard!) Here is the line you should see:

```
Command: H(alt, I(nitialize, M(onitor, U(ser restart [ ]
```

Notice that there is no question mark on this extension because there are no further activities in the Command menu.

The last item on a menu (generally enclosed in square brackets ("[ ]") is a **version number**. This number indicates which version of a p—System component you're using. A typical version number on the Command menu might be "IV.13". If you have this legend on your command line, the major version of your p—System is IV.1, and you have variation "3" of that.

In this book, we have deleted the version numbers from the menus we show, so as not to confuse you. Most of the directions we provide in this book should work for any Version IV p—System. Where there are exceptions to this general rule, we use footnotes to alert you.

The sequence of menu portions that you see each time you type "?" may be different from that shown above. If so, your p—System has a different activity set or has been configured for some other screen width than 80 columns. The p—System always shows as many activity names as it can within the defined screen width. If there are more activities to show, the "?" appears to remind you.

It is not necessary for an activity to be visible on the menu in order for you to use it. You can select any of the activities of a menu, no matter which part of it is visible.

To prove that, select the F(ile activity from the Command menu by typing F. This activity allows you to do housekeeping operations involving the files on your diskettes and a variety of other useful tasks. After some disk activity, a new menu ("Filer") appears:*

```
Filer: G(et, S(ave, W(hat, N(ew, L(dir, R(em, C(hng, T(rans, D(ate,? [ ]
```

One of the activities that can be selected from this menu is Q(uit. Try typing Q. You should shortly see the Command menu again. You have now left the F(ile housekeeping activity altogether.

---

* *IV.2 users, note:* The Filer menu is different from that shown. The G(et, S(ave, W(hat and N(ew activities are no longer there. This comment applies to all subsequent references to the Filer menu. We will explicitly note any situations where these differences affect the key sequences you type.

When you typed "Q", just now, you probably waited until you could see, by the presence of the Filer menu, that the p–System was waiting for your next selection. Many p–System implementations have a capability called **type ahead**, which allows you to type characters into the p–System even if it is still working on responding to earlier characters you typed. Thus, for instance, you could type "F" and "Q" in quick succession. After the Filer menu was displayed as a result of the "F", the p–System would immediately process the "Q", and leave the Filer.

If you don't have type ahead on your p–System, you must wait to type each key until the p–System has responded to your previous typing. If you don't wait, some of your input may be lost. If this happens, you (and the p–System!) may get confused.

Just so you know where you stand on type ahead, we suggest the following simple experiment. Type F Q in quick succession. If the p–System briefly enters the Filer and returns to the Command menu immediately, you probably have type ahead support. If the p–System stays in the Filer (as if you hadn't typed "Q", for Q(uit), then you probably don't have type ahead.

You're probably not very concerned, right now, about typing many menu selections in quick succession. You may happen to do so by chance, however, and then wonder why the p–System ignored some of the keys you typed. We did this small experiment here to prepare you for that possibility. Even if this experiment indicates you have the type ahead capability, it's usually not a good idea to get too many characters ahead of the p–System's responses, since you may make mistakes that might be difficult to recover from. Furthermore, all p–Systems have some limit on how far ahead you can get in your typing.

Now we return to consideration of the Command menu. Another activity there is X(ecute, which allows you to execute programs. Type X:

```
Execute what file? _
```

You haven't seen this kind of question from the p–System before. Previously, you were given a menu of possible activities from which you could make a choice by typing a single letter. Now you are being asked to answer a question. You are expected to enter the name of the program you want to X(ecute. This kind of question is called a **data entry prompt**, or simply **prompt**. Your response to a prompt tells the computer what you want it to do.

We are not prepared yet to actually execute a program, but we take this opportunity to experiment with data entry prompts and show you how they work.

Here is the procedure for responding to a data entry prompt:

- Type in the sequence of characters that make up your response.

- If you make a mistake, use the ⟦bs⟧ key to erase the incorrect characters; then type the characters you want.
- When you're satisfied with the response you've typed, press the ⟦ret⟧ key to signal the p–System that your response is ready for processing.

If you don't remember how to type ⟦bs⟧ and ⟦ret⟧, the notes you put in the front inside cover (earlier in this chapter) should help. When you know where those keys are, try typing an x. It is displayed on the screen after the "?", and the **cursor** moves over to the next character position. The cursor is a marker that indicates where the next character that you type is put on the screen. Physically, its appearance varies among brands of computers and brands of displays. (For instance, it may be a solid block or an underline that flashes.) On your computer, the cursor looks like the character position right after the "x" you just typed! Now type two more x characters, followed by three ⟦bs⟧ keys. All the characters you typed are now gone.

Now type zzzz followed by a ⟦ret⟧. It is conventional in the p–System for the name of a program file to have ".CODE" on the end of it, so the p–System automatically adds that pattern to the name you entered and tries to find that file. That search is unsuccessful, as the p–System succinctly reports:

```
Command: E(dit, R(un, F(ile, C(omp, L(ink, X(ecute, A(ssem, D(ebug, ? [ ]
No file zzzz.CODE
```

Notice that the Command menu has returned.

What if you mistakenly select an activity that involves a data entry prompt? It is usually safe to provide an **empty** entry by simply typing ⟦ret⟧. Try this with the X(ecute activity. After typing X to invoke X(ecute, type an immediate ⟦ret⟧ to the data entry prompt. The p–System simply returns to the Command menu.

It's time to begin exploring what can be accomplished in the F(ile activity. Type F to recall the Filer menu. The activity we want to try out is V(olumes (abbreviated "V(ols" on the menu). As you can see, there is no such activity visible on the Filer menu. When you check the menu extension with "?", however, you should see the V(olumes activity listed.

1.5 p–SYSTEM VOLUMES

Invoke V(olumes in the Filer menu with a V. After a short pause, your screen should look something like this:

```
Filer: G(et, S(ave, W(hat, N(ew, L(dir, R(em, C(hng, T(rans, D(ate,? [ ]
Vols on-line:
  1    CONSOLE:
  2    SYSTERM:
  4 #  SYSTEM:    [320]
  6    PRINTER:
Root vol is - SYSTEM:
Prefix is   - SYSTEM:
```

You are back in the Filer menu, but there is new information on the screen: a list of **on—line volumes**. What is an on—line volume? For that matter, what is a volume?

One meaning of **volume** is "a p—System diskette." In the display above, the volume named SYSTEM: is the disk from which the p—System was loaded——the **system disk**. On your display, the name on that line (after the "4 #") may not be SYSTEM:, but it is still the name of **your** system disk. (Another name for system volume is **root volume**. The second—to—last line on the screen identifies the current system volume. It is probably the volume that is loaded in drive #4:. On some systems that have lots of main memory and RAM disk support, the system volume may be the RAM disk.)

An **on—line volume** is one that is accessible to the p—System. Try opening the cover door of the drive containing your system diskette. Then invoke the V(olumes activity again. The new list of on—line volumes has no entry for your system diskette because the System cannot read a diskette when the drive door is open. Each time you select the V(olumes activity, the p—System does an inventory of the accessible volumes and displays a list of those it finds.

If you have at least two disk drives, try a further experiment: Remove your system diskette from the drive and put it into another drive. (Be sure you close the drive cover after you put the disk in.) If you try the V(olumes activity again, the name of your disk should return to the list. This time, however, the number just to the left of it is different. If your computer has two disk drives, that number is probably 5. Now return your system disk to its original drive in preparation for the next operation.

Each p—System volume has a number associated with it in addition to a name. This is a **device number**. In the on—line volumes list, the device number is listed just before the corresponding volume name. Device numbers 4 and 5 represent the first two disk drives available with a p—System.

There are two categories of p—System volumes. Diskettes are in one category: **storage volumes**. Each storage volume (such as SYSTEM: in the list above) is identified in an on—line volumes list with a "#" and a number in brackets (320 in this case). This number indicates the total size of the volume in **blocks**.* Each block holds 512 characters. (The fact that

---

* *IV.0 users, note:* This volume size information does not appear in on—line volumes lists.

storage volumes are made up of blocks leads to the use of "blocked volume" as a synonym for "storage volume." The "blocked volume" terminology is still used in many p–System documents and programs.)

The key characteristic of storage volumes is that they can store information on a long–term basis. Each storage volume has its own private name, which is part of the stored information it contains. It is this private name that shows up on the on–line volumes list.

The second category of volumes is **communication volumes**. These volumes have no storage capability, but simply serve as channels for information. We deal further with communication volumes in a later section. For now, we concentrate on storage volumes. Sometimes we skip the "storage" and just use "volumes," or get very concrete and use "diskettes."

1.6 DIRECTORIES AND FILES

Information on a p–System volume is divided into **files**, and a **directory** keeps track of the name of each file, the date on which it was created, and various other housekeeping information, including the file's size and location on the volume.

The L(ist directory activity (abbreviated "L(dir" on the Filer menu) can be used to find out what files are on a particular volume.

Invoke the L(ist directory activity now by typing L. You are immediately asked to enter the name of the volume for which you want a directory listing. Ordinarily you enter a volume name (*including a colon*) in response to this prompt. You can look at the **default volume**, however, by simply entering : ⟦ret⟧.

```
List directory of what volume? : ⟦ret⟧
```

The current default volume is your system disk. This will always be the case, unless you explicitly select a different default volume (by using one of the Filer activities described in Chapter 6, for instance). A **directory listing** is produced as a response to your request and looks something like this:*

```
Filer: G(et, S(ave, W(hat, N(ew, L(dir, R(em, C(hng, T(rans, D(ate,? [ ]
SYSTEM:
SYSTEM.PASCAL     125 13-Jun-82
SYSTEM.FILER       37 13-Jun-82
SYSTEM.MISCINFO     1 30-May-82
SYSTEM.INTERP      28  8-Apr-82
SYSTEM.EDITOR      47  1-Apr-82
SYSTEM.LIBRARY     29  5-Jul-82
6/6 files<listed/in-dir>, 273 blocks used, 47 unused, 47 in largest
```

---

* *IV.2 users, note:* Directory listings are done in two columns rather than in one column as shown. This comment applies throughout the book.

In this example directory listing, the name of the system disk is SYSTEM:. Your system volume name may be something else, and other details of your display may be different from those shown.

A directory listing shows, for each file on the volume, its name, its size (in blocks), and the calendar date on which the file was created or last modified.

Look at the top line of your display. If it contains the phrase "Type space to continue", then the number of files on the volume is greater than the number of lines available on your screen. In this case, you can press ⟦space⟧ (several times, if necessary) until you don't get the "Type space to continue" message as the top line.

Whenever the p–System lists the directory of a volume containing a large number of files, it displays a full screen of files at a time. For each batch, you are prompted to "type space" to continue to the next batch. If you aren't interested in any more batches, you can type ⟦esc⟧ to cancel the listing process.

1.7 RUNNING PROGRAMS

Now that you have had a basic exposure to the concept of files, it's time to try running programs. If you're in the Filer menu, use the Q(uit activity to return to the Command menu.

You have already run one program during the exercises of this chapter––the Filer. The Filer is stored in the file SYSTEM.FILER, and the p–System provides a shorthand way to invoke it: you just type F in the Command menu.

For most programs, however, the invocation process is slightly more complicated. The main reason is that there are so many possible programs you might want to use that it is impossible to assign a single letter code in the Command menu for each one. Instead, the Command menu provides an X(ecute activity which allows you to enter the name of any program that you want to use.

It is easy to get confused between the X(ecute activity and the R(un activity, since we often use **running** as a synonym for **executing** when dealing with programs. (See, for example, the title of this section!)

In the p–System Command menu, however, there is a subtle but important distinction between these two activities. R(un is only used when you're developing new programs. R(un is described in Chapter 3; you shouldn't need it until then. (If you don't ever do program development with the p–System, you may never use R(un!)

Go ahead and invoke the X(ecute activity now. As you may recall from the early part of this chapter, the X(ecute activity is intended to be used with program files that have names that end in ".CODE". In fact, X(ecute is so sure that you will be invoking code files, that it adds ".CODE" to any name you provide in response to the data entry prompt.

What happens if you try to execute a file that doesn't have ".CODE" at the end of its name? The following screens show you what happens. Go ahead and try it, yourself.

```
Execute what file? system.filer [ret]
```

```
Command: E(dit, R(un, F(ile, C(omp, L(ink, X(ecute, A(ssem, D(ebug,? [ ]
Illegal file name system.filer.CODE
```

After the suffix is added, the file name is 17 characters long. The p–System limits file names to 15 characters in length. Therefore the file name is illegal.*

In a later section of this chapter, we show you how to create a file that does end with the usual suffix (".CODE"). In order to execute the file SYSTEM.FILER right now, however, we need some way to disable the automatic addition of the suffix. Try invoking X(ecute again, and putting a period after SYSTEM.FILER:

```
Execute what file? system.filer. [ret]
```

Success! The Filer is invoked and displays its familiar menu. When you need to execute a program file that doesn't end with the .CODE suffix, you can respond to the X(ecute prompt with the file name, followed by a period. You may never need this fact again, but it sure was handy here.

Why did the p–System look on your system volume for the SYSTEM.FILER file? Because it is the default volume. The ":" response you used earlier with the L(ist directory activity referred to the default volume as well. In both cases, the default volume was the system volume.

You can also enter an explicit volume name in connection with a file name. Q(uit the Filer and invoke X(ecute again. This time, put the name of your system volume in front of the program file name. (Your system volume's name was listed at the top of the directory listing you produced in the previous section. Return to the Filer and refresh your memory, if necessary.) Here's how your screen might look:

```
Execute what file? system:system.filer. [ret]
```

As soon as the Filer menu appears, Q(uit to return to the Command menu.

The default volume is also known as the **prefix** volume, since the p–System puts its name in front of a file name to make a complete file specification. Thus, even when you entered simply SYSTEM.FILER above, the p–System acted as though you had explicitly designated the system volume.

---

* *IV.0 users, note:* The error message shown is "No file system.filer.CODE" rather than that displayed above.

You can find out what the current default volume is by invoking the V(olumes activity and looking for the "Prefix is" line on the resulting display. Look back to the on–line volumes list at the beginning of Section 1.5, for an example.*

A volume can also be designated by the number of the device in which it is mounted. In the on–line volumes list you did earlier, your system disk appeared as device #4. Therefore the following response to the X(ecute prompt is equivalent to the two you just tried:

```
Execute what file? #4:system.filer. [ret]
```

To summarize, when responding to a prompt that requests a file name (in X(ecute or other activities) you can:

- indicate the volume by entering the number of the device in which the volume is mounted (e.g., #4:SYSTEM.FILER.), or
- enter the name of the volume name explicitly (e.g., SYSTEM:SYSTEM.FILER.), or finally,
- omit the volume designation altogether, as long as you intend to refer to the default volume.

Now that you know how to invoke programs, you also need to know how to stop them. Most of the time, of course, you should simply use the orderly exit procedure that is built into the program (for example, the Q(uit activity in the Filer menu). Sometimes, however, you simply must leave a program without going through the normal exit procedure. One reason, for instance, is if a program is clearly out of control (yes, sometimes that happens!).

The [break] key addresses this need. To experiment with it, use any of the ways you know to enter the Filer and then press [break]. (Check the inside front cover if you don't remember how to produce [break]. *Note: the p–System [break] key is very likely to be different from the key labelled "Break" on your keyboard. Be careful!*) On some kinds of computers, you need to type a character (say, [space]) after hitting [break] to make sure that the [break] is accepted by the p–System.

When the [break] takes effect, the bell on your computer sounds, and a message appears on the bottom line of your screen:†

---

* *IV.2 users, note:* You also have the option of using the Command menu's S(et activity to learn the current prefix volume.

† *IV.0 users, note:* The message takes three lines and starts after the location of the cursor on the screen. Since the cursor was on the first line, the message starts on the second. The interpretation of the message and your expected response are essentially as described here.

```
Filer: G(et, S(ave, W(hat, N(ew, L(dir, R(em, C(hng, T(rans, D(ate,? [ ]











Program interrupted by user--Seg PASCALIO P#18 O#306 <space> continues
```

This is called an **execution error message**. It means that something has caused the p–System to halt the program that was executing. In this case, the cause was your typing the ⟦break⟧ key, but other causes that really are errors are also possible.

The first portion of the error message identifies the error ("Program interrupted by user", in this case). On some systems, due to main memory limitations, the textual error message (such as "Program interrupted by user") does not appear. Instead, an error number ("8", in this case) is shown. If this happens on your computer, you can check Appendix B, "Execution Errors," to get the textual message. Appendix B also provides possible reasons and recovery actions for each of the various types of execution errors.

The error message also provides **error coordinates** that indicate where the program was executing when it was interrupted. If you're running a program developed by someone else, you probably can't do much with those error coordinates. You should, however, note them down, if you want the supplier of the program to help you diagnose what went wrong.

After the error coordinates, the error line indicates how to go on. Type ⟦space⟧ to do that. After some disk activity the Command menu returns, along with a notice that the p–System has reinitialized itself (since the unexpected interruption may have left it in an unhealthy state):

```
Command: E(dit, R(un, F(ile, C(omp, L(ink, X(ecute, A(ssem, D(ebug,? [ ]
System re-initialized
```

Another similar kind of message occurs when the p–System needs to load a section (or **segment**) of a program from a volume that is no longer on–line. This circumstance can easily arise, for instance, if you remove a program disk from a one–drive computer in order to do something with a data disk.

A "segment needed" message also appears at the bottom of your screen and might look like this:*

```
Need segment MYSEG:  Put volume MYVOL in unit 4 then type <space>
```

This message indicates that the p–System has unsuccessfully attempted to load the program segment MYSEG from the volume MYVOL. You are requested to restore that volume to unit 4 and then type ⟦space⟧. After you do so, the p–System tries again to load MYSEG (presumably with more success) and operation of the program continues. Unlike the execution error messages described above, these "segment needed" messages do not cause termination of the program and re–initialization of the p–System.

You should now know enough about running programs in the p–System to get started on productive personal computing. As for the other topic of this chapter (managing files), there are additional aspects to cover.

1.8 BACKING UP YOUR p–SYSTEM DISKETTES

The next section introduces the first of many Filer activities that can modify disks, not just examine them. The use of these activities increases the risk that you might unintentionally damage your p–System disks. Replacing your copy of the p–System would certainly be inconvenient, and possibly expensive, as well. Therefore, take time right now to make an extra (back up) copy of your p–System disk or disks (if you haven't already done so).

The details of making back up copies are somewhat machine–dependent. Therefore you will deal with this task during your next visit to the appendices.

One of the operations that you may use during the back up process is **disk formatting**. Formatting a disk involves having the system write some necessary control and address information on the disk surface, and is (on most computer types) a necessary step before a new diskette can be used with any software.

Formatting is done by a utility program. The details of how you run that program are usually different on each kind of personal computer. (For some computers, you don't need to do the formatting operation at all, because you can get disks that are already formatted.)

You should turn now to the appropriate computer–specific appendix and follow the directions in the section "Making Back Ups."

---

* *IV.0 users, note:* This message appears at the current location of the cursor and is spread across three lines, but contains roughly the same information. Your response should be as discussed above.

1.9 CHANGING THE CALENDAR DATE

Having just returned from a trip to the appendices, you should now be using the p–System on the new copy of the p–System diskette that you just made.

One of the first things to do whenever you begin a session with the p–System is update the calendar date maintained by the System. During the first session with the p–System on a particular day, use the D(ate activity in the Filer menu to tell the system the correct date. Enter that activity now. (You may need to enter the Filer, first.)*

Keeping the date current is important because whenever you create or modify a file, the current date is stored with the file name in the volume directory. As you begin to do more work with the p–System, the dates associated with files will become very important to you. They can tell you, for instance, whether a data file stored on a diskette is the current version of that file, or one that is out–of–date.

Here is the prompt produced by the D(ate activity:

```
Date set: <1..31>-<JAN..DEC>-<00..99>
Today is 1-Jan-85
New date? _
```

This activity does two things. First, it tells you the p–System's notion of the current calendar date. Second, this activity allows you to enter a new date if you want to.

The line "New date?" is a data entry prompt. If you don't want to change the date, you can simply press ⟦ret⟧. The p–System returns to the Filer menu.

If you do want to change the date, read the line that starts "Date set". The date format is day, month, year, with two "–" separators:

- The day should be in the range 1 to 31,
- a three character abbreviation for the month should be used, and
- a two–digit year is expected.

Try entering the current date in the indicated format. If the structure of your entry is acceptable, the p–System reports the new date as shown in the following screen. If the System cannot interpret your entry, it reconfirms the old date.

```
Today is 1-Jan-85
New date? 2-jan-85 [ret]
The date is 2-Jan-85
```

---

* *IV.2 users, note:* You also have the option of using the Command menu's S(et D(ate activity. That activity is functionally equivalent to the Filer's D(ate activity described here.

When you establish a new date, it is recorded on the system disk, and remains there until you change the date again. Until that time, whenever you start up the p—System with the same system disk, the same date is used.

There is a handy short cut that should simplify your use of the D(ate activity. The p—System allows you to enter just the day (if only that has changed) or just the day and month. Try it! First change just the day, and then try the day and month. After your experimentation, be sure to re—establish the correct date.

1.10 MOVING FILES AROUND

Now you're ready to start using the T(ransfer activity, which is the Filer's principal tool for moving files around. This section describes only a few of the capabilities of T(ransfer. Additional aspects are discussed later in this chapter and in Chapter 6.

Invoke the L(ist directory activity on your system volume (which should be your default volume): L : ⟦ret⟧. The last line of the directory listing gives a summary of the space situation on the volume and might look something like this:

```
6/6 files<listed/in-dir>, 273 blocks used, 47 unused, 47 in largest
```

Your summary line is probably different, but make a mental note of your "blocks unused" number. These are the blocks on your volume that are available for the storage of additional files.

Now invoke the T(ransfer activity. You are immediately asked what file you want to transfer:

```
Transfer what file? _
```

You are going to copy the file SYSTEM.FILER on your system disk. Type SYSTEM.FILER ⟦ret⟧. The Filer responds with another data entry prompt, requesting that you specify where you want SYSTEM.FILER to be put:

```
Transfer what file? SYSTEM.FILER ⟦ret⟧
To where? _
```

When you type FILER.CODE ⟦ret⟧, some disk activity occurs; then the Filer reports:

```
Filer: G(et, S(ave, W(hat, N(ew, L(dir, R(em, C(hng, T(rans, D(ate,? [ ]
To where? FILER.CODE ⟦ret⟧
SYSTEM:SYSTEM.FILER     --> SYSTEM:FILER.CODE
```

What you've done is put another copy of SYSTEM.FILER on your system disk, with a new name: FILER.CODE.

When you choose a name for a new file, be sure it has fifteen or fewer characters. For program files, the suffix ".CODE" should generally be present, leaving ten characters for you to choose. It's simplest if you stick to alphabetic letters (A to Z) and digits (0 to 9) in the file names you create. Chapter 4 defines legal file names in greater detail and indicates the special characters that are also valid. This information is summarized on the back inside cover of this book.

Check the directory of your system disk to see how that has changed. Type L : ⟦ret⟧. If you compare the new FILER.CODE entry in the directory with the SYSTEM.FILER entry, you should find that both the size and the date on the new file match those on the old file. T(ransferring a file doesn't change its date (since the contents are unchanged).

You should also notice that the unused space (reported in the summary line) has been reduced by the size of the new file, FILER.CODE.

What if you want to move a file to a different volume, and retain the original file name? You could, of course, type the same name twice, but the p—System makes life easier for you by providing a special symbol that you can use in place of an explicit destination file name when you simply want to reuse the old name on the new file. The screen below shows you how to do such an operation, which results in a file SYSTEM.FILER on a hypothetical volume MYVOL:

```
Transfer what file? SYSTEM.FILER [ret]
To where? MYVOL: $ [ret]
SYSTEM.FILER    ---->    MYVOL:SYSTEM.FILER
```

When you use "$" in place of a destination file name in the T(ransfer activity, the Filer uses the source file name for the new file. (Note that you must still specify the destination **volume**.)

What happens if you choose a destination file name that conflicts with a file already on the destination volume? Since there cannot be two files on a volume with the same name, the Filer asks you to settle the matter. For example:

```
Transfer what file? SYSTEM.MISCINFO [ret]
To where? $ [ret]
Remove old SYSTEM:SYSTEM.MISCINFO? _
```

If you answer "Y" for "Yes," the old version of the destination file (SYSTEM.MISCINFO in this case) is removed, and a new copy of the file is made on your default disk. Answer "No," and the T(ransfer operation is canceled. You can try doing the example T(ransfer shown above if you'd like.

This kind of Yes/No question is like a menu in that a single character response is expected, and no ⟦ret⟧ is necessary. In this menu, however, the options are implicit!

What if there isn't room (on the destination volume) to store the file you're transferring? The following screens show an attempted transfer to a hypothetical MYVOL: volume that is already crowded:

```
Transfer what file? SYSTEM.FILER [ret]
To where? MYVOL:NEWFILER.CODE [ret]
```

```
Filer: G(et, S(ave, W(hat, N(ew, L(dir, R(em, C(hng, T(rans, D(ate,? [ ]
No room on vol
```

The Filer indicates that there is no room to store a copy of the Filer program on MYVOL:.

If you get this "No room on vol" message, you can often make room on the destination volume by removing any unnecessary files (an operation which is explained in a later section).

1.11 TEXT FILES AND COMMUNICATION VOLUMES

So far we've only dealt with files that contain programs——the **code files** whose names usually end in ".CODE". These files contain encoded computer instructions and are not directly readable by ordinary mortals. There is another variety of files called **text files** that contain readable characters. Not surprisingly, the names of these files generally end in ".TEXT".

To experiment with a text file, you must create your own. There are many ways to create a text file; here is one that should prove useful in its own right.

Invoke the L(ist directory activity (by typing L) and respond to its prompt as follows:

```
List dir of what volume? : ␣ DIRECTORY.TEXT [ret]
```

After some disk activity, the System returns to the Filer menu, as usual, but instead of the usual directory listing on the screen, the phrase "Writing." appears. The reason is that this expanded version of the L(ist directory request has caused a textual version of the directory of your system volume to be stored in the file DIRECTORY.TEXT.

Invoke L(ist directory again, but this time request a conventional display of your system directory. The resulting display should contain a file description item that looks something like this:

```
DIRECTORY.TEXT      4  2-Jan-85
```

A text file has indeed appeared there. That file contains the directory listing that would ordinarily have appeared on your screen just a few moments ago. Note that the date shown for DIRECTORY.TEXT is the current date that you set earlier in this chapter. Also, the size of your file depends on the size of your directory listing, and may be larger than the four blocks shown above.

You can look at the contents of DIRECTORY.TEXT using the T(ransfer activity:

```
Transfer what file? DIRECTORY.TEXT [ret]
To where? CONSOLE: [ret]
```

Your screen should now contain a directory listing of your system volume with a final line that looks like this:

```
SYSTEM:DIRECTORY.TEXT ----> CONSOLE:
```

For this T(ransfer operation, the destination was the console screen rather than a file on a diskette. Just as with previous T(ransfers, the p–System reported the source and destination of the operation after it was completed. This accounts for that last line.

It may surprise you that the file DIRECTORY.TEXT doesn't appear on this list. The reason is that when the directory listing contained in DIRECTORY.TEXT was made, there was no DIRECTORY.TEXT file! Once the DIRECTORY.TEXT file has been created by the p–System, the fact that it represents a directory listing is entirely forgotten. To the p–System, the file is simply a collection of characters. Therefore, there is no attempt to update the text file when the **real** directory is updated to include the new file.

This was your first use of the communication volume CONSOLE:. You can use the V(olumes activity to see the other communication volumes available. (They don't have the "#" marks.)

```
Filer: G(et, S(ave, W(hat, N(ew, L(dir, R(em, C(hng, T(rans, D(ate,? [ ]
Vols on-line:
  1    CONSOLE:
  2    SYSTERM:
  4 #  SYSTEM:    [320]
  6    PRINTER:
Root vol is - SYSTEM:
Prefix is   - SYSTEM:
```

One of the standard p–System communication volumes is PRINTER:. If that is listed on your screen, you probably have a printer device attached to your computer. If PRINTER: doesn't appear in your V(olumes list, it may be because you don't have a printer, or possibly because it is not turned on and readied for operation. On some computers, PRINTER: may appear on the list even though the printer is not ready to print. Check your printer for readiness.

If you do have a printer, and it is ready to be used, T(ransfer the file DIRECTORY.TEXT to the volume PRINTER:.

Your printer should produce a printed copy of the directory listing you saw earlier. If the Filer waits before printing anything, it may be because your printer isn't ready to print––check the manual for your printer if necessary. If you can't get the printer to work, and the p–System continues to wait, you may have to restart the entire p–System and not try to use the printer again until you know how to make it work.

It is often quite useful to have a printed list of the files on a diskette. As you accumulate a larger collection of diskettes, it gets harder to remember what is on each one. A printed directory listing, tucked into the diskette envelope, can be very helpful. Is there a more direct way to produce a printed directory listing? Yes, there is: you could type L : , PRINTER: [[ret]].

Just as with storage volumes, you can use the device number style of referencing communication volumes. CONSOLE: is equivalent to #1:, while PRINTER: is equivalent to #6:. If you like, try transferring DIRECTORY.TEXT to #1:, instead of to CONSOLE:.

Which is the better approach, using the name of a volume or the corresponding device number? In the case of communication volumes, it is simply a matter of convenience. Some people feel more comfortable with the name, since it is more meaningful. Others are more concerned about the number of keystrokes they use!

In the case of storage volumes, there is an important difference between these two approaches. When you use the device number style of volume reference, you refer to *whatever volume is installed in that device.* This may or may not be the one you intended. If you use the volume name, however, this potential source of confusion and mistakes is eliminated.

You should use the name style of volume reference (at least initially).

Now that you've seen several ways to create new files on a volume, it's time to find out how to remove them.

1.12 REMOVING FILES FROM A VOLUME

Just as with the files in an ordinary file drawer, files on a diskette volume occasionally need to be discarded. A particular file may contain obsolete information or may have been created by mistake. Whatever the motivation, it is important to keep in mind that removing a file from a storage volume has one important difference from taking a file folder out of a file drawer and throwing it in the wastebasket: *It's very hard to take the diskette file out of the wastebasket again if you change your mind!*

So, be cautious in your "housecleaning" on a diskette.

Invoke the R(emove activity (on the Filer menu) now. Respond to the resulting prompt as follows:

```
Remove what file? FILER.CODE [[ret]]
SYSTEM:FILER.CODE              --> removed
Update directory? _
```

Now you have one last chance to change your mind. If you type "N" (for "No") to this question, the removal operation is canceled. If you type "Y", you indicate your approval for the removal and the file FILER.CODE is no more. Type Y.

The p–System generally asks for verification when you request an operation where a mistake could have serious consequences. This is one of the ways that the System is designed to help you avoid costly mistakes.

Notice that you are back in the Filer menu. Check the directory of your system volume to see if FILER.CODE has indeed disappeared. (Type L : [ret].)

What if you try to delete a file that isn't there? Try R FILER.CODE [ret] again:

```
MYVOL:SYSTEM.FILER - File not found <source>
```

The aspects of the T(ransfer and R(emove activities that you've seen so far are sufficient to do most things you'll need to do. However, if you should need to transfer or remove many files at once, the methods you know could get a bit tedious. The next section introduces some short cuts for such multi–file operations.

1.13 MULTI–FILE SHORT CUTS

When you want to remove many files from a volume, it is rather inconvenient to have to repeatedly type "R", followed by the name of one of the files and [ret]. It's easy to forget the names of the files you want to discard, so you may have to get a printed copy of the directory of the volume, or you may have to invoke the L(ist directory activity frequently to refresh your memory.

There is a better way! To try it, type R ? [ret]. You are telling the p–System that you want to remove files from the default volume, but that you don't want to go through the tedious process of naming each file you want to delete. Instead, you are requesting the system to ask you, for each file on the volume, whether you want to remove that file. The Filer responds by asking you a question something like this (in which the file named is probably different from that shown):

```
Remove what file? ? [ret]
Remove SYSTEM:SYSTEM.PASCAL? _
```

Now the Filer is waiting for another of those yes or no answers. Type Y. The Filer goes on to ask the same question about each of the files on your volume. Type N in response to each such query. Then the Filer gives you the familiar chance to change your mind:

```
Remove what file? MYVOL: ? [ret]
Remove SYSTEM:SYSTEM.PASCAL? Y
Remove SYSTEM:SYSTEM.INTERP? N
Update directory? _
```

If you answer "Y" to this question, all the files selected individually for removal disappear from the volume. Since you definitely don't want to remove any files from your system volume, answer N.

By the way, if you wanted to apply this process to some other volume (say, MYVOL:), you would invoke the R(emove activity and respond to its prompt like this: MYVOL:? [ret].

This kind of multi–file capability is available in the T(ransfer activity also. It is very useful for making back up copies of an important group of files. Just as with the R(emove activity, you are asked about the transfer of each file on a designated volume. For instance, if you wanted to transfer some of the files from your default volume to a volume called MYVOL:, the following use of T(ransfer would be an easy way:

```
Transfer what file? ? [ret]
To where? MYVOL: $ [ret]
```

This response indicates that some of the files from the default (system) volume are to be transferred to MYVOL:. Just as with the single file T(ransfer you did earlier in the chapter, the special "$" symbol means "don't change the names of the source files when they are transferred to the destination volume." You would next be asked about the T(ransfer of each file on the system volume.

The capability of the p–System to support multi–file operations is much more general than described here. One property of these multi–file operations that is particularly useful is the ability to use the special key [esc] to cancel a series of questions about specific files. The full story is told in Chapter 6.

1.14 DEALING WITH CROWDED OR DAMAGED VOLUMES

Have you ever tried adding a file folder to a drawer that is almost full already? Usually you have to compress the existing files together so that the new one will fit. This wouldn't be necessary if it were practical to take the sheets of paper in the new file folder and slip them in wherever they would fit. Unfortunately, that would make it rather difficult to find the information from that folder when needed.

A similar situation occurs in storage volumes maintained by the p–System. The information in a p–System file must be kept together, too. As a volume is used, and files are added and removed, they can get spread around on the volume with unused space between them. Sometimes there is not enough space available in one place to store a new file on a volume.

Remember the summary line produced by the L(ist directory activity? In addition to showing the total unused space on a volume, that line also indicates the size of the largest single area. That largest area sets the limit on the size of a file that can be added to that volume. Consider, for instance, the following summary line for a 100–block volume:

```
3/3 files<listed/in-dir>, 48 blocks used, 52 unused, 36 in largest
```

In this case, the size of the largest file that can be added is 36 blocks. An attempt to add a larger file (such as SYSTEM.EDITOR, which is well over 50 blocks in size), would result in a "No room on vol" message just like we discussed earlier.

The *total* unused space on the volume described above is 52 blocks so it could hold a 50–block additional file if that unused space were collected together.

How can you gather the unused areas on a volume into a single large area? The Filer activity K(runch is designed to do exactly that. We defer detailed description of K(runch to Chapter 6, except for the following important caution:

> Don't *ever* stop the p–System, remove a disk, or turn off your computer during a K(runch operation. You might interrupt the operation at an inappropriate time and lose one or more files from your disk. If by accident you do interrupt a K(runch operation, refer to Chapter 6, where the topic of recovering a damaged volume is dealt with in considerable detail.

What if there still isn't enough room on a volume even after K(runching? The obvious solution is to remove some files (making sure, of course, that you can do without them first!).

Another Filer activity that is useful with crowded volumes is E(xtended directory list. It shows you where each of the unused areas on a volume is and also provides additional information about the files on the volume. We leave the details of this activity to Chapter 6.

One other housekeeping aspect of the use of disks needs to be mentioned here. Just as a phonograph record can become warped or scratched, it is possible for areas of a disk to become unusable for storing or retrieving information. This may result from a physical deformity, a speck of dust, or some other cause. Blocks on the disk that are not usable by the p–System are called **bad blocks**. If the p–System has trouble doing some operation, such as a T(ransfer, it may be due to bad blocks on a disk.

In Chapter 6, the B(ad block scan and X(amine activities of the Filer menu are described. These activities are useful in diagnosing and correcting the existence of bad blocks on a p–System volume.

Another way the p–System helps you recover from disk failures is the **duplicate directory** facility. When you create a p–System volume, you can choose to have the p–System maintain an extra copy of your directory information on the volume. If one copy gets damaged, the other copy serves as a back up source of information about the files on that volume. In Chapter 6, we describe the p–System tools that are available to work with duplicate directories.

1.15 USING SINGLE–DRIVE PERSONAL COMPUTERS

Though the p–System is considerably more convenient to work with on a personal computer with at least two disk drives, it can certainly be productively used on a one–drive computer, as well. The ideal one–drive computer for p–System use contains enough main memory so that you can use part of that space for a RAM disk. If you can use the RAM disk for important parts of the p–System (such as the operating system, the Filer, and perhaps the Editor) those components are always conveniently and speedily available. It's almost as good as having a second drive!

Remember the "segment needed" message that we described in Section 1.7? Such a message is displayed by the p–System when you need to restore a volume containing a needed code segment to a particular disk drive. In most circumstances, it is simple to respond to this message and continue with your p–System use.

The use of some programs, however, may involve considerable shuffling of data disks in and out of your disk drive. An example of such a program is the Filer (particularly when you use it to copy disks, perhaps for back up purposes). It can get hectic responding to Filer prompts to put various disks in a single drive while dealing with segment needed messages at the same time. Fortunately, the Filer provides for this circumstance with a handy activity: F(lip Swap/Lock.

When you invoke F(lip Swap/Lock (by typing F in the Filer menu), all the segments of the Filer are loaded in main memory. Thereafter, the disk containing the Filer is not needed to invoke any Filer activity so you can use your single drive freely for other disks.

If you don't have enough main memory, there may not be room to load the Filer segments and you receive a message so indicating. In this case, develop a habit of having the Filer disk in your drive when you invoke a Filer activity (so that the p–System can fetch any segments needed for that activity before you remove the Filer disk).

This concludes our discussion for this chapter about managing p–System files. We also have dealt with the running of programs. The last topic of this chapter is how to acquire the p–System programs you want to use.

1.16 ACQUIRING p–SYSTEM APPLICATION PROGRAMS

If you've ever browsed among the offerings of a personal computer software outlet, you may have noticed that each software package in the inventory is usually specifically intended for one brand (and often one particular model!) of personal computer. Even if a particular product is offered for more than one computer, there's usually a separate version for each computer variety.

There are two reasons for this. First, most personal computer software is not very **portable**. That is, it cannot handle the differences between the physical computer hardware used in different brands of computers. The result: software must be specifically tailored to a particular computer and once this tailoring is done, it won't run on other kinds of computers.

Second, there are incompatibilities between personal computer brands in the way information (including application programs) is recorded on diskettes. Even when two dissimilar computers both use the same size diskette (often the 5–1/4 inch size), there may still be differences in the details of information recording. The result: even when software portability is achieved, these mismatches in distribution media make it impossible for a single software package to be used on many different personal computers.

The p–System addresses both these problems (lack of software portability and distribution medium mismatches) to a greater degree than any other widely available software environment for personal computers.

First, p–System application programs can be completely portable to any personal computer that has the p–System installed.

Second, the distribution medium mismatches are minimized (at least for computers using 5–1/4 inch diskettes) by the popularity of the diskette format used with IBM PC–based p–Systems.

You may wonder why all this is important to you. After all, if you only have one kind of computer, why should it matter whether a software package can run on other computers? What if the only kind of computer you care about is yours?

One answer is that you should benefit if an application developer does not have to adapt an application specifically for your brand of computer, since the cost of development and distribution can be substantially reduced. This cost reduction should (we hope) be passed on to you in a lower price for the product, or perhaps in greater capabilities. Without the simplifications of the p–System's portability, the developer may choose not to make the product available at all for your computer!

In addition, there may be benefits of portability that haven't yet occurred to you. For one thing, you may want to replace your current computer by a different one eventually. Wouldn't it be pleasant to continue to use the same software on the new machine?

If you use a personal computer in your work, are there other people in your organization who also use personal computers, but of different kinds? The portability of the p–System offers the hope that productive sharing of software can occur (both for software that is developed by your organization and for software that is acquired from others).

But you can't begin to reap all these benefits unless you find application programs that meet your needs. You can start looking in the usual places like retail computer stores and personal computing magazines. If those sources don't turn up the application programs you need, check the *p–System Applications Catalog* or the USUS *Software Source Directory* mentioned at the beginning of this chapter.

Once you have decided to acquire a particular application, you need to be aware that the p–System's portability is not completely automatic: application developers must still take care in their programs to make sure that portability is not compromised. Similar care is needed in documentation and packaging of an application if it is to realize the portability that is possible in the p–System.

You should tell the potential supplier of your application what kind of personal computer you use and something of its configuration (for instance, how much main memory it has). You should also mention the version of the p–System that you use. If the application depends on specific features of a particular version, it's important to know if you have that version. You should also check on the application's use of "real numbers." Section 1.17 discusses the issues in this area.

After this discussion about the hardware and software that you have, the conversation can turn to the application you want to acquire. In addition to the natural discussion about what the application can do for you, you may want to raise the following questions:

- Is the software specifically offered for your brand and model of computer? If the answer is "yes," the developer has probably tested the software directly on your kind of computer and made sure that any peculiarities of that computer are dealt with by the software and the documentation that accompanies it.

- Is the software offered for other computers that use the same size diskettes as yours? If so, it may be relatively straightforward to access the software with your computer. If not, the biggest challenge may be in getting the software converted to a diskette format that your computer can read. The software vendor should be able to advise you.

The answers to these questions may determine whether it is practical to acquire the software for use on your computer.

1.17 APPLICATIONS THAT USE REAL NUMBERS

There is one other issue you should discuss with the potential supplier of an application program. You should ask whether the program you're interested in uses **real numbers**. In computer jargon, real numbers are those that can have fractional parts, such as "4.531" or "6.92". In the same vein, an **integer number** cannot have a fractional part. Examples of integer numbers are "58" and "21237".

The simplest situation is if the program you want to use doesn't use real numbers. Then you don't need to worry about the issue at all.

If the program does use real numbers, then you need to be aware that the p–System can support two sizes of real numbers. However, only one size is supported by a particular p–System configuration. You have to make sure that the size assumed by the program you want to use is the same as the size for which your p–System is configured. Some p–System suppliers allow you to choose either size; other suppliers make the choice for you. The computer–specific appendices to this book (or comparable information from your p–System supplier) should tell you what freedom you have in this area.

The two sizes supported are known as "two–word" and "four–word." A p–System "word" has room to store two characters, or bytes. Real numbers either occupy two of these words, or four of them. The size difference determines how big the real numbers can be, and how precisely they can be represented. For instance, with the two–word format, a program usually can't distinguish numbers that have the first six or more digits in common. So the dollar figure $5,345,789.20 would be treated as essentially the same as the dollar figure $5,345,786.73. For some kinds of programs, this limitation poses no problems. For other kinds of programs (in the accounting area, for instance) the four–word format is highly preferable, since as many as 15 digits can be distinguished. The basic question is whether your preference is for precision or compactness in the real numbers processed by your applications.

Some application suppliers provide programs in both sizes so you can make your own choices.

2

EDITING TEXT

2.1 INTRODUCTION

This chapter shows you how to use the p–System to manipulate text files like the DIRECTORY.TEXT file that you created in Chapter 1.

Of course the text that you deal with will be much more interesting and useful than the simple list of file names in DIRECTORY.TEXT. Business plans for a new company, human readable forms of computer programs, or even a PhD thesis, a letter to your Mom, or a book report –– all these can be stored as text files on p–System volumes.

Why should you work with these kinds of text using your computer and the p–System rather than manual methods involving pencil and paper or typewriter? If your interest is in developing p–System programs, you have no real alternative, since the p–System must be able to process your program, and it can't do that unless the program is stored in a file.

For other kinds of text, the main reason for using the p–System is convenience. The p–System includes an **Editor** program that allows you to create a text file and then later review and modify it very easily. When you are satisfied with the contents of the file, you can print it out on paper with just a few commands to the p–System. Alternatively, you can use a text formatter program to do the printing, just as we did with this book. If changes are needed, you can use the Editor again and then print the revised text. This approach is a big improvement over typing all that text again on a typewriter (especially since you're likely to produce a new set of typographic errors in the process)!

We've talked enough about the joys of text editing. It's time to do some! If you aren't already looking at the Command menu on your computer screen, do whatever you must, to get to that state. (If you need to start up the p–System again, refer back to the appropriate computer–specific appendix, or to your p–System documentation.)

To follow along in this chapter, you need to have the Screen–oriented Editor. To see if you have it, type E to invoke the E(dit activity from the Command menu. You're in luck (and you should go on to the next section), if your screen ends up looking like this:

```
>Edit:
No workfile is present. File? (<ret> for no file ) _
```

If, instead, your screen has the message "Cannot find SYSTEM.EDITOR", then you need to find the file containing the Editor and use the T(ransfer activity in the Filer to copy the editor file to some available on–line volume. Once you have installed the Editor, invoke it by typing E in the Command menu. When you see the screen above, go on to the next section.

Some runtime configurations of the p–System don't have the Editor at all. If this is your situation, you can still read this chapter and see how useful the Editor would be if you had it!

2.2 LOOKING AT AN EXISTING TEXT FILE

Your first experience with the Editor involves a text file that already exists. (You guessed it: DIRECTORY.TEXT!) Later you will create a text file from scratch.

After the Editor program is started up, your screen should look like this:

```
>Edit:
No workfile is present. File? (<ret> for no file ) _
```

With the "File?" question, the Editor is requesting that you designate the file you want to work on. Since this is a data entry prompt, and since the file you're going to edit is DIRECTORY.TEXT, enter DIRECTORY [ret]. Only text files can be edited, so the ".TEXT" suffix is omitted.

Now the Editor goes to the system diskette and gets the DIRECTORY.TEXT file (or whatever file you designate in response to the "File?" prompt). The file is copied from the disk into the Editor's **workspace** in main memory so that you can work with it. DIRECTORY.TEXT is still out on the disk; a copy of it is made in main memory. When the copying is done, a screen something like the following appears:

```
>Edit: A(djust C(opy D(el F(ind I(nsert J(ump K(ol M(argin P(age ? [ ]
SYSTEM:
SYSTEM.PASCAL     125 13-Jun-82
SYSTEM.FILER       37 13-Jun-82
SYSTEM.MISCINFO     1 30-May-82
SYSTEM.INTERP      28  8-Apr-82
SYSTEM.EDITOR      47  1-Apr-82
SYSTEM.LIBRARY     29  5-Jul-82
6/6 files<listed/in-dir>, 273 blocks used, 47 unused, 47 in largest
```

First notice the familiar menu structure on the top line of the screen. This is the Edit menu. Later, we explore the activities on this menu.*

Also notice that the contents of the file DIRECTORY.TEXT are displayed on the screen below the menu. (The details shown on your screen reflect your system volume, and may differ from those shown above.)

This editor is called "screen–oriented" because it uses the display screen of your computer as a **window** into the workspace. When you want to look at or modify a portion of a workspace, you move the window so that you can see the portion of interest, and then use the activities on the prompt line to make changes (or whatever). Figure 2.1 shows this concept.

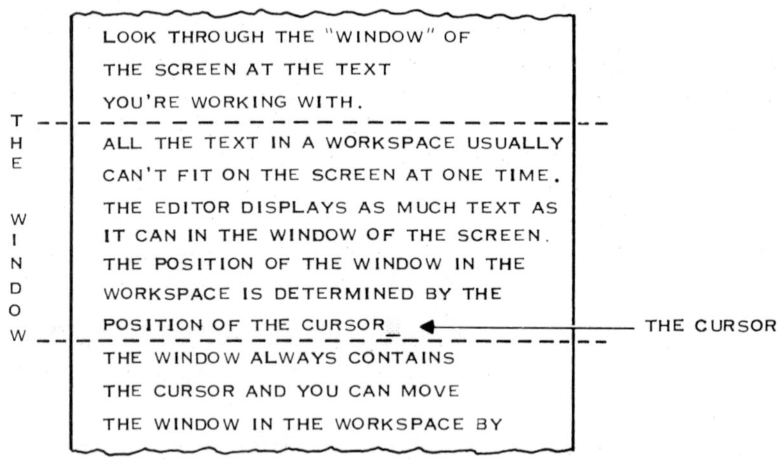

Figure 2.1

The window only highlights a general area of the workspace for attention. How can you point to a specific letter or word within the window? The answer involves the cursor, which we talked about earlier in connection with data entry prompts. You should see it right now on the

---

* *IV.0 users, note:* The Edit menu is different from that shown above. There is no question mark at the end of the menu, so there is no menu extension. There are, however, menu items that aren't shown. In fact, the Version IV.0 Editor has all the activities that the Version IV.1 Editor has.

first character of the line just below the menu on your screen. (A cursor is also shown in Figure 2.1.) You can think of the cursor as a pointer into the workspace you're editing. When you want to do some editing action, such as removing a word, your first step is to move the cursor to point to the word. As you move the cursor in the workspace, the Editor generally moves the window so that you can see the area where the cursor is pointing.

There are special keys which you can use to move the cursor. Some of these you've used already, but they have a slightly different function when used for cursor movement.

The ⟦space⟧ bar can be used to move horizontally on a line. Each ⟦space⟧ moves the cursor to the right by one position. If you space past the end of a line, the cursor moves to the beginning of the next line. Go ahead and ⟦space⟧ past the first line of the directory information in your workspace.

You can move the cursor to the left with ⟦bs⟧. Notice that when you use ⟦bs⟧ for this purpose, characters aren't erased as you backspace over them; only cursor movement occurs. What happens if you backspace through the beginning of a line? Try it! As you may have expected, you end up at the end of the previous line.

Another familiar key, ⟦ret⟧, moves the cursor towards the end of the workspace like ⟦space⟧, but by leaps of a line at a time, rather than small steps of a character at a time. Each time you type ⟦ret⟧, the cursor moves to the beginning of the following line.

The arrow keys, which you haven't used before in this book, also move the cursor. The ⟦left⟧ arrow key has the same effect on the cursor as described above for ⟦bs⟧. The ⟦right⟧ arrow key acts like the ⟦space⟧.

You can think of the characters in your workspace as beads on a string. Lines of text are separated from each other by line separator characters. These separators are also like beads on the string, but they are invisible on the screen. Consider, for instance, this simple workspace:

```
>Edit: A(djust C(opy D(el F(ind I(nsert J(ump K(ol M(argin P(age ? [ ]
 LINE1
  AND
LINE TWO
```

Figure 2.2 shows the characters of this workspace as "beads on a string." The normally invisible line separator characters are shown, and the position of the cursor is indicated by an upward pointing arrow designating the "A" in the second line. This corresponds to the position of the cursor in the workspace above.

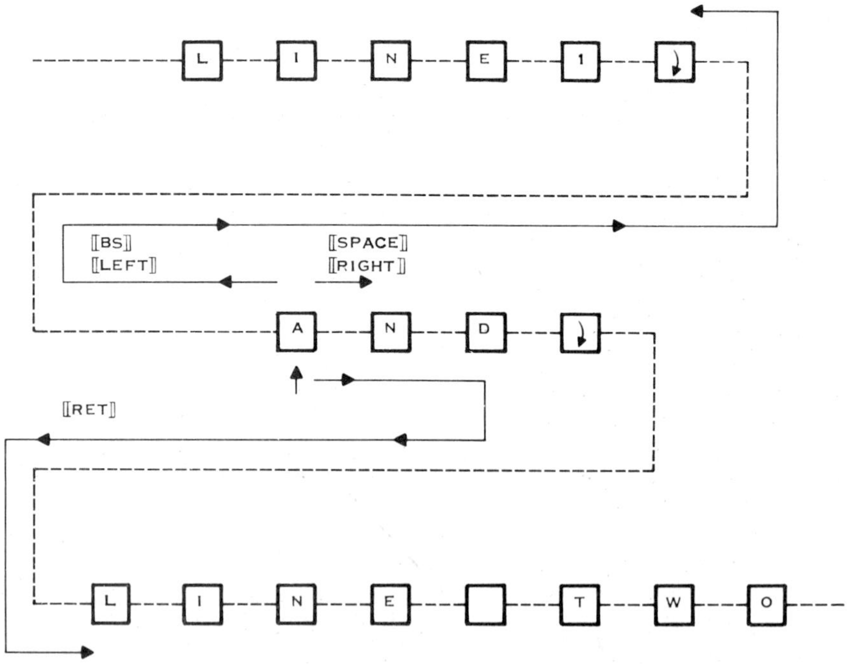

Figure 2.2

The cursor movements that would result from pressing any of five special keys (⟦bs⟧, ⟦left⟧, ⟦space⟧, ⟦right⟧, ⟦ret⟧) are shown.

The ⟦up⟧ and ⟦down⟧ arrow keys move the cursor, also, but they cause movement vertically, rather than along the imaginary string of Figure 2.2.

If you want to exercise your understanding of the cursor movement commands, try traversing a square on the screen using the cursor. It should be easy. Imagine how much more tedious the job would be if you couldn't use the vertical arrow keys.

You've probably seen enough of DIRECTORY.TEXT by now. You can leave the Editor by invoking the Q(uit activity. When you type Q, you should see the following screen:

```
>Quit:
     U(pdate the workfile and leave
     E(xit without updating
     R(eturn to the editor without updating
     W(rite to a file name and return
```

In this chapter we are only concerned with the last three of these options. The R(eturn activity is useful if you press "Q" by mistake. It puts you right back in the Editor as if you hadn't typed "Q" at all. Try typing R Q, to exercise the R(eturn item and get back to the Quit menu.

The E(xit activity is used when you haven't modified the workspace, implying that the file stored on disk does not need to be updated. For instance, you may have been simply inspecting the text. E(xit is also used if you have made modifications to the workspace but want to discard them and leave the file on disk (DIRECTORY.TEXT in this case) as it was before you entered the Editor. Go ahead and invoke E(xit. You should soon be out of the Editor and back in the Command menu. Since the next topic is the use of the Editor to create a new file, you should immediately reinvoke the E(dit activity.

2.3 CREATING A NEW TEXT FILE

This time when the prompt "No workfile present. File?" appears, you should simply press ⟦ret⟧, indicating that there is no existing file you want to edit, since you are going to build one yourself. Now the main edit menu appears, but the screen below it is empty. You're looking through the window of the screen at an empty workspace.

I(nsert is the activity that allows you to enter text. Type I You could not see a clod , and the screen should look like that shown next:

```
Insert: Text {<bs> a char,<del> a line} [<etx> accepts, <esc> escapes]
You could not see a clod,
```

You are now inserting text. The cursor is immediately after the comma, indicating where the next character you type goes. What if you wanted "cloud", rather than "clod"? Just as with data entry prompts, you can use ⟦bs⟧ to correct errors. Type ⟦bs⟧ ⟦bs⟧ ud , and the error should be fixed.

The Insert prompt is somewhat different from other prompts you've seen. In this activity, you can type any arbitrary text that you want to add to the workspace--the word "text" in the prompt is intended to remind you of that. You can also use ⟦bs⟧ to delete a character you just typed--"<bs> a char" is intended to remind you of that. Furthermore, you can delete an entire line, but we leave the description of that possibility to Chapter 5. The last two special key possibilities in the prompt are discussed below.

Now enter the remainder of the following small excerpt from Lewis Carroll's poem "The Walrus and the Carpenter" in *Through the Looking Glass.* Use ⟦ret⟧ to end each line. Here is the screen after you press ⟦ret⟧ on the last line:

```
Insert: Text {<bs> a char,<del> a line} [<etx> accepts, <esc> escapes]
You could not see a cloud, because ⟦ret⟧
No cloud was in the sky: ⟦ret⟧
No birds were flying overhead-- ⟦ret⟧
There were no birds to fly. ⟦ret⟧
_
```

Now you have two alternatives. First, you could conclude that this little bit of poetry was not what you wanted to insert at all. In this case, typing the ⟦esc⟧ key would discard the text you entered and you would be back in the Edit menu with an empty screen.

The second possibility is to complete the insertion by typing the ⟦etx⟧ key. (If you need to, check the inside front cover for the details on typing the ⟦etx⟧ and ⟦esc⟧ keys on your system.) Go ahead with ⟦etx⟧, and you return to the Edit menu.

Imagine you're Lewis Carroll for a moment. You're not quite happy with these four lines as they stand: they start out rather abruptly; another couple of lines at the beginning could help considerably. Move the cursor to the beginning of the first line (⟦up⟧⟦up⟧⟦up⟧⟦up⟧ should do it) and type I. The Editor doesn't know the size of the insertion you want to make, so it first opens up as much space as it can on the line where the cursor is:

```
Insert: Text {<bs> a char,<del> a line} [<etx> accepts, <esc> escapes]
                                          You could not see a cloud, because
No cloud was in the sky:
No birds were flying overhead--
There were no birds to fly.
```

You can now enter new material. One possible new line is "'The time has come,' the Walrus said,". Enter that and see how it looks. Notice that the new line goes *before* the character on which the cursor appeared ("Y"). The cursor really points *between* characters. Since that is impossible to show accurately on most computer display screens, the character immediately after the real position of the cursor is highlighted. When an insertion is made in the workspace, the characters ("beads") after the cursor are moved down to make room for the inserted material. Figure 2.3 shows some character beads on a string——before, during, and after an insertion. In each case, the location of the visible cursor is shown by an arrow.

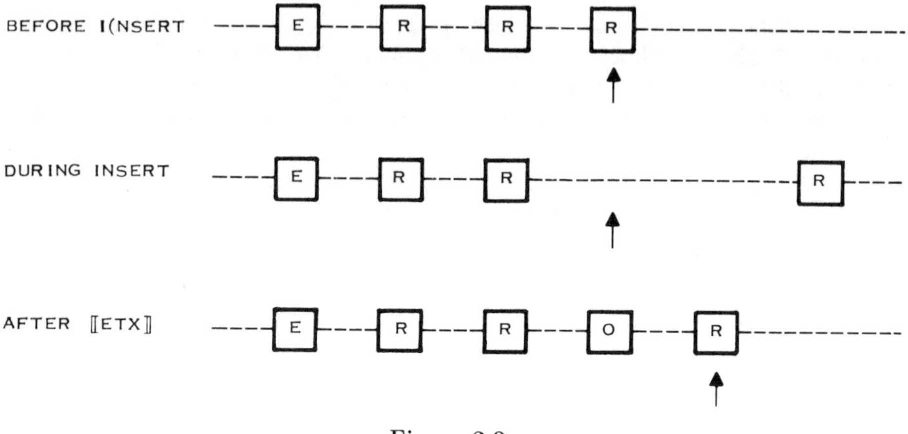

Figure 2.3

Even though you're not Lewis Carroll, it should be clear after you've entered this new line that it doesn't quite work. Here's your chance to use the ⟦esc⟧ key to discard an insertion. When you type ⟦esc⟧, the offending line vanishes, and you're back with the original four lines.

Maybe the best idea is to use the words that Lewis Carroll actually wrote. Type I to invoke I(nsert; then enter the two new lines that are shown at the top of this screen:

```
>Edit: A(djust C(opy D(el F(ind I(nsert J(ump K(ol M(argin P(age ? [ ]
The sea was wet as wet could be, ⟦ret⟧
The sands were dry as dry. ⟦ret⟧
You could not see a cloud, because
No cloud was in the sky:
No birds were flying overhead--
There were no birds to fly.
```

Now press ⟦etx⟧ to accept the insertion. The next section describes how you can save the results of your work so far.

2.4 SAVING THE WORKSPACE ON DISK

When Lewis Carroll wrote these lines in 1872, he wasn't using a personal computer and didn't have to worry about power failures or other technical catastrophes. You do. As a result, it is prudent to stop periodically during a long editing session and write a copy of your workspace from main memory onto a disk file. Usually you wouldn't do this after only six lines of input, but poetry is hard work, and it's time for a break.

To save a copy of your workspace on disk, invoke the Q(uit activity and its W(rite option. The screen should look like this:

```
>Quit:
Name of output file (<cr> to return)  ->_
```

When you enter a file name here, you can leave off the .TEXT suffix just as you did on entry to the Editor.

You need to choose a name for this file. How about "WALRUS"? Respond as follows:

```
>Quit:
Name of output file (<cr> to return)  ->WALRUS ⟦ret⟧
```

The Editor reports the results of the copy–to–disk operation, including the number of **bytes** ("characters") that were contained in your workspace. The Editor then queries you on the next step:

```
>Quit:
Writing..
Your file is 1003 bytes long.
Do you want to E(xit or R(eturn to the Editor?_
```

Type E to E(xit the Editor. We'll re–enter the Editor momentarily and copy "WALRUS" into the workspace again from disk.*

Sometimes a Q(uit W(rite operation can go wrong. For instance, you might pick a file name that had too many characters or was illegal in some other way. Chapter 5 discusses (in the "Leaving the Editor" section) the possible problems and what you can do about them.

Now that you know how to *insert* text, the next step is learning how to *delete* text.

2.5 DELETING AND MOVING TEXT

One of the pleasures of using a personal computer to write poetry is that it's easy to experiment with various arrangements of the lines of a poem. Let's try some modifications to our "Walrus and the Carpenter" excerpt. Let's exchange the second and the fourth lines. That probably won't be an improvement from an aesthetic point of view, but it will be an enlightening exercise.

Enter the Editor and respond to the "File?" question with WALRUS [ret]. After some disk activity, the immortal lines should reappear below the Edit menu.

There isn't a specific operation in the Editor for moving material from one place to another. What you do instead is delete text from one place and copy it in at the new location. A special facility called the **copy buffer** allows you to avoid retyping the text during this process.

Move the cursor to the beginning of the second line by typing [ret]. Invoke the D(elete activity by typing D. The Delete menu appears:

```
>Delete: <> <Moving commands> {<etx> to delete, <esc> to abort}
The sea was wet as wet could be,
The sands were dry as dry.
You could not see a cloud, because
No cloud was in the sky:
No birds were flying overhead--
There were no birds to fly.
```

The position of the cursor when you enter Delete is called the **anchor**. The cursor moving keys, such as [space], [bs], [ret], and the arrow keys, are operational in Delete. Whenever you cause the cursor to move away from the anchor, text disappears; if you move towards the anchor, that text reappears. This works on either side of the anchor. Figure 2.4 shows what happens.

---

* *IV.2 users, note:* You can use the Editor's W(rite activity to periodically write your workspace to disk. If you've created a workspace from scratch, you'll have to specify a file name where the workspace is to be stored; otherwise, the single W saves your workspace on disk and returns to your previous cursor position.

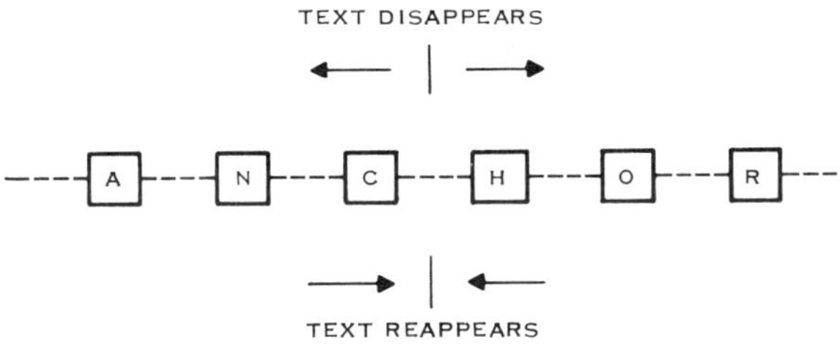

Figure 2.4

You can see this behavior in action by typing ⟦space⟧ several times. Each ⟦space⟧ causes a character to disappear. Now try a few ⟦bs⟧ keys; for each one, a character reappears until you reach the anchor. If you continue, characters start disappearing again.

Since what we really need to do is delete the entire "sands were dry" line, ⟦space⟧ back to the anchor. You could now delete the characters of this line individually with ⟦space⟧, but it is simpler to use ⟦ret⟧ to do it in one step. Go ahead and do that.

At any point during Delete, you have the option to type ⟦esc⟧ and leave the workspace just as it was when you invoked D(elete. Alternatively, you can type ⟦etx⟧ and cause the deletion to take effect. Now that the line we wanted to get rid of has disappeared, it's time to type ⟦etx⟧. The resulting screen shows that you have succeeded:

```
>Edit: A(djust C(opy D(el F(ind I(nsert J(ump K(ol M(argin P(age ? [ ]
The sea was wet as wet could be,
You could not see a cloud, because
No cloud was in the sky:
No birds were flying overhead--
There were no birds to fly.
```

There is still the matter of copying the deleted line into its new location. For that, we make use of the C(opy activity. The Editor has saved the line you deleted in its **copy buffer**. If you now move the cursor to the place you want the text to go, the C(opy activity allows you to place it there. Type ⟦down⟧ C; this screen should result:

```
>Copy: B(uffer  F(rom file  <esc>
The sea was wet as wet could be,
You could not see a cloud, because
No cloud was in the sky:
No birds were flying overhead--
There were no birds to fly.
```

The Copy menu shows two possible choices: "B" causes the contents of the buffer to be inserted where the cursor was on entrance to C(opy; "F" allows text to be copied in from another file. Type B. You did it! Now use the same approach to move the "No cloud was in the sky" line so that it becomes the second line of the poem. How does it feel to be an author? (Or at least an editor!)

Text is stored in the copy buffer when any of the following actions occur:

- When you exit the Delete menu with ⟦etx⟧, the designated text disappears and is saved in the copy buffer. You just made use of this feature.
- When you exit the Delete menu with ⟦esc⟧, the designated text is not deleted, but it is stored in the copy buffer, anyway. This facility can be used to make a duplicate copy of a section of text.
- When you exit the Insert menu with ⟦etx⟧, the inserted text is stored in the copy buffer, and can be reinserted elsewhere in the workspace.

When you ⟦esc⟧ from Insert, the copy buffer is cleared. If you're using the copy buffer to move some text, be careful not to invoke I(nsert before you have placed the text in its new position.

We think Lewis Carroll would have enjoyed the concept of the copy buffer. We can see the sequel: *Alice's Adventures in the Copy Buffer.*

If you want to do any further experimentation with your workspace, do it now. When you're ready to go on to other material, there is one more thing you need to know about the Q(uit W(rite activity. When you invoke it this time, the screen is different from last time:

```
>Quit:
$ writes to WALRUS.TEXT
Enter output file name (<cr> returns) ->_
```

This time, the Editor knows that the workspace was copied from the file WALRUS.TEXT. The Editor now gives you a shorthand way to write the workspace out to that file. If you simply type $ ⟦ret⟧, you'll save five letters of typing and the mistakes you might have made in the process. Go ahead and do that; then E(xit the Editor.

A Q(uit W(rite operation on a file replaces an existing version of that file by a new one containing the workspace. Therefore you should be sure, when you use Q(uit W(rite, that you really want to discard the previous version of the file.

In the next section we create a larger file and explore some other capabilities of the Editor that are very useful with larger files.

2.6 SHORT CUTS FOR TEXT CREATION

We are going to create text from scratch again, so enter the Editor (with E) and type ⟦ret⟧ to the "File?" question. Invoke the I(nsert activity and enter the text shown in this screen:

```
>Edit: A(djust C(opy D(el F(ind I(nsert J(ump K(ol M(argin P(age ? [ ]
99 bottles of beer on the wall, [ret]
99 bottles of beer; [ret]
If one of those bottles should happen to fall: [ret]
There'd be 98 bottles of beer on the wall. [ret]
[ret]
_
```

Be sure to do an extra [ret] on the last line to insert an empty line and an [etx] to accept the insertion.

As you probably know, there are many verses to this song——one hundred to be exact! Each one starts with one less bottle available. We are now going to test your text–entering stamina by adding the next ten or so verses to the one you've already entered.

Before you panic and/or rebel, we should tell you that it won't be as hard as it sounds. Using the conveniences of the Editor simplifies the task dramatically.

If you entered all the text above in a single invocation of the I(nsert activity, then those lines are stored away now in the copy buffer.

If you did more than one Insert or a Delete, those operations modified the copy buffer, so you need to go to the top line of the text, and type D [ret][ret][ret][ret][ret][esc] to set the copy buffer.

Type C B. The screen should look like this:

```
>Edit: A(djust C(opy D(el F(ind I(nsert J(ump K(ol M(argin P(age ? [ ]
99 bottles of beer on the wall,
99 bottles of beer;
If one of those bottles should happen to fall:
There'd be 98 bottles of beer on the wall.

99 bottles of beer on the wall,
99 bottles of beer;
If one of those bottles should happen to fall:
There'd be 98 bottles of beer on the wall.


_
```

Type the same two characters ("CB") three more times, and you have the first five verses (except for little details like the correct numbers in each).

The next step is to go back and get all the numbers right. (Don't worry, there are short cuts for this task, as well.)

The first need is to get back to the beginning of the workspace. You could type [bs] a great many times. Alternatively, you could type [up] somewhat fewer times. Either approach would be rather awkward. In the next section, we describe some additional facilities in the Editor for moving the cursor around; these are particularly applicable (and necessary) when workspaces start to get large like this one.

2.7 MORE ON CURSOR MOVEMENT

One very useful cursor movement concept is **repeat factors**. A repeat factor is a number that you type before pressing a cursor movement key. If you type "5", and then [ret], the Editor acts as if you typed [ret] five separate times.

If you don't type an explicit repeat factor before a cursor movement key, the Editor only performs the cursor movement once. If you do type a number, it won't appear on the screen: you'll just see the results when the cursor makes a large leap rather than a small step. The repeat factor only applies to the very next activity or special key, and can have any value between 1 and 9,999.

Try it! Experiment with the [up] and [down] keys, using various repeat factors. Notice that no matter what repeat factor you use, you can't move down past the end of the workspace or up past the beginning.

There is a special repeat factor, "/", which means "as many as possible." When you type "/" [ret], the Editor moves the cursor all the way to the end of the workspace. Similarly, "/" [up] moves the cursor to the beginning of the workspace.

There are more direct ways to accomplish these movements: the J(ump activity allows you to leap directly to the beginning or end of the workspace with just two keystrokes. Invoke J(ump now, by typing J. This menu should appear on the top of your screen:

```
>JUMP: B(eginning E(nd M(arker <esc>
```

The purpose of the B(eginning and E(nd options should be clear by now. Try them out if you'd like. We postpone discussion of the M(arker option until Chapter 5.

One remaining cursor movement operation needs to be introduced in this chapter: the P(age activity, which moves the cursor by a distance that is approximately the size of the display screen. P(age is very handy for browsing through the workspace.

What if you want to P(age backwards in the workspace? Look at the first (leftmost) character on the menu line of the screen. It is the Editor's **direction indicator**. The ">", which should be there now, indicates that forward motion (towards the end of the workspace) is assumed by the Editor. To change to backward motion, press the < key (left angle bracket, usually the shifted version of the comma key). You should see the direction indicator change to "<". If you invoke P(age next, the cursor leaps towards the beginning of your workspace. Try exercising P(age in both directions.

This direction indicator affects more than the P(age activity. If the direction is backwards, [space] acts like [bs], and [ret] moves to the end of the previous line, rather than the beginning of the next line. The arrow keys and [bs] are unaffected by the Editor's direction status.

You can change the Editor's direction indicator whenever you can use the cursor movement keys such as the arrows, ⟦space⟧ and ⟦bs⟧. You can also type the comma key or the minus key as a substitute for typing "<", and the period key or the plus key, instead of ">".

The period and comma are available in this context because on many keyboards, "<" is the shifted version of the comma, and ">" the shifted version of the period.

You now know many ways to move the cursor, including several equivalent approaches to each kind of cursor movement. Each user of the Editor develops a style of cursor movement in which some of these approaches are emphasized and others are virtually ignored. In the style we use in our own work, for instance, we rarely change the Editor's direction indicator, except in connection with the P(age activity.

Now back to the original problem: changing the numbers in each verse from "99" or "98" to the appropriate ones. You could, of course, use the cursor movement keys you have seen above to put the cursor on each "99", delete those two characters and insert a "98" (or a "97", or a "96"...), but there's got to be a better way!

2.8 FINDING AND REPLACING TEXT PATTERNS

One better way involves the F(ind activity on the Edit menu, which allows the Editor do the work of finding each occurence of "99". If the cursor isn't already at the beginning of the workspace, use J B to move the cursor there. Also make sure that the direction indicator is pointing forwards, ">". Then invoke F(ind, and the following prompt appears on the top line of your screen:*

```
>Find[1]: L(it <target> => _
```

You are now expected to enter a **target** text pattern; that is, the one you wish to find. The pattern (or "string") should be bounded on each side by a **delimiter** character, such as "/". Any character that isn't a letter or number is fine, as long as the same one is used on both ends of the string and does not occur within the string. Here are some valid strings with delimiters around them:

/99/
/tropical "blend"/
"ways/means"
:"Hello!":

---

* *IV.2 users, note:* The F(ind prompt has two additional items: C(ase and I(d. You can ignore these items in this chapter.

Normally, F(ind only discovers occurrences of the target that are "isolated words" (that is, character sequences surrounded on both sides by blanks or special characters). For instance, if the target is "the", the word "thereafter" is ignored by F(ind. The description of F(ind in Chapter 5 has details on finding "embedded" patterns of this sort.

Type /99/; the cursor should leap to the end of the first "99" in the current direction (forwards). Since this instance of "99" is just fine as it stands, you need to go on. Fortunately there is a short cut that saves you typing "99" again. When you search for the same string twice in a row (or more), you can type "F" to select F(ind, and then "S" (for "same"), instead of typing the string again. Even more conveniently, it turns out that repeat factors work for the F(ind activity just as they do for the simpler cursor movement operations. Remember the "[1]" in the Find menu? That was the repeat factor for that invocation of F(ind. (Recall that an absent repeat factor is assumed to be one.)

We can combine these two shorthand tricks and type 2FS to skip to the character after the third "99" in the workspace. (In that short–hand sequence, the "2" is a repeat factor, the "F" invokes F(ind, and the "S" indicates that "99" should be sought again.)

We want to change that "99" to a "98". The following sequence should do the job:

D [bs][etx]	Delete one character backwards.
I 8 [etx]	Insert an "8".

Here is the interesting part of the resulting screen:

```
>Edit: A(djust C(opy D(el F(ind I(nsert J(ump K(ol M(argin P(age ? [ ]
99 bottles of beer on the wall,
99 bottles of beer;
If one of those bottles should happen to fall:
There'd be 98 bottles of beer on the wall.

98_bottles of beer on the wall,
99¯bottles of beer;
If one of those bottles should happen to fall:
There'd be 98 bottles of beer on the wall.
```

F(ind is certainly a handy activity for this job, but it would be preferable if you didn't have to do the explicit I(nsert and D(elete operations. And you don't if you use the R(eplace activity (abbreviated "R(plc" on the menu). With this activity, you can replace occurrences of one string of characters (called the target, just as in the F(ind activity) with another (called the **substitute**). When you use R(eplace, the Editor F(inds the first occurrence of the target string you specify and replaces it by the substitute string.

Invoke R(eplace now, by typing R; the following prompt appears:*

---

* *IV.2 users, note:* The R(eplace prompt has two additional items: C(ase and I(d. You can ignore these items in this chapter.

```
>Replace[1]: L(it V(fy <targ> <sub> => _
```

Ignoring for this chapter the "L(it V(fy", this prompt is requesting that you specify the target and substitution strings. What you need to do is replace "99" by "98", so type /99/ /98/ and make sure the replacement is done.

To complete conversion of the second verse, type R /98//97/. Here is the interesting portion of the resulting workspace:

```
>Edit: A(djust C(opy D(el F(ind I(nsert J(ump K(ol M(argin P(age ? [ ]
99 bottles of beer on the wall,
99 bottles of beer;
If one of those bottles should happen to fall:
There'd be 98 bottles of beer on the wall.

98 bottles of beer on the wall,
98 bottles of beer;
If one of those bottles should happen to fall:
There'd be 97_bottles of beer on the wall.
```

It should be clear now that you could go on to do similar operations to correct the rest of the verses. Even though the use of R(eplace would simplify that job compared to doing it with I(nsert and D(elete, the task would still be somewhat tedious.

A further simplification can be achieved by using repeat factors with R(eplace. Just as with F(ind, the repeat factor is shown inside square brackets in the R(eplace menu. With R(eplace, the repeat factor determines how many instances of the target string are replaced by the substitute string. When the "infinite" repeat factor ("/") is used, the result is that *every* occurrence of the target string that is found in the current direction of cursor movement is replaced by the substitution string. (See Section 2.7 for a discussion of the infinite repeat factor.) The following sequence uses repeat factors with R(eplace to complete the corrections on the first five verses of *99 Bottles of Beer.*

2 R /99//97/	Correct the two 99's in the third verse.
R /98//96/	Correct the 98 in the third verse.
2 R /99//96/	Correct the two 99's in the fourth verse.
R /98//95/	Correct the 98 in the fourth verse.
2 R /99//95/	Correct the two 99's in the fifth verse.
R /98//94/	Correct the 98 in the fifth verse.

At last you're done!

You certainly want to save this masterpiece on disk. Go ahead and do that now, using the Q(uit W(rite activity, and choosing some appropriate file name (say, "99BOTTLES"). Remember to complete the entry of the file name with [ret]. When the writing is done, type R to R(eturn to the Editor for one more experiment with this workspace.

The exercise below is intended to eliminate any confusion you may have about the difference between the effects of Q(uit E(xit and Q(uit W(rite. Here is the sequence:

J B	Move cursor to start of workspace.
/ R .beer..Coke.	Replace *all* "beer" by "Coke".
Q E	Q(uit E(xit.*
E	Re–enter the Editor and get
99BOTTLES [ret]	the file 99BOTTLES.TEXT. If you chose a different name in the Q(uit W(rite, above, use that name.

The screen you see in the Editor should have lots of "beer" and no "Coke" at all! The conclusion: *The work you do with a workspace in the Editor is not saved on disk, and is lost forever, if you use Q(uit E(xit to leave the Editor.*

In the next section we use the creation of another small workspace to show you how the Editor helps you in entering text where the indentation structure is important (as in outlines, for example). To prepare for that exercise, leave the Editor now (via Q(uit E(xit, Q E).

2.9 ENTERING OUTLINE–STRUCTURED TEXT

The Editor is quite handy for working with text in which the indentation of a line shows its position in a structure. One example of such text is an outline. Another potential example is a computer program.

We are indebted to *The Official Preppy Handbook* for an example of an outline to work with in this and subsequent sections. The word "preppy" was made famous by Erich Segal's best–selling novel, *Love Story.* The least interesting definition of "preppy" is a young man in college who had his high school training in a private "prep school." Selections from the *Handbook's* Table of Contents are shown below:

---

* *IV.2 users, note:* You should press Q E Y for Q(uit, E(xit, Y(es because the Editor asks you to verify that you want to exit even though you have made changes to your workspace. Because of this change, this exercise is less important than it is for Version IV.1, since the possibility for careless error is much reduced.

THE RIGHTS OF BIRTHRIGHT: The Years at Home.
  Prep on All Fours: The Proper Pet.
  Regulating the Cash Flow: Well–to–Dos and Don'ts.
THE ROOT OF ALL PREP: The Years at School.
  Preparing to Prep: Picking the School for You.
    Boarding vs. Day
    Single–Sex vs. Coed
  Breaking the Rules: The Importance
    of Getting Kicked Out.

Enter the Editor with an empty workspace (by typing E ⟦ret⟧ from the Command menu). Then invoke I(nsert and type in the first line of the table of contents above. On the second line, type ⟦space⟧ twice at the beginning. When you finish that line and type ⟦ret⟧, notice that the Editor places the cursor under the "P" of the previous line.

This behavior is called **automatic indentation**. When you type spaces at the beginning of a new line, the Editor assumes that means you are establishing a new indentation level at the first non–space character you type. On your next line, the Editor automatically indents the cursor to that new indentation level.

After you enter the third line, the Editor initially aligns the cursor with the beginning of the previous line. The same principle you used above allows you to change the indentation in the other direction. If you type ⟦bs⟧ twice and then the "THE ROOT OF ALL PREP" line, another new indentation position is established. Go on in this way to do the entire selection. When you're done, type ⟦etx⟧ to confirm the insertion.

Remember, if you want to change the indentation on a line, you must type ⟦space⟧ or ⟦bs⟧ immediately after terminating the previous line with ⟦ret⟧.

This concludes our introduction to the aspects of the Editor that are useful for working with programs and with ordinary text like memos and books. If you are only interested in using the Editor to develop programs, you may skip the rest of this chapter and go right to Chapter 3. You may want to come back and read the rest of this chapter at some point. The last section "Printing Text Files," is likely to be of interest to you even if you use the p–System solely for programming.

2.10 PARAGRAPH–ORIENTED TEXT

So far we have dealt with text that has lines as a natural structural unit. We've seen poems, song lyrics and outlines. There are many kinds of text, of course, where paragraphs are the natural unit of structure, and line boundaries are simply determined by the left and right margins that have been established. In this section we introduce you to the Editor activities which are useful for manipulation of text that is paragraph–oriented.

You have just entered portions of a Table of Contents into your workspace. Imagine now that each of those lines is a sentence in a paragraph and that you need to get them to look more like a paragraph than a set of independent lines. As an exercise, we're going to go ahead and fill this imagined need.

There are two ways to proceed: the easy way (using facilities built into the Editor for just this kind of task) and the hard way (using Editor facilities that you already know about). We spend a little time on the hard way, first. (If you haven't already typed ⟦etx⟧ to accept the insertion of the Table of Contents, do so at this point.)

The principal foundation of this more difficult approach is that two lines can be merged into one by deleting the invisible line separator that divides them. You can delete that character by moving the cursor to the end of a line (right after the last character), invoking D(elete, pressing ⟦space⟧ (to move one character), and closing with ⟦etx⟧. If you apply this process at the end of the first line of the outline, you should get this result:

```
>Edit: A(djust C(opy D(el F(ind I(nsert J(ump K(ol M(argin P(age ? [ ]
THE RIGHTS OF BIRTHRIGHT: The Years at Home.Prep on All Fours: The Proper Pet.
  Regulating the Cash Flow: Well-to-Dos and Don'ts.
THE ROOT OF ALL PREP: The Years at School.
  Preparing to Prep: Picking the School for You.
    Boarding vs. Day.
    Single-Sex vs. Coed.
  Breaking the Rules: The Importance
    of Getting Kicked Out.
```

Since there is ordinarily some space between sentences, you need to insert a space character at the position of the cursor to complete the transformation. (Type I ⟦space⟧ ⟦etx⟧.) If you apply this same process to the next pair of lines, the following display results:

```
>Edit: A(djust C(opy D(el F(ind I(nsert J(ump K(ol M(argin P(age ? [ ]
THE RIGHTS OF BIRTHRIGHT: The Years at Home. Prep on All Fours: The Proper Pet.
  Regulating the Cash Flow: Well-to-Dos and Don'ts. THE ROOT OF ALL PREP: The Ye!
  Preparing to Prep: Picking the School for You.
    Boarding vs. Day.
    Single-Sex vs. Coed.
  Breaking the Rules: The Importance
    of Getting Kicked Out.
```

You probably have a "!" on the right–hand margin of your screen, just like that shown above. When the Editor cannot display a line completely, it substitutes a "!" for the last character that it can show (in our case the 80th). The location of the "!" on your screen depends on what line width your display can handle.

The entire line (without the "!") is still in the workspace. What we need to do now is break this over–sized line by inserting a line separator (just as we deleted one earlier). Move the cursor right to the "T" in "The". Typing 22 ⟦right⟧ should do it. Then type I ⟦ret⟧⟦etx⟧ to complete the first few lines of your painful transformation of the line–oriented workspace to a paragraph orientation:

```
>Edit: A(djust C(opy D(el F(ind I(nsert J(ump K(ol M(argin P(age ? [ ]
THE RIGHTS OF BIRTHRIGHT: The Years at Home. Prep on All Fours: The Proper Pet.
  Regulating the Cash Flow: Well-to-Dos and Don'ts. THE ROOT OF ALL PREP:
  The Years at School.
  Preparing to Prep: Picking the School for You.
    Boarding vs. Day.
    Single-Sex vs. Coed.
  Breaking the Rules: The Importance
    of Getting Kicked Out.
```

Now, for the easy method! We need to change the Editor to a different mode of operation: a mode designed specifically for paragraph–oriented text. We deal with this mode change in the next section.

2.11 CHANGING EDITOR MODES

Type S E to invoke S(et E(nvironment. This activity allows you to change certain aspects of the Editor's behavior and get at useful information. You should see a display like the one that follows.

```
>Environment: {options} <spacebar> to leave
     A(uto indent   True
     F(illing       False
     L(eft margin   1
     R(ight margin  80
     P(ara margin   6
     C(ommand ch    ^
     S(et tabstops
     T(oken def     True

     2301 bytes used, 16020 available.

     Patterns:


Editing: unnamed
Created January 2, 1985; last updated January 2, 1985 (revision 0).
Editor Version [ ].
```

In this screen the first group of lines (ending with "T(oken def") deals with options that affect the Editor's operation in various ways. The values of these options can be modified. You choose the option you want to change by typing the first letter of its name. You can return to the Edit menu by typing ⟦space⟧.

The rest of the display provides information on the status of the Editor and the current workspace. For instance, it shows the name of the file from which this workspace was copied and how many characters (or "bytes") of information are in the workspace.

We deal with all these options and status values eventually in this book. For now, we are concerned about only two of the options: "A(uto indent" and "F(illing". These options determine whether the Editor is better suited to line–oriented text entry or to paragraph–oriented entry.

A(uto indent controls the automatic indentation that you saw in the previous section. If A(uto indent is True, the placement of the cursor at the beginning of a new line occurs as you saw it earlier. If A(uto indent is false, the cursor simply starts at the left margin.

F(illing determines whether the Editor treats text as paragraph–oriented or line–oriented. You've already seen the Editor's behavior when F(illing is False. When F(illing is True, the Editor attempts to keep text within the left and right margins you've established. It breaks lines wherever necessary (between words) to maintain the margins.

When A(uto indent is False, and F(illing is True, the Editor makes handling of paragraph–oriented text very simple. To reach this blissful state, type A; the previous setting of A(uto indent is erased, and the Editor awaits the new value. All you need to type is the first letter: F, and the Editor does the rest. Typing F T sets F(illing to True in a similar fashion.

We go back now to the Edit menu to try the easy way of turning the outline into a respectable looking paragraph. Before you leave the Environment menu, take note of the values of the L(eft margin, R(ight margin, and P(ara margin options. They indicate that text is to be kept between columns 1 and 80, and that the first line of a new paragraph is to start on column 6. These values determine the appearance of the text when you return to the Edit menu. Do so now, by typing ⟦space⟧.

2.12 WORKING WITH PARAGRAPH–ORIENTED TEXT

Why hasn't there been any change in the appearance of your workspace? The answer is that the Editor only applies the margin restrictions automatically when new text is being entered. To apply the margins to existing text in your workspace, you have to invoke the M(argin activity. Do that now by typing M; the screen should go blank for a few moments; then the following display should appear:

```
>Edit: A(djust C(opy D(el F(ind I(nsert J(ump K(ol M(argin P(age ? [ ]
     THE RIGHTS OF BIRTHRIGHT: The Years at Home.  Prep on All Fours: The
Proper Pet. Regulating the Cash Flow: Well- to-Dos and Don'ts. THE ROOT OF ALL
PREP: The Years at School. Preparing to Prep: Picking the School for You.
Boarding vs. Day. Single-Sex vs. Coed. Breaking the Rules: The Importance of
Getting Kicked Out.
```

As you can see, the outline has become a paragraph. Now let's play with the values of the margin options and see what effects they have. Return to the Environment menu with S E. Just as before, you select an option for modification by typing the first letter of its name. Try R. The Editor awaits your entry of a new value for the R(ight margin option. For this option, and the other numeric options, you can enter a value as a simple integer (with four digits or fewer), followed by ⟦ret⟧. Try 65 ⟦ret⟧. Leave the other values as they are and return to the Edit menu with ⟦space⟧.

Once again you need to invoke M(argin to apply the new margin values to your workspace. When you do so, this screen results:

```
>Edit: A(djust C(opy D(el F(ind I(nsert J(ump K(ol M(argin P(age ? [ ]
     THE RIGHTS OF BIRTHRIGHT: The Years at Home.Prep on All
Fours: The Proper Pet. Regulating the Cash Flow: Well-to- Dos
and Don'ts. THE ROOT OF ALL PREP: The Years at School.
Preparing to Prep: Picking the School for You. Boarding vs.
Day. Single-Sex vs. Coed. Breaking the Rules: The Importance of
Getting Kicked Out.
```

When you insert text, the Editor automatically applies the current margins. As you enter words, the Editor checks each one to see if it goes past the right margin. If so, the entire word is moved down to the next line. You can continue typing without worrying about when to press ⟦ret⟧. You can see this facility in action by using I(nsert to add a few sentences to the outline/paragraph in your workspace. (You may need to J(ump E(nd, first.) Be sure to close the insertion with ⟦etx⟧.

When you do an I(nsert within a paragraph, the Editor automatically reformats the remainder of the paragraph after you close the insertion. This automatic reformatting does not occur, however, when D(elete is used within a paragraph.

The Editor uses a very simplified notion of "word" when it makes decisions about where to break lines during automatic margin control. It takes a word to be a group of one or more letters bounded on each side by a space or a hyphen ("–"). Therefore "DIRECTORY.TEXT" would be treated as one word, and moved in its entirety to the next line if the right margin were threatened. On the other hand, "p–System" would be considered two words, and broken at the hyphen if necessary.

Paragraphs can be separated by one or more blank lines. When you're I(nserting, and you signal a paragraph break by typing ⟦ret⟧ twice, the Editor starts the cursor on the new line at the P(ara margin. When you invoke the M(argin command, it only modifies the paragraph that contains the cursor. No matter where the cursor is pointing in the paragraph, M(argin reformats the entire paragraph.

Experiment with the handling of paragraph boundaries by inserting a few strategically placed ⟦ret⟧s to make several paragraphs. Also try adding some new paragraphs, if you like. You'll see how the process works.

You can also prove to yourself that different margin restrictions can be applied to different paragraphs. For each of two paragraphs you've entered, follow these steps:

- Invoke S(et E(nvironment and change some or all of the margin options (L(eft, R(ight, or P(ara).
- Move the cursor to the paragraph you'd like reformatted with those margins, and type M for M(argin.

Here is one way your workspace could end up:

```
     THE RIGHTS OF BIRTHRIGHT: The Years at Home.Prep on All Fours:
The Proper Pet. Regulating the Cash Flow:

   Well-to- Dos and Don'ts. THE ROOT OF ALL PREP: The Years at
     School. Preparing to Prep: Picking the School for You.

         Boarding vs. Day. Single-Sex vs. Coed. Breaking the
         Rules: The Importance of Getting Kicked Out.
```

For the three paragraphs shown on the previous page, the margin settings were:

Paragraph Number	Left Margin	Right Margin	Paragraph Margin
1	1	70	6
2	6	65	4
3	10	65	10

Table 3.1

Notice that a P(aragraph margin smaller than the L(eft margin setting can be used to create "bulleted" paragraphs.

The Editor keeps no record within the workspace of the margin settings that you have applied to a particular paragraph. Therefore, you must be careful to use M(argin (or do an I(nsertion!) within a paragraph only when the current margin settings are appropriate for that paragraph. Fortunately, even if you forget this warning occasionally, it is not hard to recover. (Just invoke S(et E(nvironment, adjust the margin settings, and use M(argin to reformat the paragraph.)

Just as you can have paragraphs with different margin settings in a single workspace, you can also have portions that are line–oriented rather than paragraph–oriented. One application of this capability is the inclusion of tables like Table 3.1. The Editor includes specific support for tables of this sort, including settable tab stops and the K(olumn activity. We aren't able to go into these facilities in this introductory chapter, but you may want to look over the relevant sections of Chapter 5.

You must be very careful when you work with a mixture of line–oriented and paragraph–oriented material. If you do an I(nsert or M(argin in a line–oriented section when F(illing is True, the filling operation destroys the line structure and is likely to cause you much grief. For example, consider the screen below, which shows the text from Table 3.1 after an accidental M(argin operation.

```
>Edit: A(djust C(opy D(el F(ind I(nsert J(ump K(ol M(argin P(age ? [ ]
Paragraph Left Right Paragraph Number Margin Margin Margin 1 1
70 6 2 6 65 4 3 10 65 10
```

We recommend that you set F(illing to False when you are working with line–oriented material. That will keep the Editor from doing automatic filling during or after an I(nsertion. Furthermore, if you accidentally type "M" and invoke M(argin, the Editor will disallow the operation.

We are now done with this Table of Contents workspace. Unless you want to save it for some perverse reason, leave the Editor now with Q(uit E(xit. (If you want to save the workspace, do so, and then leave the Editor.)

Now you have all the basic tools for doing simple text processing using the UCSD p–System. The next section provides some suggestions about one particular kind of text processing: producing memorandums.

2.13 PRODUCING MEMOS

We use the p–System ourselves for much of our professional work. When we write programs, we certainly use the p–System for that. But we also write design documents, as well as technical and administrative memos, using the facilities you've learned about in this chapter and the previous one. The purpose of this section is to pass on to you some approaches we've found for simplifying this use of the p–System.

If you write many memos, it becomes tedious to type, over and over, the heading portions that are shared by all memos. There is also the issue of setting up the Editor's environment (including margins, paragraph– vs. line–orientation, and so on).

Our solution to this problem is to prepare a "starter" file (which we call START.TEXT) in which all this work has been done. We'll show you in a moment how to build one of these files.

Here is how you can use START.TEXT, once you have built it. When you start a new memo, your first step is to invoke the Editor and request that the START.TEXT file be copied into the workspace. You can then modify that text appropriately for the specific memo you're preparing, and enter the memo, itself. Using the Q(uit W(rite activity, you can then write the workspace out to disk, with a file name specific to that memo.

Enter the Editor now with an empty workspace. (If you forgot to leave the Editor at the end of the previous section, do that first, with Q E.) You're going to build a START.TEXT file using the conventions we have found convenient for our memos. Later you can modify it, if you like, to suit your style.

The first job is to set up the Editor environment. We'll leave the Editor in line–oriented (rather than paragraph–oriented) mode, so that entry of the heading lines is easy. Just before you enter the text of a particular memo, you will switch to paragraph orientation.

To choose unindented paragraphs and a right margin of 65, invoke S(et E(nvironment and type R 65 ⟦ret⟧ P 1 ⟦ret⟧. Then return to the Edit menu with a ⟦space⟧.

Since the Editor environment is saved on disk along with the workspace when you Q(uit W(rite, setting these options now will save you some time on each memo.

Now I(nsert the heading lines shown in the screen below. The lines should be preceded by several ⟦ret⟧s and separated from each other by a blank line. The contents of your workspace after you close the I(nsertion with ⟦etx⟧ are shown.

```
⟦ret⟧
⟦ret⟧
MEMORANDUM⟦ret⟧
⟦ret⟧
⟦ret⟧
⟦ret⟧
To: ⟦ret⟧
⟦ret⟧
From:               Mark Overgaard and Stan Stringfellow ⟦ret⟧
⟦ret⟧
Date: ⟦ret⟧
⟦ret⟧
Subject: ⟦ret⟧
_
```

Now you may see why we left the Editor in line–oriented mode. If the heading lines were treated as a single paragraph, the use of I(nsert to enter the addressee would result in this screen:

```
MEMORANDUM


To: Addressee From: Mark Overgaard and Stan Stringfellow Date: Subject:
```

Given the blank lines between heading items, the actual effect of such an insertion would simply be the compression of the first heading line, but you don't want that either. Naturally you would put your name after "From:" if you were preparing a START.TEXT file for yourself.

The "MEMORANDUM" line would certainly look much better if the word were centered. There is an easy way to center a line in the Editor, but it uses an activity that hasn't been introduced yet: A(djust. We leave a full description of A(djust to Chapter 5.

All you need to know right now is that to center a line, you should move the cursor so that it's somewhere in the line. Then type the sequence A C ⟦etx⟧, which invokes A(djust, causes the C(entering of the line, and accepts the adjustment. The completed START.TEXT workspace is shown below.

```
                              MEMORANDUM


To:

From:               Mark Overgaard and Stan Stringfellow

Date:

Subject:
```

All that remains is to save the workspace on disk. Type Q W START ⟦ret⟧ to do that. Then E(xit the Editor.

Now we use the START.TEXT that you've created to send a small memo from us to you. Unfortunately, you're going to have to do the entering of this memo!

Enter the Editor and copy the file START into the workspace. (E START ⟦ret⟧ should do the job.) Move the cursor so that it is immediately after the "To:". Then follow this sequence of Editor input:

I ⟦tab⟧⟦tab⟧	Enter I(nsert and move to Addressee position.
Gentle Reader ⟦etx⟧	Memo is addressed to YOU!
2 ⟦ret⟧ 5 ⟦space⟧	Prepare to enter Date,
I ⟦tab⟧⟦tab⟧	
Jan. 2, 1985 ⟦etx⟧	and then do it.
2 ⟦ret⟧ 8 ⟦space⟧	Prepare to enter Subject,
I ⟦tab⟧	
Best Wishes ⟦etx⟧	and do it!
J E	Prepare to enter the memo, itself.

Before you enter the memo, type SE AF FT ⟦space⟧ to use S(et E(nvironment to establish paragraph–oriented mode. I(nsert the memo as shown below (with an initial ⟦ret⟧ to separate the text of the memo from the heading).

```
                         MEMORANDUM


To:               Gentle Reader

From:             Mark Overgaard and Stan Stringfellow

Date:             Jan. 2, 1985

Subject:          Best Wishes

We hope this is only the first of many memos you prepare with the
UCSD p-System.
```

The last step is to copy the memo from the workspace out to disk. Invoke Q(uit W(rite. Don't yield to the temptation to enter "$" ⟦ret⟧ in response to the prompt. You don't want to modify the starter file. Instead, respond with BESTWISHES ⟦ret⟧; then E(xit. You've written your first p–System memo!

2.14 PRINTING TEXT FILES

Now that you know how to compose memos and letters, the remaining question is: "How can you print them?" There are several ways to print text files in the p–System. They range from the simple use of the T(ransfer activity in the Filer to the use of a sophisticated text formatter program like the one used to produce the master copies of this book.

In between these two extremes is a very convenient tool for routine printing: the Print utility.*

This utility can print your text files, and in the process, do useful things like inserting page breaks and putting a heading on each page. In addition, Print allows you to control other aspects of the printing process, including the spacing between lines (that is, double spacing or single spacing) and the number of lines printed on each page.

Let's try out Print on the memo you wrote in the previous section. If Print is on your system disk, then typing X PRINT ⟦ret⟧ should suffice to invoke it. If that doesn't work, scout around on your p–System disks to find PRINT.CODE; you may want to T(ransfer it to your system disk, since you'll probably be using it often. If you can't find the program, you may have a version of the p–System that was produced before Print was included.

Print produces a full screen menu that looks like this:

```
Print [ ]: Select an option (type "?" for help):

        I(nput-->
        O(utput--> PRINTER:
        G(o.  Print the input file on the output.
        A(dvance.  Skip to the next page on the output.
        M(ake script file for setting current parameters.
        Q(uit.  Leave this program.

No      D(ouble-space the lines?
No      N(umber the lines?
No      S(top before each page for single sheet loading?
Yes     U(se ASCII formfeed characters between pages?

1       F(irst page number
1       T(op Margin size in lines
3       B(ottom Margin size in lines
66      P(age size in lines (total: includes margins and heading)

\       E(scape sequence start-character
.       C(ommand line start-character

        H(eader--> Page \page.  File is "\file".  Printed on \date.
```

Even though the activities of this menu are listed on different lines, the approach to using it is similar to the one–line menus used in other parts of the p–System. There are two kinds of activities in this menu. One kind allows you to determine the setting of an option that guides subsequent print operations. (These are similar to the S(et E(nvironment options.) The

---

* *IV.0 users, note:* The Print utility is not offered with Version IV.0 (or even some early releases of Version IV.1). In these systems, the only simple and standard means for printing text files is the Filer's T(ransfer activity.

other kind causes an immediate action. For instance, you could use an option activity (I(nput, in fact) to choose a file to print, and an action activity (G(o) to start the printing.

Let's try I(nput. When you invoke it, directions appear on the top line of the screen and the cursor is placed after "I(nput-->" to await your entry of the name of a file to print. Enter the response: BESTWISHES ⟦ret⟧.

To print BESTWISHES, you need only select G(o. Before you do, however, make sure that you have paper in your printer and that it is ready to print. When the printer is ready, invoke G(o, and watch the printing of your first p–System memo. As the top line of the screen indicates, you can temporarily suspend the printing by typing ⟦space⟧, and cancel it by typing "Q". Try ⟦space⟧ if you like. The resulting prompt should be self–explanatory.

The printed version of BESTWISHES looks just like it did in the Editor's workspace, except that there is a header line at the top of the page that contains a page number, the input file name, and the current date. Print allows you to design your own header line. We discuss that below.

After the memo is printed, the paper should advance to the end of the page. If it doesn't do that, try the following recovery procedure:

> It may be that your printer doesn't respond to the standard form feed character that Print uses to signal the end of a page. You can tell Print not to use the form feed character by typing U N. Do that, and try printing BESTWISHES again. (You may need to advance the paper manually to the top of the next page.) If the new setting of the U(se form feed option results in success, be sure to establish that setting whenever you print a file in the future.

If you have to load each sheet of paper into your printer individually, then there's at least one more option that you need to change from its initial setting:

- Use S Y to indicate to Print that you need a chance to load paper before each page.
- Also, you may have to position the printing mechanism an inch or so into the page in order to make contact with the pinch rollers. If so, you'll want to modify your P(age size option. Assuming that your printer puts six lines on an inch of paper, the lost inch at the top of the page implies that your P(age size should be 60 lines for an 11–inch page, rather than 66 lines. Change that option if necessary.

Figure 2.5 shows how the layout of pages produced by Print is controlled by the P(age size, T(op margin, and B(ottom margin options. Try printing BESTWISHES with several different settings of these options to see what you prefer. You can even set P(age size ridiculously small (say

10 lines), to see what effect that has. Remember that each time you press "G" for G(o, the printing of the I(nput file is guided by the option settings at that time.*

```
----------------------------
-------- T(OP MARGIN -------
----------------------------
THIS IS THE HEADING LINE.
---------BLANK LINE---------
THIS IS THE FIRST LINE OF TEXT
ON THE PAGE. IT IS FOLLOWED
BY ADDITIONAL LINES UNTIL THERE
ARE ONLY B(OTTOM MARGIN LINES
LEFT ON THE PAGE. THESE LINES
ARE LEFT BLANK, AND PRINTING
BEGINS ON THE FOLLOWING PAGE.
----------------------------
----------------------------
------ B(OTTOM MARGIN -----
----------------------------
```

Figure 2.5

If the standard heading line that you've seen on the printouts so far is not to your taste, you can change it by setting the H(eader option. For instance, typing "H", followed by ⟦ret⟧, would erase the header altogether (though two lines on the page would still be used, just as always).

If you want a heading line, but don't like the specific arrangement of the standard line, you can rearrange it. First you need to know something about **escape sequences**.

In any line processed by Print, the **escape sequence flag character** has a special meaning. If the word after the flag is one of the standard Print escape sequences, then some other string is substituted for the escape sequence when that line is printed. For instance, if the escape sequence "\date" is found, the current p–System date replaces it in the printed version. Similarly, "\page" is replaced by the current page number, and "\file" by the name of the file being printed.

---

* *IV.2 users, note:* Print has an additional menu item, L(eft margin, that you can use to shift printing right on the page. Try experimenting with this possibility, as well.

This escape sequence facility is very useful in the heading line. You could, for example, set the heading line to "Best Wishes--Page \page" to get heading lines of the form: "Best Wishes--Page 1" and "Best Wishes--Page 2".

Escape sequences can also be useful within a memo, as well. Remember the START.TEXT file that you created above to serve as the starting point for writing memos? You could modify the "Date:" line in that file to have "\date" instead of any particular date. Then whenever you printed a memo based on START.TEXT, the printed version would contain the current date without explicit effort on your part.

Print has several more capabilities that we don't detail here. For instance, you can have **command lines** inside the file being printed. These can change the header line on the fly, cause an explicit page break, or perform other useful functions. It is also possible, with the M(ake script activity, to record the non-standard option settings that you routinely use in a **script file**. When you use this script file to invoke Print, those option settings are automatically established. This facility could save you considerable inconvenience. Chapter 9 directs you to further reading on these and other aspects of the Print utility.

3

DEVELOPING PROGRAMS

3.1 INTRODUCTION

In Chapter 2, we showed you how to edit text using the p–System. We didn't try to guide you on the content of the memos or other material you might be planning to write. Similarly, in this chapter, we get you started in p–System program development, but have little to say about the content of those programs or about the languages in which they are written.

Much of what you need to know to develop programs on a particular computer system has nothing to do with the composition of programs, or with the details of a computer language. You need to know how to enter the program into the computer, and how to "compile" it (or translate it from human terms to machine terms) and then how to run it after this translation has been done. Many programming texts ignore these logistic details because they are intended to be used in various programming environments that may be very different from each other. Unfortunately, it is often these practical matters that are most troublesome for beginners. That's where we come in. This chapter, along with the previous chapters on editing text and using existing programs, is intended to get you to the point where you are comfortable with the logistic aspects of developing p–System programs. We leave the descriptions of the content and structure of programs to other books.

If you are already a relatively experienced programmer in a language supported by the p–System, a quick pass through this chapter, supplemented by appropriate language reference manuals, should allow you to do productive program development with the p–System.

If you don't yet know how to program, you will need a tutorial on programming in the language of your choice. Several such tutorials are listed in Chapter 9. These books can take you on from where this chapter leaves off.

Even though we're not trying to tutor you on the details of any particular language, we do need to provide you with some basic background on what computer languages are and why they are necessary. For instance, why can't we communicate with computers in ordinary English (or Papuan or Burmese)?

3.2 COMPUTER LANGUAGES

There are many areas where the capabilities of computers are superior to the corresponding abilities of humans. One example is the speed with which computers can do arithmetic. Another example is their unwavering attention to detail.

There are also many areas where human proficiencies far surpass the current capabilities of computers. One of these areas is the understanding of "natural" languages (such as English or Japanese). There are all sorts of subtleties and potential ambiguities that humans can easily untangle, but which would totally befuddle a computer. Consider, for instance, the sentence: "Time flies like a bullet."

There are many possible interpretations of this sentence. For instance, if "time" is an adjective, "flies" a noun, and "like" a verb, this sentence would be a description of the preferences of a particular variety of flies. On the other hand, it could be a prescription for how to do timing measurements on flies: "You time flies just like you time a bullet, of course!"

People can use common sense and contextual clues to sort out which of several possible meanings for a sentence is intended. Computers are short on common sense.

Communication with computers, therefore, occurs in languages specifically designed for that purpose. These languages are very strict in their definitions of the meanings of words and sentences. They are also close enough to natural languages (using words like "begin" and "if") that they are quite comprehensible to humans.

Even though these computer languages are extremely restricted compared to natural languages, they are still much more complicated than the fundamental built–in capabilities of typical small computers. Therefore, it is usually necessary to have a translation process that converts the language text that is suitable for human consumption into a sequence of much more primitive operations that a computer can do directly. This translation process is called **compilation**, and the translator is a program called a **compiler**. During the translation process, the compiler also checks that the program obeys the rules that govern the structure of programs in the language (called its **syntax**).

Next, we list the steps involved in developing and running a program in one of these languages. After that, Figure 3.1 restates this process (with a slightly different viewpoint) in diagram form.

- Use the Editor to create the text representation of the program. This representation (which is too complicated to be executed directly by the computer) is called the **source text**, and is stored in the **text files** that you read about in Chapters 1 and 2.
- Use a compiler to translate the source text to **object code** that can be executed by the computer. This object code is stored in **code files** like those you used in Chapter 1. If errors of syntax are found during the compilation, return to the Editor to fix them in the source text and try the compilation again.
- Run the program object code and test whether it performs as intended. If not, return to the Editor to change the source text of the program and start another cycle of compilation and testing.
- After the program has successfully passed your tests, save it away for later use.

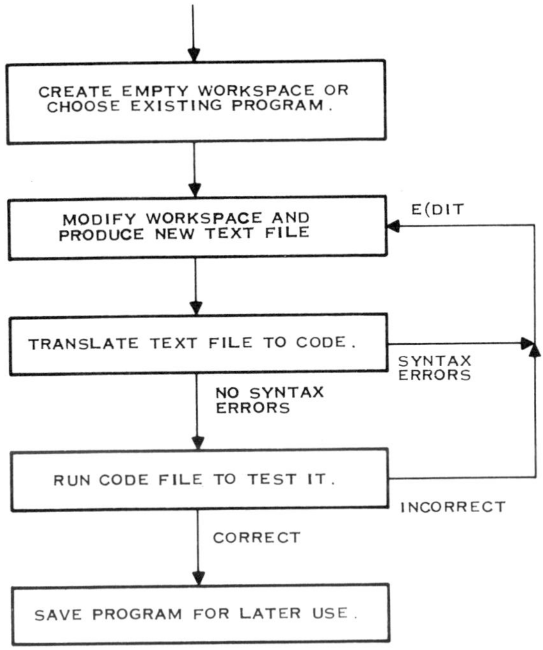

Figure 3.1

3.3 LANGUAGES SUPPORTED BY THE p–SYSTEM

The three principal languages supported by the p–System are UCSD Pascal, FORTRAN, and BASIC. Your choice of language for a particular program will be determined by your needs and experience.

UCSD Pascal is a variant of the language Pascal, which was first defined in 1968 by Swiss computer scientist Niklaus Wirth. Pascal is the most modern of the three languages. Originally designed for teaching programming, it is now probably the dominant language for introductory computer science courses (at least at the University level). In addition, Pascal is very widely used in industrial and business applications, particularly on microcomputers.

UCSD Pascal was originally the only language supported by the p–System. It is still the case that all major high level p–System components (such as the editors and file handler) are implemented in UCSD Pascal. It is generally the language of choice for new programs written specifically for the p–System environment.

FORTRAN is a mature language (first used in 1953) which has achieved dominance in the area of scientific applications of computers. The p–System implementation of FORTRAN is a subset of FORTRAN–77 (which is named after the year in which the definition was finalized). The main attraction of FORTRAN is the large number of programs that already exist, particularly in the area of numerical analysis. This momentum means that most new scientific programs are also written in FORTRAN. If you want to apply computers to scientific or engineering pursuits, you should probably be familiar with FORTRAN.

Like Pascal, BASIC was also originally designed for beginning programmers. (The name is an acronym for "Beginner's All–purpose Symbolic Instruction Code.") BASIC is very widely used (particularly on small computers). In most implementations of BASIC, the style of use is more interactive and immediate than the scenario described above: the computer directly "interprets" the source of your BASIC program without the complicating compilation step.

However, the BASIC in the p–System is implemented by a compiler, just as UCSD Pascal and FORTRAN–77 are. Because of this, p–System BASIC is probably no more suitable for beginner use than UCSD Pascal, and may be less so. The principal benefit of p–System BASIC is the ability to import existing BASIC programs from other software environments into the p–System environment.

In that p–System BASIC is not particularly suitable for beginners, we don't deal with it explicitly in this book. The rest of this chapter provides details for using UCSD Pascal and FORTRAN–77 in the p–System. Two separate sections cover the details of setting up and then using each of these two languages.

Before you can start using either language, however, you need to check that there's enough room on your system disk to store the programs you'll be working on. You need an area of at least 20 blocks to do the programs in this chapter. If you go on to write larger programs later, with the approach used in this chapter, you may need additional space.

Invoke the Filer now, and see what your situation is in this regard. Type F L * [ret]. The summary line of the resulting directory listing tells you the size of the largest area on your system disk. If that number is 15 or greater, you should be all right. If that number is smaller than 15, or if you go on later to work on larger programs, you may need to free up some space.

You may have added several files to your system disk in the exercises of the previous chapters (with names like DIRECTORY.TEXT, WALRUS.TEXT, 99BOTTLES.TEXT, and so on). If those files are taking up needed space on your system volume, use the R(emove activity to get rid of some or all of them.

If that effort doesn't yield sufficient space, you may be able to move some files off your system volume. In Chapter 4, in a section called "System

Files," we describe the files that are typically on a system disk and that must stay there, and those files you can move to other volumes.

As soon as you have enough space available, go on to the next section (if you'll be using UCSD Pascal), or to the section after that (if you'll be using FORTRAN).

3.4 USING PASCAL IN THE p–SYSTEM

Before you can use UCSD Pascal, you should have the Pascal compiler on an on–line volume with the name SYSTEM.COMPILER. The first part of this section helps you get your p–System set up to meet that requirement. After this step is completed, you can go on to do some simple Pascal programming.

Setting Up for Pascal

Assuming you have acquired the Pascal compiler, the simplest situation is if it is already on your system disk with the name SYSTEM.COMPILER. This is probably true, for instance, if all your p–System software is on a single disk. If so, skip this subsection and go right on to do your first Pascal program.

Alternatively, your Pascal compiler may have been delivered on a separate disk (probably labelled "Pascal" or something similar). Locate that disk now.

For simplicity of configuration steps below, we assume that your personal computer has at least two disk drives and that you can use one of them to hold the disk containing the Pascal compiler. (If you have only one drive and don't have the compiler already on your system disk, you should put it there. We can't give you step–by–step directions for doing that, however. The remainder of this subsection assumes you have two drives.)

First, make sure you have made a back up copy of your Pascal disk (using the same procedures you used earlier to back up your system disk). After setting the master copy of the Pascal disk aside, mount the second copy in a disk drive.

Next, check the directory of your Pascal disk to see what the compiler is called. If it is not called SYSTEM.COMPILER, invoke the C(hange activity of the Filer to change the name. If the original name is (say) PASCAL.CODE on volume PASCAL:, the following interaction with C(hange should do the trick:

```
Change what file ? PASCAL:PASCAL.CODE [ret]
Change to what ? SYSTEM.COMPILER [ret]
PASCAL:PASCAL.CODE  --> SYSTEM.COMPILER
```

One more chore: if your system disk does not contain a file named SYSTEM.SYNTAX and your Pascal disk does, use the T(ransfer activity to move the file to your system disk:*

```
Transfer what file ? PASCAL:SYSTEM.SYNTAX ⟦ret⟧
To where? $ ⟦ret⟧
PASCAL:SYSTEM.SYNTAX      --> SYSTEM.SYNTAX
```

Your set up operation is now complete. Leave the Pascal disk mounted during your work in this chapter with the Pascal language. Type Q to leave the Filer.

Using Pascal

Now you're ready to try your first Pascal program in the p–System. The first step is to use the Editor to enter your program into the computer. Invoke the Editor and type ⟦ret⟧ to the "File?" question. Then use I(nsert to put the simple Pascal program below into your workspace. Remember that you can use the auto–indentation feature of the Editor to do the two lines starting with "writeln". The other lines should be on the left margin in your workspace. When you enter the third line, replace "<your name>" by your real name (for example, Raoul or Millicent).

```
program MyFirst;
begin
  writeln ('Congratulations, <your name>,');
  writeln ('on your first Pascal program!');
end.
```

Each of the "writeln" (pronounced "write–line") statements causes a line containing the text inside the quotes to be written to your computer display when the program is run.

Compare your workspace with the original program above to make sure that all the details are correct. You should particularly check:

- that the left and right parentheses, "(" and ")", are matched,
- that the congratulatory messages are marked at both ends by single quotes,
- that the semicolons (;) are placed as shown above, and
- that there is a period after the "end".

When your survey of this checklist is completed, write your workspace out to disk by invoking the Q(uit activity and its U(pdate option (by typing Q U). After the Editor confirms the writing of your workspace to disk, it returns you to the Command menu.†

* *IV.2 users, note:* This transfer operation is not necessary for you. SYSTEM.SYNTAX can be on any on–line volume.

† *IV.2 users, note:* Before that confirmation can occur, you need to do some extra steps. First, you see an additional prompt asking you to name the output file. Respond to it with: MYFIRST ⟦ret⟧. The file goes on your

What you need to do now is run the program you've just created. It must be compiled first, however. Fortunately the R(un activity (which you should invoke now by typing R) takes care of causing the compilation to occur before it attempts to run the program. You should see the following screen:‡

```
Compiling...
Output file for compiled listing? (<cr> for none) _
```

The Compiler can produce an annotated **listing** of your program containing the source lines, along with line numbers and other information produced by the compiler. This prompt asks you to indicate where that annotated listing should be put. Enter a simple ⟦ret⟧ to indicate that no listing is needed.

If you made no typing errors in entering the program, some disk and screen activity occurs, and the following screen eventually appears:

```
Command: E(dit, R(un, F(ile, C(omp, L(ink, X(ecute, A(ssem, D(ebug,?[ ]
Congratulations, Millicent,
on your first Pascal program!
```

Consider yourself congratulated! You are now back in the Command menu, with the leftover output of your first program on the screen.

If you don't see a display like the one above, it's probably because you made a small typing error in entering your program. When the compiler detects such errors (called **syntax errors**), it sounds your computer's bell and stops. If this happens to you, we suggest you read on through the end of this section without typing anything further. After you know more about syntax errors and how to handle them, come back and deal with this one by going back in the editor and making sure that your workspace matches the original program exactly.

---

system disk (which is currently the default volume).

Now press S to select S(et, followed by W to select W(orkfile. A prompt asks for the new **workfile** name. Enter MYFIRST ⟦ret⟧.

Now press Q to quit the S(et activity and return to the Command menu. You have now established a workfile containing the program you are working on. Various p–System functions (such as E(dit) that you invoke from now on will apply automatically to that workfile. In p–System versions before IV.2, the workfile mechanism is different and there is no need to explicitly name the workfile at this point. Further discussion of workfiles occurs later in this chapter.

‡ *IV.0 users, note:* The prompt shown above does not appear, so you don't need to respond. Rather, the compilation process begins immediately. Be on the lookout for similar situations later in the chapter where you are directed to type an unnecessary ⟦ret⟧.

During the compilation process, considerable screen activity occurred. At one point, your screen probably looked something like this:

```
Command: E(dit, R(un, F(ile, C(omp, L(ink, X(ecute, A(ssem, D(ebug,?[ ]
Output file for compiled listing? (<cr> for none) [ret]

Pascal Compiler - release level [ ]
<    0>..
MYFIRST
<    2>..

4 lines compiled.

MYFIRST.
```

The main purpose of the screen output produced during compilation is to keep you posted on the Compiler's progress (and, particularly, to convince you that progress is occurring!). The compiler makes two "passes" across the program. In the first pass, it writes a dot to the screen for each line it processes, and a line number in angle brackets at the beginning of each line of dots. The compiler completes the first pass by reporting the total number of lines in your program.

The remainder of the display is produced by the second pass, where dots are also used to indicate progress.

Let's return to the Editor and make some modifications to the program. This time when you enter the Editor, your program is automatically read into the workspace.*

This next program shows you one way in which p–System programming ability can be useful to you. Say you happened to win $10,000 in a contest, and that you could choose the number of months over which the payment of the prize would be spread. The program presented below will prompt you for a number of months, and then calculate and display the minimum amount of the monthly payment for you. We realize that this calculation could also be done in your head or with the aid of any $10 calculator, but this program should prove a useful exercise, nevertheless.

Use D(elete and then I(nsert to change the second "writeln" statement and add four new lines as shown on this screen:

```
>Edit: A(djust C(opy D(el F(ind I(nsert J(ump K(ol M(argin P(age ? [ ]
program MyFirst;
begin
  writeln ('Congratulations, <your name>,');
  writeln ('on your $10,000 win!');
  writeln ('Payments over how many months? '); [ret]
  readln (months); [ret]
  monthly := 10000 div months; [ret]
  writeln ('You would get at least $', monthly , ' per month.'); [ret]
end.
```

What is the purpose of these new statements? When you run this program, the "readln" statement allows you to enter a number of months at the keyboard. The value you enter is stored in the **variable** "months".

---

* *IV.2 users, note:* You must press [ret] to confirm your workfile name before it is read into the workspace.

The variable holds (or "remembers") the number you type in so that it can be used in the subsequent calculation.

The next line accomplishes the main purpose of this program. The total amount of the prize money ($10,000) is divided by the number of months, and the result stored in another variable, called "monthly".

The final line reports the results to you on the screen. When the variable "monthly" is named in a "writeln" statement, the number stored in the variable is written to the screen, along with other text in the statement.

This completes your second program. As before, check each line for agreement with the printed version above.

Now Q(uit U(pdate from the Editor and invoke R(un again. As before, the p–System conveniently goes ahead and invokes the Compiler.

Whenever you Q(uit U(pdate from the Editor, the p–System assumes you must have changed something in the source text (otherwise, why would you be saving a copy on disk?). Therefore, when you indicate your program is to be run, the p–System automatically calls the Compiler first, to translate your new program into machine understandable terms.

After you type [ret] to refuse the offer of the production of a listing, the behavior of the Compiler should initially be just as it was in the previous compilation. But then the bell on your computer sounds and the following display appears:

```
Compiling...
Output file for compiled listing? (<cr> for none) [ret]

Pascal Compiler - release level [ ]
<   0>..
MYFIRST
<   2>...
  writeln ('Payments over how many months? ');
  readln (months <---
Undeclared identifier
Line 6
Type <sp> to continue, <esc> to exit, or 'e' to edit
```

The Compiler has detected a syntax error: a place in your program where the structure rules that govern Pascal programs are violated. The error is "Undeclared identifier" and the "<–––" indicates the point in the program where the error was detected.

The syntax rules of the Pascal language require that all variables used in a program must be **declared** or named, before they are used. Names of variables or other objects in Pascal programs are referred to as **identifiers**. The identifier "months" was not declared in your program. We show you how to fix that problem shortly.

Textual error messages like that shown here are only displayed if the file SYSTEM.SYNTAX (which contains those messages) is present on your system disk. If the file is not present, then an error number is given (without a corresponding message), and you should look in Appendix C, "Syntax Errors," for the text of the error message. If you are missing the file SYSTEM.SYNTAX, your screen shows "Error #104" instead of "Undeclared identifier".

You have three choices at this point, as indicated by the menu:

- You can type ⟦space⟧ to continue the compilation. (You may want to see if there are any other syntax errors in the program.)
- You can type "e" to return to the Editor, presumably to fix the problem and try again.
- Finally, you can choose ⟦esc⟧ to give up on the compilation altogether and return to the Command menu.

Choose the edit option. In a short while you should be back in the Editor with the following screen displayed:

```
Undeclared identifier: Type <sp>
program MyFirst;
begin
  writeln ('Congratulations, <your name>,');
  writeln ('on your $10,000 win!');
  writeln ('Payments over how many months? ');
  readln (months);
  monthly := 10000 div months;
  writeln ('You would get at least $', monthly , ' per month.');
end.
```

On the top line of the screen is the same error message you saw during compilation. The cursor is positioned at the place in the workspace where the error was detected by the Compiler. The Editor waits for you to type ⟦space⟧, indicating that you have seen the error message. After the ⟦space⟧, you're all set to fix the error!

You need to declare the variables "months" and "monthly". To do so, move the cursor to the start of the "begin" line (JB ⟦ret⟧ should do it), and insert the following line: var months, monthly : integer; ⟦ret⟧.

This construct names the variables "months" and "monthly" so that the compiler knows about them before it begins translation of the program. The "integer" part of the line indicates that these variables can only hold whole numbers, like "31", but not "57.3".

After fixing the error, Q(uit U(pdate and R(un. This time the compilation should succeed and your program should begin running. When it asks you for a number of months, try entering 6 ⟦ret⟧. The minimum monthly payment is immediately reported as $1666 (which is not the exact payment for a six month spread because this particular program can only calculate in whole numbers——no fractions).

When your program completes and the Command menu returns, you can R(un the program again. Notice that this time no compilation is needed, since no changes have been made to the text of the program. Feel free to pursue your fantasies of fabulous monthly incomes by trying various payment rates.

This concludes your initial experience with Pascal programming. The next section provides a similar treatment of FORTRAN–77. You should skip that and resume reading in Section 3.6, "p–System Workfiles."

3.5 USING FORTRAN IN THE p–SYSTEM

The first part of this section helps you get your p–System set up for FORTRAN. After this step is completed, you can go on to do some simple FORTRAN programming.

Setting Up for FORTRAN

Before you can use FORTRAN, you must have the FORTRAN compiler on an on–line volume with the file name SYSTEM.COMPILER. You also need to have a **runtime library file** for FORTRAN available, as well. (The runtime library file contains program sections that are needed during the running of a FORTRAN program.)

Assuming you have acquired the FORTRAN compiler, the simplest case is if it already resides as SYSTEM.COMPILER on your system disk. This is probably true if, for instance, all your p–System software is contained on a single disk. If you have a FORTRAN SYSTEM.COMPILER on your system disk, skip this subsection and go on to do some FORTRAN programming.

Alternatively, your FORTRAN compiler may have been delivered on a separate disk (perhaps labelled "FORTRAN," or something similar). Locate that disk now.

If you need to do some FORTRAN set up, you may have a choice to make for both the compiler and the runtime library. Remember the discussion of real numbers and their sizes in Chapter 1 (Section 1.17)? We mentioned that the p–System supports two sizes of real numbers (two–word and four–word), but only one size at a time. A particular FORTRAN compiler/runtime library set also supports only one of these sizes, either two–word or four–word. You need to choose the set that matches the real number size for which your p–System is configured. If both sizes have been provided by your p–System supplier, it is likely that the files in one set have "2" in their names, while the files in the other set have "4" in theirs. For example, one set might have the file names FORTLIB4.CODE and FORTRAN4.CODE. Unless your documentation specifically directs otherwise, select the four–word set for your use, since most p–Systems are initially configured that way.*

For simplicity of configuration steps below, we assume that your personal computer has at least two disk drives and that you can use one of them to hold the disk containing the FORTRAN compiler. (If you have only one drive and don't have the compiler already on your system disk, you should put it there. We can't give you step–by–step directions for doing

---

* *IV.2 users, note:* A single FORTRAN compiler is provided that works with both sizes, so no choice is necessary. You do, however, need to choose the right runtime library.

that, however. The remainder of this subsection assumes you have two drives.)

First, make sure you have made a back up copy of your FORTRAN disk (using the same procedures you used earlier to back up your system disk). After setting the master copy of the FORTRAN disk aside, mount the second copy in a disk drive.

Use the Filer's L(ist directory activity to list the files on your FORTRAN disk. Note the names of the compiler/runtime set that you intend to use. If the compiler is not SYSTEM.COMPILER, invoke the C(hange activity of the Filer to change the name. If the original name is (say) FORTRAN.CODE on volume FORTRAN:, the following interaction with C(hange should do the trick:

```
Change what file ? FORTRAN:FORTRAN.CODE [[ret]]
Change to what ? SYSTEM.COMPILER [[ret]]
FORTRAN:FORTRAN.CODE   --> SYSTEM.COMPILER
```

To complete the installation, you need to inform the p–System about the appropriate runtime library by assuring that a **library text file** names it. If you want to know in general about library text files, see Chapter 4. It is sufficient right now for you to know that you need a text file containing a line in it designating your FORTRAN runtime file.

The default library text file is "USERLIB.TEXT". If such a file exists on your system volume, you need to add one line to it. If such a file does not exist on your system volume, you need to create a file containing that same line.

Enter the Editor and respond with USERLIB ⟦ret⟧ to the "File?" prompt. If such a file exists, it is read into your workspace. If the file doesn't exist, a prompt requests a valid file name. Respond with a ⟦ret⟧ to enter the Editor with an empty workspace.

Now insert the line mentioned above. Typing the following text should do that (if you substitute suitable names for the FORTRAN volume and the appropriate runtime library file):

I FORTRAN:FORTLIB.CODE ⟦ret⟧ ⟦etx⟧

Now store the workspace on your system disk as USERLIB.TEXT and leave the Editor, by typing the input sequence that follows.

Q W USERLIB ⟦ret⟧ E

There is one last chore you need to do. If your system disk was configured for Pascal programming, it may contain a file called SYSTEM.SYNTAX. This file contains error messages that may be produced by the Pascal compiler when it processes a Pascal program. Since you're doing FORTRAN programming, this file is not needed, and can, in fact, be a hindrance. We recommend you remove it. (We assume that you have made a back up copy of your system disk, so that if you want to do Pascal programming, and need this file again, you can get it.)

Enter the sequence F R *SYSTEM.SYNTAX [ret]. If you don't have SYSTEM.SYNTAX on your system disk, the Filer reports:

```
SYSTEM:SYSTEM.SYNTAX -- File not found <source>
```

(The "SYSTEM:" will be replaced by the name of your system disk.)

If you do have SYSTEM.SYNTAX on your system disk, the Filer reports the removal and requests your confirmation. Give that confirmation with a Y:

```
SYSTEM:SYSTEM.SYNTAX  --> removed
Update the directory? Y
```

You are now ready to do some FORTRAN programming.

Using FORTRAN

The first step is to use the Editor to enter your program into the computer. Invoke the Editor and type [ret] to the "File?" question. Then use I(nsert to put the simple FORTRAN program below into your workspace. When you enter the third line, replace "<your name>" by your real name (e.g., Jane or Sebastian). The statement number (in the second line) should be on the left margin of your workspace. The FORTRAN statements themselves should start in column 7.

```
      program First
100   format (A,I5)
      write (*,100) 'Congratulations, <your name>,'
      write (*,100) 'on your first FORTRAN-77 program!'
      end
```

When this program is run, each of the "write" statements causes a line containing the text inside the quotes to be written to your computer display. The "format" statement controls the appearance of those lines.

Compare your workspace with the original program above to make sure that all the details are correct. You should particularly check:

- that the left and right parentheses, "(" and ")", are matched,
- that the congratulatory messages are marked at both ends by single quotes, and
- that each statement starts in column 7. (The "format" statement is preceded by a statement number ("100"), starting in column 1.)

In addition, whenever you write a FORTRAN program in the p–System, be sure that you don't have any extra lines after the "end" statement. If you do have extra lines, the program will not compile. An easy way to check this aspect of your program is to enter J E and then make sure the cursor is on the line immediately below the "end". If necessary, delete text or blank lines from your workspace until this condition is met.

When your survey of this checklist is completed, prepare to write your workspace out to disk by invoking the Q(uit activity. For small program development, the Q(uit U(pdate option is the most convenient. Invoke it by typing U. After the Editor confirms the writing of your workspace to disk, it returns you to the Command menu.*

What you need to do now is run the program you've just created, so invoke the R(un activity by typing R. The p–System automatically invokes the Compiler first, since the program needs to be translated before it can be run. You should see the following screen:

```
Compiling...
Output file for compiled listing? (<cr> for none) _
```

The Compiler can produce an annotated **listing** of your program containing the source lines, along with line numbers and other information generated by the compiler. This prompt asks you to indicate where that annotated listing should be put. Enter a simple ⟦ret⟧ to indicate that no listing is needed. If you made no typing errors in entering the program, some disk and screen activity occurs, and then the Command menu is redisplayed on the top line of your screen, leaving the screen output of your program below it:

```
Command: E(dit, R(un, F(ile, C(omp, L(ink, X(ecute, A(ssem, D(ebug,?[ ]
Congratulations, Sebastian,
on your first FORTRAN program!
```

Consider yourself congratulated!

If you don't see a display like the one above, it's probably because you made a small typing error in entering your program. When the compiler detects such errors (called **syntax errors**), it sounds your computer's bell and stops. If this happens to you, we suggest you read on through the end of this section without typing anything further. After you know more about syntax errors and how to handle them, come back and deal with this one by going back in the editor and making sure that your workspace matches the

---

* *IV.2 users, note:* Before that confirmation can occur, you need to do some extra steps. First, you see an additional prompt asking you to name the output file. Respond to it with: MYFIRST ⟦ret⟧. The file goes on the system volume (which is the current default volume).

Now press S to select S(et, followed by W to select W(orkfile. A prompt asks for the new **workfile** name. Enter MYFIRST ⟦ret⟧.

Now press Q to quit the S(et activity and return to the Command menu. You have now established a workfile containing the program you are working on. Various p–System functions (such as E(dit) that you invoke from now on will apply automatically to that workfile. In p–System versions before IV.2, the workfile mechanism is different, and there is no need to explicitly name the workfile at this point. Further discussion of workfiles occurs later in this chapter.

original program exactly.

During the compilation process, considerable screen activity occurred. At one point, your screen probably looked something like the one shown next:

```
Command: E(dit, R(un, F(ile, C(omp, L(ink, X(ecute, A(ssem, D(ebug,?[ ]
Output file for compiled listing? (<cr> for none) [ret]


FORTRAN-77 - (C) 1981 Silicon Valley Software, Inc.

FORTRAN Compiler [ ]

<    0>..
FIRST
<    3>...
5 lines. 0 errors.
```

The main purpose of the screen output produced during compilation is to keep you posted on the Compiler's progress (and, particularly, to convince you that progress is occurring!). The compiler writes a dot to the screen for each line it processes, and a line number in angle brackets at the beginning of each line of dots. A summary line indicates the total number of lines processed and the number of errors detected.

Let's return to the Editor and make some modifications to the program. This time when you enter the Editor, your program is automatically read into the workspace.*

The next program shows you one way in which p–System programming ability can be useful to you. Say you happened to win $10,000 in a contest, and that you could choose the number of months over which the payment of the prize would be spread. The program presented below will prompt you for a number of months, and then calculate and display the minimum amount of the monthly payment for you. We realize that this calculation could also be done in your head or with the aid of any $10 calculator, but this program should prove a useful exercise, nevertheless.

Use D(elete and then I(nsert to change the second "write" statement and add four new lines as shown on the screen that follows:

```
>Edit: A(djust C(opy D(el F(ind I(nsert J(ump K(ol M(argin P(age ? [ ]
       program First
100    format (A,I5)
       write (*,100) 'Congratulations, <your name>,'
       write (*,100) 'on your $10,000 win!'
       write (*,100) 'Payments over how many months? ' [ret]
       read (*,200) months [ret]
       mnthly = 10000 / months; [ret]
       write (*,100) 'Your minimum monthly payment is $', mnthly
       end
```

What is the purpose of these new statements? When you run this program, the "read" statement allows you to enter a number of months at the keyboard. Your response is stored in the **variable** "months". The variable holds (or "remembers") the number you type in so that it can be

---

* *IV.2 users, note:* You must press [ret] to confirm your workfile name before it is read into your workspace.

used in the subsequent calculation.

The next line accomplishes the main purpose of this program. The total amount of the prize money ($10,000) is divided by the number of months, and the result stored in another variable, called "mnthly".

The final "write" line reports the results to you on the screen. When the variable "mnthly" is named in a "write" statement, the number stored in the variable is written to the screen, along with other text in the statement.

This completes your second program. As before, check each line for agreement with the printed version above.

Now Q(uit U(pdate from the Editor, and try invoking R(un immediately, without doing a C(ompile first. The p–System conveniently goes ahead and invokes the Compiler anyway.

Whenever you Q(uit U(pdate from the Editor, the p–System assumes you must have changed something in the source text (otherwise, why would you be saving a copy on disk?). Therefore, when you indicate your program is to be run, the p–System automatically calls the Compiler first, to translate your new program into machine understandable terms.

After you type [ret] to refuse the offer of the production of a listing, the behavior of the Compiler should initially be just as it was before. But then the bell on your computer sounds and the following display appears:

```
Compiling...
Output file for compiled listing? (<cr> for none) [ret]


FORTRAN-77 - (C) 1981 Silicon Valley Software, Inc.

FORTRAN Compiler [ ]

<    0>..
FIRST
<    3>......
***** Error number: 163 in line 8
<sp>(continue), <esc>(terminate), E(dit
```

The Compiler has detected a syntax error: a place in your program where the structure rules that govern FORTRAN programs are violated. The error is number 163, and it occurs in line 8 of your program.*

When you look up this error number in FORTRAN section of Appendix C, "Syntax Errors," or if you prefer, in your FORTRAN reference manual), you find this specific description:

Label used as format, but not defined in format statement.

The problem is that the "read" statement depends on a "format" statement labeled 200 to specify how the reading is to occur. But there is no statement 200 in the program!

---

* *IV.2 users, note:* If your has system has the FORTRAN errors file properly set up, you may see a textual error message rather than the error number shown.

You have three choices at this point, as indicated by the menu:

- You can type [space] to continue the compilation. (You may want to see if there are any other syntax errors in the program.)
- You can choose [esc] to give up on the compilation altogether and return to the Command menu.
- Finally, you can type "E" to return to the Editor (presumably to fix the problem and try again).

Choose the E(dit option. In a few moments you should be back in the Editor with the following screen displayed:

```
SYNTAX ERROR #163. Type <sp>
        program First
100     format (A,I5)
        write (*,100) 'Congratulations, <your name>,'
        write (*,100) 'on your $10,000 win!'
        write (*,100) 'Payments over how many months? '
        read (*,200) months
        mnthly = 10000 / months;
        write (*,100) 'Your minimum monthly payment is $', mnthly
        end
```

On the top line of the screen is a reminder of the error. The Editor waits for you to type [space], indicating that you have seen the error message. After the [space], you're ready to fix the error.

You need to add a "format" statement numbered 200 to control the reading of "months." Move the cursor to the end of the FORMAT statement that's in the program already, and I(nsert this new line:

[ret]200 format(I2)

This statement indicates that "months" should be entered as a two-digit whole number, such as "11" or "06", but not "5.6". When you run the program, be sure that you enter exactly two digits for this number (even if the first one has to be zero).

After fixing the error, Q(uit U(pdate and R(un. This time the compilation should succeed and your program should begin running. When it asks you for a number of months, enter 06 [ret]. The monthly payment is reported as $1666 (which is not the exact payment for a six month spread because this particular program can only calculate in whole numbers——not fractions).

When your program completes and the Command menu returns, you can R(un the program again. Notice that this time no compilation is needed, since no changes have been made to the text of the program. Feel free to try various payment rates.

This concludes your initial experience with FORTRAN programming. There are two Editor activities that are not covered in Part 1, but which can be particularly useful in FORTRAN programming because statements generally start at column 7 (unless they are numbered). We suggest that you refer to Chapter 5 for descriptions of the Editor activities X(change and

A(djust. The first of these makes it easy to add statement numbers to existing statements. The second allows you to adjust indentations easily. Another useful activity is S(et tabstops within S(et E(nvironment. You could set a tab stop at column 7 and simplify your entry of FORTRAN statements.

3.6 p—SYSTEM WORKFILES

In this section we discuss an aspect of the p—System that you've already used (perhaps without knowing it) in developing your first p—System programs: the workfile facility. This p—System feature is intended to simplify program development, particularly on small programs. When a workfile exists, the Command menu activities E(dit, C(ompile, and R(un automatically apply to that workfile; you don't need to continually remember and type in a file name (as you did when using the Editor for ordinary text in Chapter 2).

Though the overall workfile concept is the same across all p—System versions, the details are quite different in Version IV.2 than in other p—Systems. Therefore we deal separately in this section with these two styles of workfile. In the first subsection, we address the workfile facility as implemented in Version IV.1 and prior p—Systems. In the second subsection, we describe the workfile style introduced in Version IV.2. Read the subsection that applies to you.

Workfiles in IV.1 and Earlier p—Systems

Let's review the development process you just used to create your first p—System program, and see how the workfile facility was making life easy for you behind the scenes:

- You started with an empty workspace and entered a small program. To write the workspace to disk, you used the Q(uit U(pdate activity. A file name must ordinarily be used when a workspace is written to disk, but the Editor did not bother you for a file name. Instead, it wrote the workspace out to a temporary file named SYSTEM.WRK.TEXT on the system disk. This file became the **workfile**.

- Back in the Command menu, you then invoked the R(un activity, which automatically invoked the Compiler. The Compiler just assumed that you wanted to translate the workfile, so it didn't bother you for a file name, either; it simply translated the contents of SYSTEM.WRK.TEXT, and put the results in another temporary file: SYSTEM.WRK.CODE, also on the system disk. (As you may recall, it is .CODE files that are suitable for direct execution by your computer.)

- The R(un activity then went on automatically to execute the program in SYSTEM.WRK.CODE.
- You then re–entered the Editor. It didn't bother to ask you what file you wished to edit, but simply read SYSTEM.WRK.TEXT into the workspace. The Q(uit U(pdate by which you left the Editor created a fresh copy of SYSTEM.WRK.TEXT on the disk, and the subsequent R(un and E(dit activities affected that new version of the workfile.

Let's invoke the F(ile activity and make sure that those temporary workfiles are actually on the system disk. Type F L : [ret]. A screen similar to the following should appear:

```
Filer: G(et, S(ave, W(hat, N(ew, L(dir, R(em, C(hng, T(rans, D(ate,? [ ]
SYSTEM:
SYSTEM.PASCAL      125 13-Jun-82
SYSTEM.FILER        37 13-Jun-82
SYSTEM.MISCINFO      1 30-May-82
SYSTEM.INTERP       28  8-Apr-82
SYSTEM.EDITOR       47  1-Apr-82
SYSTEM.LIBRARY      29  5-Jul-82
SYSTEM.WRK.TEXT      4  3-Jan-83
SYSTEM.WRK.CODE      2  3-Jan-83
8/8 files<listed/in-dir>, 274 blocks used, 45 unused, 45 in largest
```

There is indeed a code workfile and a text workfile listed. We frequently refer to these related files collectively as "the workfile," even though there are often two files (and possibly a third: the temporary listing file called SYSTEM.LST.TEXT).

The workfile can be temporary and have a SYSTEM.WRK name, or it can have an "explicit" name, such as MYFILE. In the latter case, the components of the workfile could be MYFILE.CODE and MYFILE.TEXT.

There are four activities in the Filer menu that relate to the workfile facility. Here are their names, along with brief descriptions:

- W(hat: used to find out the status of the workfile.
- N(ew: used to clear out any existing workfile.
- G(et: used to designate an existing file (or files) as the workfile. After the G(et, Command menu activities such as E(dit apply to that workfile automatically.
- S(ave: used to store temporary SYSTEM.WRK files under explicit names.

Invoke the W(hat activity now, and you should see the following screen:

```
Filer: G(et, S(ave, W(hat, N(ew, L(dir, R(em, C(hng, T(rans, D(ate,? [ ]
not named (not saved)
```

The workfile is "unnamed" (that is, temporary) and "unsaved" because you have not used the S(ave activity to give it an explicit name.

When you invoke the S(ave activity, the Filer asks you for an explicit name to use for the workfile:

```
Save as what file? _
```

Type MYFIRST [ret] to save the workfiles under the name MYFIRST on the system volume. Notice that no suffix (either .TEXT or .CODE) can be used in the response to this prompt. The screen indicates that both the .CODE and .TEXT workfiles are saved:

```
Filer: G(et, S(ave, W(hat, N(ew, L(dir, R(em, C(hng, T(rans, D(ate,? [ ]
Text file saved & code file saved.
```

Feel free to type L : [ret] to check that MYFIRST.CODE and MYFIRST.TEXT actually showed up on your system disk, and that the temporary files disappeared.

Note that MYFIRST is still the workfile. If you were to Q(uit the Filer now, and re–enter the Editor, the familiar program in MYFIRST.TEXT would be read into the workspace. What if you aren't interested in MYFIRST any more, but want to work on another program instead? The N(ew activity can clear the workfile and break any association with MYFIRST. You can see how N(ew affects the workfile by invoking W(hat, then N(ew, followed by another W(hat. You should see these screens in quick succession:

```
Filer: G(et, S(ave, W(hat, N(ew, L(dir, R(em, C(hng, T(rans, D(ate,? [ ]
Workfile is SYSTEM:MYFIRST
```

```
Filer: G(et, S(ave, W(hat, N(ew, L(dir, R(em, C(hng, T(rans, D(ate,? [ ]
Workfile cleared
```

```
Filer: G(et, S(ave, W(hat, N(ew, L(dir, R(em, C(hng, T(rans, D(ate,? [ ]
No workfile
```

In your version of the first screen above, the name of your system disk, whatever that is, should appear instead of SYSTEM.

At this point there is no workfile known to the p–System. If you were to exit the Filer and enter the Editor, the familiar "File?" question would be asked, just as it was in Chapter 2.

You can now exercise the G(et activity on the file MYFIRST. After you type G MYFIRST [ret], the Filer reports:

```
Filer: G(et, S(ave, W(hat, N(ew, L(dir, R(em, C(hng, T(rans, D(ate,? [ ]
Text & code file loaded
```

And a W(hat indicates that the "Workfile is SYSTEM:MYFIRST".

The G(et activity doesn't do any copying of files; it simply establishes some file as the workfile. Any of the Command menu activities E(dit, C(ompile, and R(un now operate on the new workfile automatically.

As a final exercise with workfiles, let's see what would happen if you modified the workfile MYFIRST. Leave the Filer with Q and enter the

Editor with E. As you would expect, the workfile is automatically read into the Editor's workspace. If you had been intending to change your program, you could do that and then Q(uit U(date. Since the p–System assumes that you have modified the workspace when you leave the Editor by Q(uit U(pdate, it is sufficient for the purposes of this exercise to simply type Q U, without making any changes at all.

Let's see what effects this excursion into the Editor has had on the workfile status.

The first check to make is L : [ret] to see what SYSTEM.WRK file(s) is (are) present. It appears that only SYSTEM.WRK.TEXT exists. This is reasonable, since you did a Q(uit U(pdate from the Editor, but no new compilation. Notice also, however, that the files MYFIRST.TEXT and MYFIRST.CODE are still on the disk, as well.

The second check is to invoke the W(hat activity. The result:

```
Filer: G(et, S(ave, W(hat, N(ew, L(dir, R(em, C(hng, T(rans, D(ate,? [ ]
Workfile is SYSTEM:MYFIRST (not saved)
```

The workfile is the permanent file SYSTEM:MYFIRST, but as the "not saved" indicates, the permanent file is now out of date. At least as far as the p–System knows, the file SYSTEM.WRK.TEXT contains the newest version of your program.

The logical next step is to S(ave this "newest version" of your program. When you invoke S(ave, the Filer asks you whether you want to retain the current name of the workfile for the new copy that is about to be made. You will see the following screen.

```
Save as SYSTEM:MYFIRST? _
```

If you respond with "N", you are able to choose a new name. Respond with a Y. Now the Filer requests confirmation that the old copy of MYFIRST.TEXT should be removed. Give that confirmation with a Y, and the screen reports:

```
Filer: G(et, S(ave, W(hat, N(ew, L(dir, R(em, C(hng, T(rans, D(ate,? [ ]
Text file saved & Code file removed.
```

What happened to the MYFIRST.CODE file that corresponded to the old version of MYFIRST.TEXT? It has been removed, since if it were left, the textfile and codefile would not be compatible with each other. (Go ahead and check, if you'd like, that MYFIRST.CODE is gone.) This is a very convenient service of the workfile facility, because it helps you avoid a lot of confusion.

The diagram in Figure 3.2 should help you remember how workfiles are used. We've taken the Figure 3.1 diagram and added the sequence of p–System activities that is involved in each of the major program development steps.

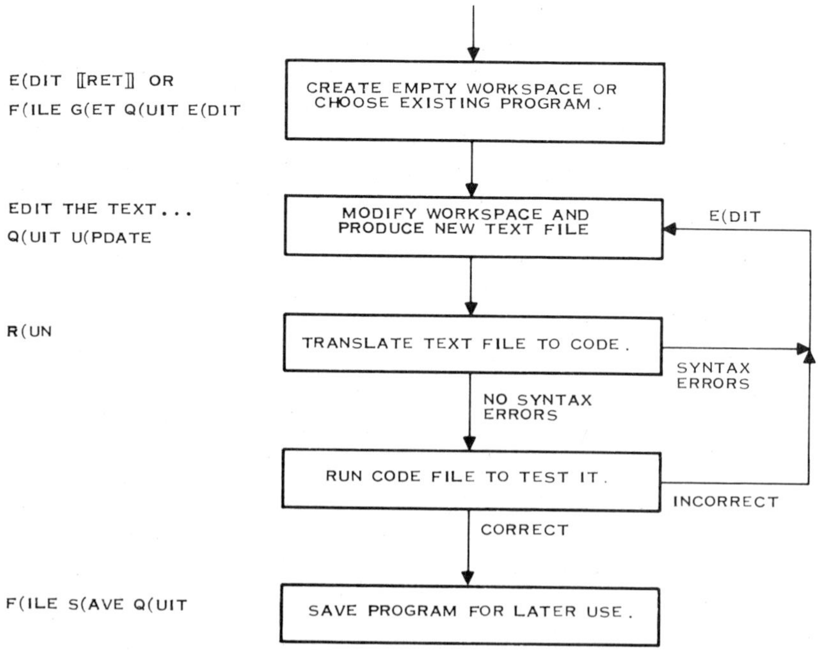

Figure 3.2

You may be wondering at this point if the workfile facility can be used for non–program text, such as the memos and poems that you worked on in Chapter 2. The answer: workfiles can be used for any text files, whether or not they contain programs.

Why then didn't we introduce the concept back in Chapter 2? The reason is that the use of workfiles doesn't necessarily offer a lot of benefits when you're working with ordinary text files: the simple Q(uit W(rite approach we used in Chapter 2 is fine.

The key observation is that the effort of designating a workfile is most worthwhile when you're going to do many operations with it (for instance, go many times through an E(dit, R(un cycle). If you're just going to E(dit, the use of G(et and S(ave doesn't save much time, and can introduce unneeded confusion. You're welcome, of course, to experiment and reach your own conclusion.

You should now know enough about workfiles to do simple program development using the p–System. Unless you're interested in the Version IV.2 style of workfiles, skip the next subsection.

Workfiles in IV.2 p–Systems

Let's review the development process you just used to create your first p–System program, and see how the workfile facility was making life easy for you behind the scenes:

- You started with an empty workspace and entered a small program. To write the workspace to disk, you used the Q(uit U(pdate activity. You needed to designate a file to be created for the workspace.
- You used the S(et W(orkfile activity to designate that file as your workfile.
- Back in the Command menu, you then invoked the R(un activity. With no further directions from you (except perhaps to decline the offer of a compiled listing), the p–System automatically compiled your program and executed the translated version.
- You then re–entered the Editor. A simple confirming [ret] caused your workfile to be read into the workspace. The Q(uit U(pdate by which you left the Editor created a fresh copy of the workfile, containing your updated workspace.

During this entire process you only typed the name of your file twice––once to create it from the Editor and once to designate the newly created file as your workfile. Workfiles mean convenience!

Invoke the F(ile activity and check the directory of your system disk. F L : [ret] should do it. You should see the files MYFIRST.TEXT (containing the source text of your first program) and MYFIRST.CODE (containing the translated object code of your first program). Now Q(uit the Filer and invoke the S(et activity. A screen like the following should appear:

```
S(et: D(ate, T(ime, W(orkfile, U(serlib, C(ompiler, A(ssembler, E(ditor,?


January 3, 1985  12:00:00

Workfile:       MYFIRST
Userlib:        *USERLIB.TEXT

Compiler:       SYSTEM.COMPILER on SYSTEM:
Assembler:      SYSTEM.ASSMBLER on SYSTEM:
Editor:         SYSTEM.EDITOR   on SYSTEM:

Prefix:         SYSTEM
Root:           SYSTEM

Real Size:      4 words (64 bits)
Spooler:        not available
File System:    SFS
Code Pool:      64k bytes
Stack/Heap:     64k bytes
```

In Chapter 4, we deal with all the activities and status information on this screen. For now, it is sufficient to confirm that the workfile is

MYFIRST. (Both the MYFIRST.TEXT and MYFIRST.CODE files are implied.)

Here is a typical scenario for using the workfile facility for program development:

- Use the S(et W(orkfile activity to designate an existing file as the workfile. No suffix (i.e. .TEXT or .CODE) is included in that designation. When you want to start a new file and cause it to be the workfile, use the Editor and its Q(uit U(pdate activity (or some other means) to create the file before you use the S(et activity to establish it as the workfile.

- Invoke the Editor. You are asked to confirm that you want to edit the workfile. Simply entering ⟦ret⟧ gives that confirmation, but you can also backspace over part of the displayed name or add characters to it (to refer to some other file) before you press ⟦ret⟧.

- When you're through editing, leave the Editor with Q(uit U(pdate. The workspace is written to disk as a new file with the same name you used on entry to the editor. The previous version of that file is removed. If there is a .CODE file corresponding to the previous version, that is removed as well. (It wouldn't do to have code and text versions of a file that are not compatible!)

- Invoke the R(un activity to compile your new file and execute it. The compilation produces a code file with the same name as the text file (except for the .CODE suffix). Naturally the code file goes on the same volume as the text file. Cycle through this E(dit, Q(uit U(date, R(un sequence until you're satisfied with the operation of your program.

- Use the S(et W(orkfile activity again to choose a new workfile. Alternatively, you can cancel the current workfile designation by responding with an immediate ⟦ret⟧ to the prompt displayed by S(et W(orkfile.

Try canceling the current workfile with S W ⟦ret⟧. Notice that the new status display indicates that no workfile is designated.

Consider how the above scenario maps into the program development process diagrammed in Figure 3.1. Notice that no explicit activities need to occur in the "SAVE PROGRAM FOR LATER USE" step, since an up–to–date copy of the workfile is always on disk (except while you're actively editing, of course).

You may be wondering at this point if the workfile facility can be used for non–program text, such as the memos and poems that you worked on in Chapter 2. The answer: workfiles can be used for any text files, whether or not they contain programs.

Why then didn't we introduce the concept back in Chapter 2? We might have if the workfile facility in all p–System versions was like the Version IV.2 set up that we've just discussed. The older style of workfile is somewhat more awkward, however, and the benefits it offers are therefore reduced.

The key observation is that the effort of designating a workfile is most worthwhile when you're going to do many operations with it (for instance, go many times through an E(dit, R(un cycle). If you're just going to E(dit a file once and then go on to E(dit the next file, the effort of designating a workfile may not pay off. You're welcome (and urged!), of course, to experiment and reach your own conclusion.

You should now know enough about workfiles to do simple program development using the p–System. The next section deals with a final aspect of developing programs.

3.7 COPING WITH EXECUTION ERRORS

You've now seen how to enter a program into the computer and translate it for execution. Another skill you need is the ability to design programs––to take a description of a problem and write a program to solve that problem. As we indicated in the introduction to this chapter, this program design skill is largely independent of the p–System, so we leave that to one of the many excellent texts on the subject.

Even after you've convinced the Compiler to swallow your program (probably after fixing some syntax errors like you did in this chapter), your program may still not do what you intended. For instance, the p–System may detect an "execution error" during the operation of your program (just as the Compiler can detect syntax errors). This section deals with that possibility.

There are many other ways in which your program may fail to operate as you intended. For instance, the program may appear to operate normally, with no errors detected by the p–System, and still produce incorrect results. A program that doesn't do what it's supposed to is said to have **bugs**. Most techniques for stamping out bugs (or avoiding them in the first place) are not specific to the p–System, so we don't go into them in this book.

In a very limited sense, the computer can check its own actions to make sure that they are legal and sensible. When one of these checks reveals a problem, your program can be brought to a screeching halt. This is called an "execution error" to distinguish it from the "syntax" errors that are caught by the Compiler during the translation process.

When one of these execution errors occurs, it will be very obvious that the program has failed, and probably quite easy to discover the unhealthy symptoms that caused it to fail. However, the task of identifying and curing the program disease that caused the symptoms may be somewhat harder.

You can watch an execution error happen by running your MYFIRST program. Yes, there is a potential error lurking in that simple program! Use the Filer to G(et MYFIRST as the workfile and R(un.* A compilation is automatically performed, since the code file that you produced earlier was removed.

When your program finally asks you the period over which you want the payment of your prize to be stretched, enter 0 ⟦ret⟧. This would correspond to immediate payment of the entire prize. Almost immediately, trouble strikes. The bell sounds, and an execution error message appears on the bottom line of your screen:†

```
Running...
Congratulations, Millicent,
on your $10,000 win!
Payments over how many months?
0 [ret]






Divide by zero--Seg MYFIRST P#1 O#83 <space> continues
```

The screen shown here corresponds to the Pascal program that you would have produced if you followed the steps in Section 3.4. Some details will be different if you did your first program in FORTRAN.

You have just watched the occurrence of an execution error. Unlike the similar experience with the ⟦break⟧ key in Chapter 1, this is an honest–to–goodness error! As you may have already known, it is not possible (at least on a mere computer) to divide zero into 10,000. The p–System detected an attempt to do so in your program and complained loudly.

You know exactly where this difficulty occurred in your program, since there is only one divide operation. In other programs, it is often the case that you could isolate the location of the execution error because of program actions (such as output to the screen) that happen just before the error is detected. Circumstantial evidence of this sort is often sufficient to pinpoint the location in your program where the execution error was detected.

When circumstantial evidence is not enough, the p–System provides a more direct way to determine the error site. Within the execution error message, just after the error identification (for instance, "Divide by zero"),

---

* *IV.2 users, note:* Since the F(iler has no G(et activity, type S W to select S(et W(orkfile, instead. Then enter MYFIRST ⟦ret⟧. To exit the S(et activity, press Q. Finally, invoke R(un as directed above.

† *IV.0 users, note:* The execution error message looks different from that shown. It occupies three lines and appears immediately below your entry.

are the error coordinates that define exactly where the error occurred (in terms of the *compiled* version of your program). These coordinate items are:

- The **segment name** (introduced by "Seg"). The "segments" of a program are major divisions within it, and each of them is named. In small programs like those you'll probably be writing, there is usually only one segment, and its name is the name of your program (such as "MYFIRST").
- The **procedure number** (which follows the "P#"). In your initial small programs, this will generally be a "1". A "procedure" is a programmer–designated logical section of a program segment. When each procedure is translated, it is assigned a number by the compiler.
- The **procedure offset** (introduced by "O#"), which designates the location in the procedure where the failure occurred. The translated procedure consists of a sequence of computer instructions. Each instruction occupies one or more **bytes** of storage space. This offset number indicates where in this series of bytes the error occurred.

These three items together constitute an "address" of the error location, just as a country code, area code, and phone number can uniquely identify a particular phone. The specific address shown above corresponds to the location of the division operation in the Pascal program from Section 3.4. If you did your first p–System program in FORTRAN, the address on your screen is different from that shown above.

Now the question is, how can you associate these error coordinates with a particular point in the text version of your program? Only then can you figure out what caused the problem. The answer lies in a compiled listing of your program. In such a listing the lines that make up your program are recorded, along with the "address" of each line, and other useful information. The next several paragraphs explain how to interpret the compiled listings produced by the Pascal and FORTRAN compilers and discover where in your program an execution error occurred.

Figure 3.3 contains a compiled listing of the Pascal program, MYFIRST. In a Pascal compiled listing, the first column of numbers is simply a line number. Of the remaining numbers on each line, the most interesting are in the third column, which contains the procedure number, and in the fifth column, which contains the procedure offset corresponding to the beginning of that line.

Given an error coordinate containing a procedure number and procedure offset, you can use these two columns to find the line where the error occurred. The error line must have a matching procedure number and an appropriate procedure offset. We have marked the error line in Figure 3.3 with an asterisk, "*". Notice that your error offset number is greater than that listed for the error line, and less than or equal to the listed offset for the line following.

```
 1   2    1:d    1  program MyFirst;
 2   2    1:d    1  var months, monthly: integer;
 3   2    1:0    0  begin
 4   2    1:1    0    writeln ('Congratulations, <your name>,');
 5   2    1:1   20    writeln ('on your $10,000 win!');
 6   2    1:1   40    writeln ('Payments over how many months? ');
 7   2    1:1   60    readln (months);
 8   2    1:1   76*   monthly := 10000 div months;
 9   2    1:1   83    writeln ('You would get at least $', monthly, ' per month.');
10   2     :0    0  end.
```

Figure 3.3: Pascal Compiled Listing

Figure 3.4 shows a compiled listing for the FORTRAN program FIRST. The first number on each line is simply a line number. The second number is the procedure offset corresponding to the beginning of that line.

In the simple programs you write initially, any execution errors will probably have a procedure number equal to two (indicating that they occurred in the main program). We won't go into the more complex case where subprograms are present. Locating the line containing the execution error, then, is simply a matter of matching the procedure offset in the error coordinate to one of the lines of your listing.

In the example listing below, we have marked the line where the error occurred with a "*". Notice that your error offset number is greater than that listed for the error line, and less than or equal to the listed offset for the line following.

```
0.      0         program MyFirst
1.      0 100     format (A,I5)
2.      0 200     format (I2)
3.      0         write (*,100) 'Congratulations, <your name>,'
4.     24         write (*,100) 'on your first FORTRAN-77 program!'
5.     49         write (*,100) 'Payments over how many months? '
6.     73         read (*,200) months
7.    100*        mnthly = 10000 / months
8.    108         write (*,100) 'Your minimum monthly payment is $', mnthly
9.    136         end
```

Figure 3.4: FORTRAN Compiled Listing

We show you in the next section how to produce one of these compiled listings. Before we can do that, though, you need to leave the error site and return to the Command menu.

As the error message indicates, you should press [space] when you're ready to go on. "Go on," in this context, means "abandon the attempt to execute this program and return to the Command menu." When you type [space], there is a pause with some disk activity while the p-System reinitializes itself (to repair any damage that might have been caused by the execution error). Then the Command menu returns.

Instead of running into an execution error, your program could fail by stumbling into an "infinite loop," in which repetition of a particular section of the program goes on indefinitely.

Imagine the consequences if this kind of difficulty were to show up in a program directing the activities of an automated bank teller. The program could get stuck in the "dispense cash" section and spew out twenty dollar bills indefinitely! In this situation, but also in your own programming work, it is sometimes highly desirable to get a program to halt unconditionally.

The ⟦break⟧ key that we introduced in Chapter 1 addresses this need very nicely. If your program appears to be stuck in an infinite loop, typing ⟦break⟧ causes an execution error, and error coordinates are given, just as with the "Divide by zero" error. (This doesn't necessarily work on every p–System implementation. On some computers, keys that you type may not be recognized by the system while a running program is doing pure calculation, with no input or output activity.)

After stopping a program with the ⟦break⟧ key, you can use the approach described above to locate the part of your program where the endless looping is occurring. (This will only work if the program is actually executing a part of your program when you press ⟦break⟧. It may be that some operating system section, or section of the FORTRAN runtime library is executing. In that case, the error coordinates shown in the execution error message will not correspond to your program at all.)

One drawback of using the ⟦break⟧ key to halt your program is that you cannot restart it. The program is aborted and the p–System re–initialized. However, there is another approach that can be used to stop and restart your program: the ⟦stop/start⟧ key. The effect of pressing this key is to suspend output to the console until you press it again. Therefore, if your program is producing output to the console when the key is pressed, the program pauses until the key is pressed again, allowing output to resume. If, however, your program is simply computing, and not producing output, then ⟦stop/start⟧ has no effect on its progress.

The final topic is how to produce a compiled listing. Invoke the Compiler (assuming your workfile is still MYFIRST) and you should soon see the familiar prompt:*†

---

* *IV.0 users, note:* If you're using UCSD Pascal, you don't have the option of requesting a listing after invoking the compiler. Instead, you need to return to the Editor and immediately enter the following text: I (*$L PRINTER:*) ⟦ret⟧.

This **compiler directive** causes compiled listing to be produced on your printer. If you don't have a printer on your computer, substitute CONSOLE: for PRINTER:. See Appendix D, "Compiler Directives," for more information on this topic.

† *IV.2 users, note:* Two additional prompts appear before the one shown. Enter ⟦ret⟧ ⟦ret⟧ to respond to them. This response confirms that you want the workfile MYFIRST.TEXT translated into a corresponding MYFIRST.CODE file.

```
Output file for compiled listing? (<cr> for none) _
```

Instead of responding with ⟦ret⟧, as you have in previous compilations, type PRINTER: ⟦ret⟧, or CONSOLE: ⟦ret⟧. Each of these responses causes a listing to be produced on the corresponding device. You should use PRINTER: if you have a printer, since a listing on paper is usually more useful than the memory of a listing flashing by on the screen.

If you do choose the CONSOLE:, you may need to use the ⟦stop/start⟧ key that was just mentioned; otherwise, the listing may go by so quickly on the display that you won't be able to read it. Also, a standard formfeed character is sent to the console at the beginning of each page. On the printer, this character causes a new page to be started. On the console, these characters may show up as strange visible characters, or may cause the screen to be cleared at the beginning of each page.

You can choose to send a listing to a disk file such as MYLIST.TEXT, rather than using CONSOLE: or PRINTER: as the destination. To do this, substitute the desired file name where CONSOLE: or PRINTER: were used above. Once a listing file is complete on the disk, you can transfer it to PRINTER: or CONSOLE:. You could even peruse the file with the Editor, but that might be a bit awkward, since the file is likely to have wider lines (up to 120 columns) than your screen can display.

4

THE OPERATING SYSTEM

4.1 INTRODUCTION

The first three chapters of this book were designed to lead you on an interesting tour of the UCSD p–System and give you a feeling for how it works. If you are fairly experienced with computers, you may have decided to skim those chapters and start here.

The next three chapters provide a more thorough and systematic discussion of the p–System. In this chapter, we cover general p–System concepts and the Command menu items. The next two chapters deal with two of the most frequently used p–System components, the Editor and the Filer.

4.2 STARTING UP THE p–SYSTEM

Before you can do anything with the p–System, you must start it running on your hardware. This process is sometimes called "bootstrapping." It is usually very easy and involves two or three steps similar to these:

- Turn your computer on.
- Place your system disk in the appropriate drive.
- Perhaps press a button or two.

Then, a greeting message and the main p–System menu is displayed. The disk that you use to bootstrap the p–System is called the **system disk**.

If you do not already know how to start the UCSD p–System on your computer, you should look at the appendix for that particular computer at the end of this book. If you are using a computer for which an appendix has not been included, consult the appendix "The p–System on Other Computers."

4.3 MENUS AND PROMPTS

When the p–System first starts running, the Command menu is displayed:

```
Command: E(dit, R(un, F(ile, C(omp, L(ink, X(ecute, A(ssem, D(ebug,? [  ]
```

Whenever a question mark is the last item on a menu, as in this case, there is more to the menu than can be displayed on the screen. If you type "?", the rest of this menu is displayed:

```
Command: H(alt, I(nitialize, U(ser restart, M(onitor [ ]
```

The Command menu is at the outermost level of the UCSD p–System. An item on this menu is selected by typing its first letter. The first letter is always in upper case and is separated from the rest of the word by a "(". For example, to select E(dit, you should type "E".

Most of the activities on this menu have menus or prompts of their own. For example, the Editor has the following main menu:

```
Edit: A(djust C(opy D(el F(ind I(nsert J(ump K(ol M(argin P(age ? [ ]
```

This menu is said to be one level below the Command menu. Several of the activities on it have menus of their own. A(djust, for instance, has a menu that looks like this:

```
>Adjust: L(just R(just C(enter <arrow keys> {<etx> to leave}
```

There is always some way to return from a lower level to a higher level. Usually, you can select Q(uit, or type ⟦etx⟧ or ⟦esc⟧, depending upon where you are. (The ⟦etx⟧ and ⟦esc⟧ keys are known as special keys and are described in the next section. We indicate special keys in this book by using the double square brackets, as shown.) Normally, the current menu tells you how to return to a higher level.

Notice that typing the same letter at different levels can have a different effect. For example, "A" selects the A(ssembler from the Command menu, but it selects A(djust from the Edit menu.

It is often the case that a prompt is displayed rather than a menu. A menu, as we just pointed out, requires that you type a single letter to select an item. A prompt requires that you type in some information, followed by ⟦ret⟧.

For example, if you select X(ecute from the Command menu, you see this prompt:

```
Execute what file ? _
```

You are expected to type in the name of a file followed by ⟦ret⟧, as shown below (with your response underlined, as usual):

```
Execute what file ? A.PROGRAM ⟦ret⟧
```

(We explain more about files below. For now we are simply concerned with how to respond to any sort of prompt.)

If you make a mistake while responding to a prompt, you can use ⟦bs⟧ to move the cursor backward. As you do this, characters are erased. You can then retype the response correctly.

There is a kind of prompt that only requires you to enter a single letter. This is one where the response is either "Y" for yes, or "N" for no. You can use lower case or upper case letters. Here is an example of one of these prompts:

```
Are there 320 blocks on the disk ? (Y/N) Y
```

Often the "(Y/N)" is not displayed, but it should be obvious from the context that a yes/no answer is required.

4.4 SPECIAL KEYS

There are several keys which have special significance to the p–System. We already mentioned several of them in the previous section.

Most computers do not have physical keys to correspond to every special key the p–System uses. Use the table in the front inside cover of this book to remind yourself how to type each of these special keys on your computer.

Often, you may need to press two keys at once in order to produce one of the p–System's special keys. For example, many computers require that you hold down the ⟦control⟧ key and type "C" in order to produce the ⟦eof⟧ key.

The Editor uses all of the keys described in this section, and more. It gives a slightly different meaning to some of them. The Editor's use of special keys is described in Chapter 5.

Here are the special keys that are used throughout the p–System:

⟦ret⟧ This key indicates that you have finished typing your response to a prompt. When it is shown on a prompt or menu, it usually takes one of these forms: <ret> or <cr>. The first version is derived from "return" and the second from "carriage return."

⟦space⟧ The space bar usually produces a blank space in the text you are typing (just as on a typewriter). There are some situations where prompts or menus require a space either by itself, or as a separator between items of input. It is shown on menus and prompts like this: <space>, <spacebar>, or <sp>.

⟦bs⟧ The back space key allows you to move the cursor backward, erasing what you have typed so far. It is usually used for correcting mistakes while responding to a prompt. It is shown on menus and prompts like this: <bs>.

⟦esc⟧ The escape key often allows you to escape (exit without doing anything) from a prompt or menu to the next higher level prompt or menu. It is displayed like this: <esc>.

⟦delete line⟧ This key erases the entire line that you have entered while responding to a prompt. It is a quick way to backspace over all of your input. It is rarely displayed as a menu item except in the Editor where it appears as <del>.

⟦break⟧ This key allows you to manually interrupt a program's execution. When this key is typed, the program that is running is immediately interrupted. An execution error message is displayed and you are asked to type ⟦space⟧ to continue. When you do, the p–System is reinitialized.

⟦stop/start⟧ This key allows you to temporarily stop the program that is currently running. (That program may be a p–System component such as the Editor or Filer.) When this key is typed, the running program is halted before the next I/O operation is performed. In order to resume execution, type ⟦stop/start⟧ again.

⟦flush⟧ This key causes output to the console to be suppressed. This means that characters normally displayed on the screen will not appear. To return the situation to normal, type ⟦flush⟧ again.

⟦eof⟧ This key signals the end of file from the console. When the keyboard is used as an input file, this key indicates that you have finished typing in the contents of that "file."

NOTE: These keys are summarized on the inside front cover of this book.

4.5 DISK FILES AND FILE NAMES

The p–System makes extensive use of disk storage. It runs on computers that use 8 inch, 5–1/4 inch, and 3–1/2 inch diskettes, as well as large capacity hard disks.

When information is stored on a disk, it is placed in a **file**. Each file is a collection of information that can be accessed, changed, removed, and so forth. There may be as many as 77 files on a disk at one time. If you have a need to place more files on one disk, you can use the **subsidiary volumes** facility (if you have p–System version IV.1 or later). Subsidiary volumes are described in Chapter 6.

There are several types of files. **Text files** are generally created by the Editor and contain textual material, such as letters, memos, poems, or human readable computer programs. **Code files** are created by the compilers and the assemblers, and contain code which can be run by the computer. **Data files** can be created in a variety of ways and may contain miscellaneous sorts of data such as names and addresses, or part names and part numbers. There are other types of files as well.

Each file has a **file name**. This name must contain 15 or fewer characters. The valid characters that may be used to make up a file name are shown in the following table:

Letters	A through Z
Numbers	0 through 9
Period	.
Underline	_
Dash	–
Slash	/
Back Slash	\

A file name may have a **file suffix** which usually indicates the type of the file. The file suffixes and the file types to which they correspond are shown below. (This book does not cover all of the file types.)

.TEXT	A text file
.BACK	A backup text file
.CODE	A code file
.SVOL	A subsidiary volume file
.BAD	A bad block file
.FOTO	A graphics image file
Any other suffix	A data file
No suffix	A data file

Usually, you are responsible for choosing the file name. Here are some valid file names:

PROGRAM.TEXT
PROGRAM.CODE
A–DATA_FILE
MY/FILE123/NEW
BAD.00192.BAD
PICTURE.FOTO
MY–VOL.SVOL

and some invalid names:

A_FILE_NAME_THAT_IS_TOO_LONG
MY,FILE

The first invalid example exceeds the 15 character limit. The second name contains an illegal comma.

A file name can be followed by an optional **size specification**. The size specification is only used when a file is created (by the Filer's M(ake activity or by a program). The size specification indicates the file's length and is bounded by square brackets. It has these forms:

FILE–NAME [number]
FILE.NAME or FILE–NAME [0]
FILE–NAME [*]

If a number is used (other than 0), the file is created to occupy that number of 512–byte blocks. The file is created in the first area on the disk that contains that many blocks. If [0] is used, or if no size specification appears, the file is created to occupy the largest unused area on the disk. If an asterisk is used, the file is created to occupy half of the largest area, or all of the second largest area, whichever is larger.

NOTE: The information presented in this section is summarized on the inside back cover of this book.

4.6 STORAGE VOLUMES AND VOLUME IDs

Disks of all types are called **storage volumes**. A storage volume is said to be **on–line** when it is placed correctly in a drive. The Filer has an activity called V(olumes which shows you all the volumes that are on–line.

Volumes are assigned **volume names**. The same characters that are valid for file names are valid for volume names. However, a volume name may have at most seven characters. Also, volume names are followed by a colon, ":". Here are some valid volume names:

A.VOL:
1234567:
BACKUP1:

A storage volume can also be referred to by the **device number** of the drive in which it is mounted. Most computers that run the p–System have at least two disk drives. These drives are assigned device numbers 4 and 5. If there are any additional drives, they are assigned numbers starting at 9. Device numbers are preceded by a number sign, "#", and usually followed by a colon. Here are some examples:

#4:
#9

An asterisk, "*", can be used to indicate the **system disk** (the disk with which you bootstrap). A colon, ":", can be used to indicate the **default disk** or **volume**. The default disk is covered in the next section.

The term **volume ID** is the generic term for volume specification. It refers to a volume name, device number, asterisk, colon, or empty volume specification (default disk).

NOTE: The information presented in this section is summarized on the inside back cover of this book.

4.7 FILE SPECIFICATION

A **file specification** consists of a volume ID, a file name, and a size specification. Any of these three may be missing from the file specification. Taken together they indicate a disk and a file on that disk. Here are some samples:

```
MY_VOL:PROGRAM.CODE
#5:LETTER.TEXT
*SYSTEM.PASCAL
DATA/BASE/2
NEWFILE[10]
#9:NEWFILE[*]
#4:
*
:
```

A volume name, by itself, should only be thought of as a file specification in the context where the volume "acts" like a file. This is the case when the volume is a source or destination for a stream of information. In the context where a volume "contains files," the term file specification does not apply.

When you use a file name without the associated volume ID, the file is assumed to reside on the **default disk** or **volume** (also known as the **prefix volume**). The default disk, at least initially, is the system disk. You can designate another disk as the default disk if you like. This can be convenient. For example, here are some miscellaneous p–System prompts. The responses all indicate files on the disk BACKUP:

Execute what file ? BACKUP:A.PROG ⟦ret⟧
Transfer what file ? BACKUP:FILE1,BACKUP:FILE2 ⟦ret⟧
Compile what file ? BACKUP:TEST ⟦ret⟧
List what vol ? BACKUP: ⟦ret⟧

If the prefix disk is BACKUP:, you can more easily respond to these prompts like this:

Execute what file ? A.PROG ⟦ret⟧
Transfer what file ? FILE1,FILE2 ⟦ret⟧
Compile what file ? TEST ⟦ret⟧
List what vol ? : ⟦ret⟧

Notice that a colon, by itself, stands for the default disk (as shown in the last example prompt).

You can change the default disk by using the Filer's P(refix activity. You can also change it using **execution option strings** (which are described later in this chapter).*

Using an asterisk, you can easily indicate the system disk in this manner:

Execute what file ? *A/PROG ⟦ret⟧
Edit what file ? *SONG–LYRIC ⟦ret⟧
List what vol ? * ⟦ret⟧

NOTE: The information presented in this section is summarized on the inside back cover of this book.

4.8 THE ARRANGEMENT OF FILES ON A DISK

In order to effectively manage files, it is important to understand how they are physically arranged on a disk. You may want to move files around, add and remove them, determine how much free space is left on a disk, and so forth. If you have a good conceptual understanding of what files look like on a disk, all of this is made easier.

At the beginning of every disk used by the p–System, an area is set aside for the **directory**. The directory contains information about the files

---

* *IV.2 users, note:* You can also use the Command menu's S(et P(refix activity to change the default disk.

that currently reside on the disk. The name of each file, its size, location, and several other pieces of information about each file are stored in the directory. The Filer's L(ist directory activity displays this information for you.

A disk may optionally contain a **duplicate directory**. A duplicate directory is a copy of the main directory which can be kept as a backup in case the main directory is lost. When you use the Filer's Z(ero activity to initialize a disk, you are asked if you want to maintain a duplicate directory. If you elect to do so, all future updates to the main directory will be recorded in the duplicate directory as well. If the main directory is somehow lost, the Copydupdir utility (described in Chapter 6) can be used to copy the duplicate directory into the main directory's location on disk. The Markdupdir utility (also described in Chapter 6) is able to create a duplicate directory on a disk if you didn't initially do so using Z(ero.

The size of a file on a disk is measured in terms of blocks. A file is always an integral number of blocks in length. The size of a disk is also measured in blocks. (In fact, a disk is sometimes called a **blocked volume**.) The first block on a disk is block 0. The next are block 1, block 2, and so forth. The highest number depends upon the storage capacity of your disk. A file is always stored on disk as a sequence of contiguous blocks. For example, a file that covers blocks 32 through 40 would be 9 blocks long.

The directory resides in blocks 2 through 5. If you are maintaining a duplicate directory, it resides in blocks 6 through 9. Blocks 0 and 1 are not used for files. On system disks, those blocks often contain bootstrap code.

Figure 4.1 gives you an idea of how files are stored on a disk. It shows a directory and several files.

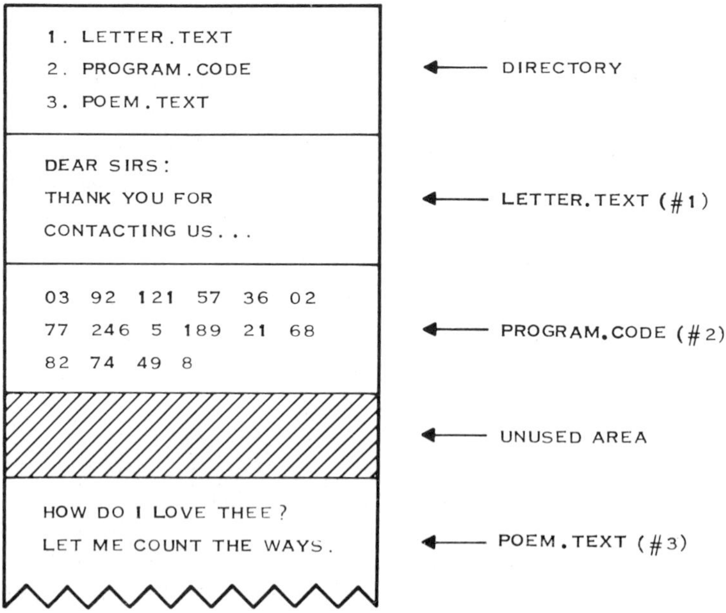

Figure 4.1

There may be unused disk space between files. The Filer's E(xtended list directory activity shows the files on disk as well as the unused space that lies between them. You may run into situations where it is desirable to move all of the files on a disk as close together as they can be. The Filer's K(runch activity does this for you. The result of using K(runch is that the unused space is consolidated into one large area. This is convenient when a large area is needed (to store a new file, for example).

On some computers, a portion of each disk is normally inaccessible to the p–System. Special utilities must be used to deal with areas of this type. For instance, an area at the beginning of the disk is often reserved for bootstrap code that won't fit in blocks 0 and 1. A utility (often called "Booter") is used to copy bootstrap code into this area.

4.9 THE SYSTEM FILES

There are several special files that are important in using the p–System. These are called **system files**. Some system files are always required and must be on the system disk. Others are only needed it you want to use the particular feature that they offer. Most of the files in this second group can reside on any on–line disk, but a few must be on the system disk. Here are the standard system files:

SYSTEM.PASCAL
SYSTEM.MISCINFO
SYSTEM.INTERP
SYSTEM.FILER
SYSTEM.EDITOR
SYSTEM.COMPILER
SYSTEM.SYNTAX
SYSTEM.ASSMBLER
xxxx.OPCODES
xxxx.ERRORS
SYSTEM.LINKER
SYSTEM.LIBRARY
SYSTEM.STARTUP
SYSTEM.MENU
SYSTEM.WRK.TEXT
SYSTEM.WRK.CODE
SYSTEM.LST.TEXT

The bulk of the p–System is contained in these files and, in several cases, their functionality is beyond the scope of this book. However, the following descriptions should provide good reference material as well as indicate how the p–System is divided up into several major components.

SYSTEM.PASCAL is the operating system. It is required and must reside on the system disk.

SYSTEM.MISCINFO contains miscellaneous information that the p–System needs so that it can correctly interface with your hardware. Most of this information pertains to your screen and keyboard. This file is required on the system disk.

SYSTEM.INTERP is the p–machine emulator which is the portion of the UCSD p–System which is specific to a particular computer (such as an IBM Personal Computer). On some computers this system file has different names such as SYSTEM.PDP–11 or SYSTEM.IBM or may depend on additional files such as SYSTEM.BIOS or SYSTEM.CONFIG. It is required on the system disk.

SYSTEM.FILER contains the Filer. The Filer manages disk files and is covered in Chapter 6. This file is only required when you want to use the Filer. It can reside on any on–line volume.

SYSTEM.EDITOR contains the Editor. The Editor is used to create human–readable text files. This system file is only required when you want to use the Editor and it can reside on any on–line volume. The Screen–oriented Editor is described in Chapter 5. If you plan to use EDVANCE (the advanced editor), you need to rename the appropriate code file

SYSTEM.EDITOR.* Chapter 8 contains a summary description of EDVANCE and Chapter 9 provides further reading suggestions concerning it.

SYSTEM.COMPILER contains a compiler. This may be the UCSD Pascal, BASIC, or FORTRAN compiler. It is only required when you want to compile a program and may reside on any on–line volume. Compilers are described later in this chapter.

SYSTEM.SYNTAX contains Pascal compiler error messages. These messages are displayed when the compiler finds syntax errors in your program text. If SYSTEM.SYNTAX is not available, you receive error numbers (instead of error messages) and you must refer to a list of compiler errors to see what the problem is. (Lists of compiler errors for Pascal and FORTRAN are provided in the "Syntax Errors" appendix.) Since this system file is only a convenience, it is never required. However, it must reside on the system disk if it is to be used. (SYSTEM.SYNTAX should not be present on the system disk if compilers other than Pascal are used.)†

SYSTEM.ASSMBLER contains an assembler. Assemblers work with machine–level languages and are briefly described later in this chapter. This file is only required when you want to assemble a file and it can be on any on–line volume.

The xxxx.ERRORS and xxxx.OPCODES files are used by the assemblers. The error file is an optional convenience. It contains English error messages which the assemblers display in place of error numbers. The opcodes file is required by the assemblers. The "xxxx" is actually an indication of a particular processor, for example: Z80.ERRORS and Z80.OPCODES, 68000.ERRORS and 68000.OPCODES, and so forth. These files can be on any on–line volume. (The 8086 assembler also requires the 8087.FOPS file if the 8087 floating point processor is to be used.)

SYSTEM.LINKER is the link editor. It is used to combine two or more assembled code files into a single code file. It can also combine assembled code files with host compiled code files. The linker is briefly described later in this chapter. It may reside on any on–line volume.

SYSTEM.LIBRARY contains separately compiled or assembled code files that can be used by your programs. There is a "long integer" package which allows your programs to use numbers of up to 36 decimal digit arithmetic. This package is usually contained in SYSTEM.LIBRARY. Applications building blocks, such as the Turtlegraphics unit, may reside

---

* *IV.2 users, note:* You can use the Command menu's S(et E(ditor activity to designate a new editor. A similar comment applies to the SYSTEM.COMPILER and SYSTEM.ASSMBLER files described below.

† *IV.2 users, note:* SYSTEM.SYNTAX is also sought on the disk containing the compiler as well as on the system disk.

Also, the other p–System languages can have textual error messages, just like the Pascal compiler can.

here. Also, the special input and output routines for FORTRAN and BASIC can be here if you intend to use those languages. SYSTEM.LIBRARY may also contain code that you write. This file is only required if you want to use the routines that are within it. It must be on the system disk in order to be used. The section "Libraries and Units," below, contains more information about SYSTEM.LIBRARY.

SYSTEM.STARTUP is an optional file that may contain any executable program. This program is automatically executed when the p–System is bootstrapped. This facility can be used, for instance, to put a company logo on the screen when the p–System is bootstrapped. (If this happens on your computer and you don't want the logo to appear, simply remove SYSTEM.STARTUP or change its name.) SYSTEM.STARTUP must be on the system disk if it is to be used.

SYSTEM.MENU is similar to SYSTEM.STARTUP. It may contain any executable program and is executed whenever the p–System is about to display the Command menu. This file is optional, but must reside on the system disk if it is to be used.*

SYSTEM.WRK.TEXT and SYSTEM.WRK.CODE are the temporary workfiles. Workfiles are described below. You can create these two files when you use the Editor and Compiler. When workfiles are in use, they always reside on the system disk.†

SYSTEM.LST.TEXT is the default destination for a compiled or assembled listing. These listings are optionally produced by the three compilers or the assemblers and contain detailed information about the code created.

4.10 WORKFILES

The p–System has some special facilities to deal with **workfiles**. Workfiles are convenient when you are developing small programs.

The Editor is used to create the human readable form of a program and store it on disk as a text file. One of the p–System compilers then takes such a text file and creates a corresponding code file that is suitable for execution. Then X(ecute or R(un is used to actually run the program.

When you are not using workfiles you must tell the Editor what file you want to edit. You must also inform the compiler what text file to compile and what code file should be produced. And, if you want to run the program, you must select X(ecute and again enter the name of the same file.

---

* *IV.0 users, note:* SYSTEM.MENU is not supported in IV.0.

† *IV.2 users, note:* Neither of these temporary workfiles (or their relative, SYSTEM.LST.TEXT) are used in IV.2.

If you are constantly making small changes in the Editor, recompiling, and rerunning a program, this can amount to a lot of typing.

Using workfiles, all of this can be done with much less typing. The Editor automatically reads a workfile into the workspace. The compiler automatically compiles it and gives the code file a standard name. And R(un automatically executes that file. You can go through this cycle of editing, compiling, and running as many times as you want without ever having to enter the name of the file that you are working with.

Though this overall workfile concept applies across all p–System versions, the details are quite different in Version IV.2 than in other p–Systems. Therefore we deal separately in this section with these two styles of workfile. First, we address the workfile facility as implemented in Version IV.1 and prior p–Systems. Second, we describe the workfile style introduced in Version IV.2. Read the subsection that applies to you.

Workfiles in IV.1 and Prior p–Systems

There are two kinds of workfiles: temporary workfiles and permanent workfiles. Temporary workfiles may be created from scratch but they may also be temporary versions of existing permanent workfiles. The temporary workfiles are:

SYSTEM.WRK.TEXT
SYSTEM.WRK.CODE
SYSTEM.LST.TEXT

SYSTEM.WRK.TEXT is created when you leave the Editor by selecting Q(uit U(pdate. SYSTEM.WRK.CODE is created by a compiler whenever you compile a workfile. Here is a typical cycle that you might go through when workfiles are used:

- Enter the Editor; modify the workspace
- From the Editor, select Q(uit U(pdate
- From the Command menu, select R(un
- See the results of your program running
- Repeat this cycle as many times as needed

Permanent workfiles (sometimes called "named" workfiles) are similar to temporary workfiles. They consist of a text file and/or code file (which correspond to SYSTEM.WRK.TEXT and SYSTEM.WRK.CODE). However, they may have any valid file names that end with .TEXT or .CODE.

It is possible to have permanent workfiles and temporary workfiles at the same time. As we mentioned, this means that the temporary workfiles are temporary versions of the permanent workfiles. The Editor can make a temporary version of a permanent text workfile. A compiler can create a temporary version of a permanent code workfile. The Filer can convert temporary workfiles to permanent status (removing the old permanent version if necessary).

The Filer has four activities that are related to workfiles: G(et, S(ave, N(ew, and W(hat. G(et allows you to designate an "ordinary" text and/or code file as the permanent workfile. N(ew clears the workfile altogether. S(ave changes temporary workfiles to permanent workfiles. W(hat tells you what the name of your workfile is (if it has one) and whether or not it has been saved.

For some experience with workfiles you should work with Chapter 3. The relevant Filer activities are covered in Chapter 6. Unless you're interested in the IV.2 style of workfiles, proceed to the next section.

Workfiles in IV.2 p–Systems

This style of workfile is very simple. To designate an existing file as your workfile, you invoke the S(et W(orkfile activity from the Command menu and enter the name of the file. No suffix (such as .TEXT or .CODE) is included in this name.

Thereafter, invocations of E(dit, C(ompile, A(ssemble, and R(un apply by default to the workfile you have designated. An invocation of R(un under these circumstances always causes the execution of the workfile (with an automatic prior compilation if necessary). The other three activities, however, request a confirmation that you indeed want to deal with the designated workfile. If you issue that confirmation (with one or more ⟦ret⟧s), the operation proceeds. Otherwise, you can choose to deal with a different file, instead, by adding additional characters before you type ⟦ret⟧ (perhaps after erasing some characters with ⟦bs⟧ or ⟦delete line⟧).

After an editing session, you can use the Q(uit U(pdate activity to leave the Editor and write the workspace to the file designated on entry to the Editor. This may be the workfile. The Editor assures that, after the source text of a program is updated by the Editor, any object code corresponding the the old version of the program is removed.

See the descriptions of the various activities mentioned above for details of these behaviors. The S(et activity is described later in this chapter along with the other Command menu activities mentioned. Editor entry and exit details are described in Chapter 5. You can get some experience using workfiles in Chapter 3.

4.11 COMMUNICATION VOLUMES

There are two types of volumes in the p–System environment: storage volumes and communication volumes. A volume is any sort of computer peripheral to which (or from which) information can be transferred. The console (screen and keyboard) is considered to be a volume. So is the printer. These volumes are communication volumes. Disks, as mentioned earlier, are storage volumes.

The distinction is that communication volumes do not store information. A printer, for example, accepts what is sent to it and prints it. But, a storage volume actually saves the information (relatively) permanently and allows later access to it.

Communication volumes have names like storage volumes except that they are standard names (unlike the names that you give to your disks). Here are the communication volumes usually available with the p–System along with the corresponding device numbers.

CONSOLE:	#1:
SYSTERM:	#2:
PRINTER:	#6:
REMIN:	#7:
REMOUT:	#8:

CONSOLE: and SYSTERM: are very similar. Both refer to the screen/keyboard. CONSOLE: echoes the characters that are typed on the screen. SYSTERM: (which stands for system terminal) does not echo those characters. PRINTER:, of course, is the printer. REMIN: and REMOUT: refer to the serial communication line (which can be used, for instance, to communicate with distant data sources over the phone). It is possible for you to have many more serial devices than these if the p–System on your computer allows it.

The device numbers can be used in place of the corresponding volume name. For example, you can use the Filer's T(ransfer activity to display a text file on the screen with either of these responses:

```
Transfer what file ? A.POEM.TEXT [[ret]]
To where ? CONSOLE: [[ret]]
```

```
Transfer what file ? A.POEM.TEXT [[ret]]
To where ? #1: [[ret]]
```

As mentioned earlier, a storage volume is on–line when it is accessible to the p–System. A communication volume is on–line when the peripheral device (console or printer, for instance) is properly connected and turned on. The Filer's V(olumes activity displays which volumes (both storage and communication) are currently on–line.

4.12 SUBSIDIARY VOLUMES

A subsidiary volume is a regular disk file which contains a directory and is treated as if it was a separate disk altogether.*

Subsidiary volumes are accessed directly just like any other volume. You don't have to specify two levels of volume names to access files on a subsidiary volume.

Subsidiary volumes are especially useful when dealing with large capacity disks. By using subsidiary volumes, such disks can be divided into logical portions. More importantly, the p–System is able to store many more files than it otherwise could on such disks. On any given volume, the p–System is able to store 77 files, which is too few to make good use of a large capacity disk. However, each subsidiary volume is able to hold 77 files of its own. This means that you could conceivably have as many as 77 times 77 files on a disk.

In Chapter 6 there is an entire section that deals with subsidiary volumes, so we won't go into any further detail concerning them here.

4.13 LIBRARIES AND UNITS

The p–System allows you to separately prepare pieces of code which can later function together as a unified program. This is referred to as **separate compilation** when you use a compiler to produce the code. (An assembler can also be used as we discuss later.) The separately compiled portions of a program are called **units**.

A program may use several units. Units, themselves, may use other units. The program or unit which uses other units is called the **client**. If it is a program, it may also be called a **host**. You can combine a host program with all of its units into a single executable code file if you wish.

Alternatively, you can leave the units in one or more disk files called **libraries**. If the p–System is correctly informed about the whereabouts of these libraries, it can find all of the necessary units when a program is executed. You might want to use libraries (instead of placing all of the units directly into the host's file) if the units are used by several clients. In this way, the disk space required by the units is not duplicated for every program or unit which uses them.

The main library is called SYSTEM.LIBRARY and must be on the system disk if it is to be used. Any units that you place in SYSTEM.LIBRARY are available for clients to use. A unit can be inserted into SYSTEM.LIBRARY (or into a client program or unit) using the Library utility which is briefly discussed in Chapter 8.

It may be convenient for you to have several libraries. To designate a code file as a library, you should use a **library text file**. A library text file is an ordinary text file that contains the names of code files which you want to designate as libraries. The standard library text file is USERLIB.TEXT

---

* *IV.0 users, note:* This facility is not supported in Version IV.0.

and should reside on the system disk. For example, you can use the Editor to place the following lines in a text file:

INIT.UNITS.CODE
MY.LIB
#5:MORE.UNITS.CODE
#5:SYSTEM.LIBRARY

You can then name that file USERLIB.TEXT and place it on the system disk. The four files are designated as libraries, along with the standard SYSTEM.LIBRARY on the system disk. The .CODE suffix is appended to these names if necessary.

It is possible to use other library text files besides USERLIB.TEXT. This can be done with execution option strings which are described under the X(ecute activity, below.*

The assembler can also separately produce portions of a host program or unit. These portions are known as **external routines**. External routines must be bound directly into the client program or unit that needs them. The L(inker, which is briefly described in this chapter, is used to do this.

4.14 REDIRECTION

Normally, the p–System is used by a person typing on a keyboard and watching the screen. However, it is possible to **redirect** the p–System's input (to come from someplace other than the keyboard) and/or its output (to go to someplace other than the screen).

You can, for example, create a **script file** which contains characters that you would normally type in response to p–System prompts and menus. If you then redirect the p–System's input to that file, it reads those characters one at a time and selects the corresponding activities. There are many instances in which repetitive tasks can be automated in this manner.

The X(ecute activity is used to redirect input and output. This is accomplished using a facility called **execution option strings** (covered under X(ecute, below).

You can use the M(onitor activity to assist you in creating script files. It causes the p–System to monitor and store away the keys that you type from the keyboard. The resulting script file can be used by X(ecute to duplicate those actions. M(onitor is also described below.

---

* *IV.2 users, note:* You can also use the Command menu's S(et U(serlib activity to establish a new user library text file.

4.15 ERROR MESSAGES

Error messages are displayed by the p–System and its various components under certain circumstances. For example, you may inadvertently take a disk out of its drive before some necessary code is read from it into main memory. Or, a program that you are compiling might not be syntactically correct. There are many other possibilities as well.

Syntax errors for the compilers along with the operating system, Filer, and Editor error messages are listed in the appendices to this book. There are two types of operating system errors that are important enough to introduce here.

The p–System often needs to read code from a disk file into main memory. If you have removed a disk when code is needed from it, you receive a message like this (usually on the bottom line of the screen):*

```
Need segment MYSEG:  Put volume MYDISK in unit 5 then type <space>
```

In this example, MYSEG is the name of the code segment that is required. MYDISK is the name of the volume that contains that code and 5 refers to device #5:, where the disk should be placed. Usually, you don't need to concern yourself about the code segment name. Just place the disk in the indicated drive and press [space].

If an error occurs while a program is running, the operating system produces an **execution error** message. If, for example, a program attempts to divide a number by zero (which is an illegal operation), an error message similar to this appears:†

```
Divide by zero -- Seg MYSEG  P# 3  O# 125  <space> continues
```

The pieces of information displayed in this message show where the error occurred in the program and are called **error coordinates**. If this kind of error occurs, you should note the error coordinates and then type [space]. The p–System reinitializes itself and displays the Command menu. Unless you are debugging the program, the error coordinates are probably not important to you. However, they may be important if you choose to seek help from the supplier or developer of the program.

---

* *IV.0 users, note:* This message appears on the screen at the current location of the cursor and is spread across three lines, but contains roughly the same information. Your response should be the same as discussed above.

† *IV.0 users, note:* This message appears at the current location of the cursor (rather than necessarily on the bottom line) and is spread across three lines. Its content and your response should be essentially as described above.

4.16 NOTATIONAL CONVENTIONS

There are several notational conventions used in Part 2 of this book for referring to volumes and files. The following generic terms, with hyphens, are used:

FILE–SPEC
FILE–NAME
VOLUME–ID
VOLUME–NAME:
SIZE–SPEC

FILE–SPEC refers to "file specification," and SIZE–SPEC refers to "size specification." These generic terms may appear together, like this:

VOLUME–NAME:FILE–NAME
FILE–NAME SIZE–SPEC

When more than one file or volume are referred to, self–explanatory conventions such as these are used:

FILE–NAME–1
FILE–NAME–2
etc.

NEW–VOLUME–ID
OLD–VOLUME–ID

Multiple number signs are used to indicate a numeric value:

Scan for ### blocks (Y/N) ?
Block ## is bad

Prompt and menu responses are underlined and may contain extraneous words such as "or":

```
Execute what file ? FILE-SPEC [ret]
Throw away current workfile ? Y or N
```

Some prompts are shown with several responses. This means that you can respond in any of the indicated ways:

```
Dir listing of what vol ? VOLUME-ID [ret]
                          FILE-SPEC [ret]
                          VOLUME-ID , FILE-SPEC [ret]
```

4.17 THE COMMAND MENU

Whenever the p–System is booted or initialized, the Command menu is displayed. Also, whenever a program finishes execution, or a p–System component (such as the Editor or Filer) is exited, this menu reappears. It provides a platform from which all programs, including the major p–System components, may be selected. The Command menu looks like this:

```
Command: E(dit, R(un, F(ile, C(omp, L(ink, X(ecute, A(ssem, D(ebug,? [ ]
```

Typing "?" displays the rest of of it:

```
Command: H(alt, I(nitialize, U(ser restart, M(onitor [ ]
```

The activities on this menu are covered in this section in alphabetical order. This section is intended as reference material as well as general interest reading.

A(ssemble

An assembler translates the assembly language for a particular microprocessor into machine code consisting of the basic computer instructions. These instructions do such things as add two numbers, store the result in a memory location, compare two numbers, and so forth.

The high–level languages that the compilers accept have more elegant and powerful capabilities. This means that programming in Pascal, for example, can be a lot less tedious than programming in assembly language. There are two reasons why assembly language is attractive to use in certain circumstances, however.

The first is that machine–level code executes faster than the **p–code** which is a compiler's output. P–code is a powerful and compact "pseudo code" that can run on any computer on which the p–System is installed. It is executed by the p–machine emulator (which is written in the assembly language of the host computer). Because of this emulation approach, p–code doesn't run as fast as machine–level code. Therefore, you may want to write time–critical portions of a program in assembly language.

The second attractive attribute of assembly language is that it is very fundamentally close to the computer hardware on which it runs. One implication of this is that you can perform low–level machine–specific tasks which are much more difficult (if even possible) to perform from high–level languages. Plus, assembly language can run with or without the underlying p–System because it is directly executed by the processor. A drawback of machine–level code is that it is specific to a particular processor. This means, for example, that you can't move the assembler's output for an 8086–based computer to a 68000–based computer.

In order to use an Assembler, its code file must be named SYSTEM.ASSMBLER (notice the missing "E") and placed on–line. Also, there is an opcodes file and an errors file that must be on–line. These have names that depend upon the processor you are using (e.g., 8086.OPCODES and 8086.ERRORS, Z80.OPCODES and Z80.ERRORS, and so forth).*

When you select A(ssemble, you are asked what file to assemble. You should enter the name of the text file which contains your assembly language source. You should not include the ".TEXT" because that suffix is assumed:

```
Assemble what text ? MY.PROC [ret]
```

This response causes the file MY.PROC.TEXT to be assembled. The next prompt asks you to give the name that you want the code file to have. You should not include the ".CODE" in your response:

```
To what code file ? MY.PROC [ret]
```

This response causes the output file to be called MY.PROC.CODE. If, instead, you answer this prompt with a dollar sign:

```
To what code file ? $ [ret]
```

the code file is given the name which corresponds to the text file. In this case it is still MY.PROC.CODE.

You should be careful if you enter the text file with a volume name, such as VOL2:MY.PROC, and then use the dollar sign for the code file. In this case, the code file is not necessarily placed on the same volume as the text file. Rather, it is placed on the prefixed volume. For example, if the prefix is VOL1:, responding like this:

```
Assemble what text ? VOL2:MY.PROC [ret]
To what code file ? $ [ret]
```

creates the code file VOL1:MY.PROC.CODE.

Next the Assembler prompts you for a listing file:

```
Output file for assembled listing (<cr> for none) _
```

An assembled listing shows your original text along with the machine code that was generated and other information. The details of assembled listings are beyond the scope of this book. In response to this prompt, you can enter a file specification, in which case the assembled listing is placed in that file. If you enter CONSOLE: or PRINTER:, the listing is displayed or printed, respectively. If you simply type [ret], no listing is produced.

As the assembling process proceeds, dots are displayed on the screen. Each dot represents one line of your source text.

The resulting code file is generally linked, using the Linker, to a high level host program. Unless this is done, the assembly language code can't be executed within the p–System environment. However, it is possible to use

---

* *IV.2 users, note:* You can use the Command menu's S(et A(ssembler activity to designate a different Assembler file.

the **Compress** utility on the assembled code file. This modifies your code file so that it can run without the underlying p–System. It is also possible to link assembled code files together. (You should consult Chapter 9 for further reading suggestions concerning all of these topics.)

C(ompile

C(ompile starts a compiler. The p–System has compilers for Pascal, BASIC, and FORTRAN. You should make sure that the compiler that you want to use is named SYSTEM.COMPILER and resides on an on–line volume. When you are using BASIC or FORTRAN, you also need to have the runtime support package in a library. Chapter 3, Sections 3.4 and 3.5, describe the steps you need to take in order to use Pascal or FORTRAN.*

If you do not have a workfile, you are asked what file you want to compile. This is assumed to be a text file so you should not include ".TEXT" in your response. For instance:

```
Compile what file ? MY.PROG [ret]
```

compiles the file MY.PROG.TEXT.

Next you are asked what you would like to call the code file that is produced. This is assumed to be a code file, so you should not include the .CODE suffix in your response. For example:

```
To what code file ? MY.PROG [ret]
```

causes the resulting file to be called MY.PROG.CODE. If you answer this prompt with a dollar sign like this:

```
To what code file ? $ [ret]
```

the resulting code file is given the name that corresponds to the text file, in this case MY.PROG.CODE. Using a dollar sign not only reduces typing, it saves you from possibly making a confusing mistake by entering an incorrect name, such as MY.PRUG.

You should be careful if you enter the text file with a volume name, such as VOL2:MY.PROG, and then use the dollar sign for the code file. In this case, the code file is not necessarily placed on the same volume as the text file. Rather, it is placed on the prefixed volume. For example, if the prefix is VOL1:, responding like this:

```
Compile what text ? VOL2:MY.PROG [ret]
To what code file ? $ [ret]
```

---

* *IV.2 users, note:* You can use the Command menu's S(et C(ompiler activity to designate a new compiler.

creates the code file VOL1:MY.PROG.CODE.

If you have a workfile, neither of these two prompts is displayed. Instead, the p–System assumes that you want to compile the workfile and that you want the code file to be called SYSTEM.WRK.CODE (the temporary code workfile).*

Next, you are asked if you want a listing of the compiled text:†

```
Output file for compiled listing? (<cr> for none) _
```

If you simply type ⟦ret⟧, no compiled listing is produced. You can enter a disk file name, in which case a file is created on disk which contains the listing. You can also answer this prompt with a communication volume such as PRINTER: or CONSOLE:. These two responses send the listing to the printer or the screen respectively. Here is an example of a Pascal compiled listing:

```
Pascal Compiler IV.1 version   1/ 1/83                              Page 1

   1   2    1:d     1  Program Listing_Example;
   2   2    1:d     1  Var One, Two, Three: Integer;
   3   2    1:d     4      An_Array: Packed Array [0..255] Of Char;
   4   2    1:0     0  Begin
   5   2    1:0     0  {This is an example of a compiled listing}
   6   2    1:1     0  For One:=1 To 200 Do
   7   2    1:2    15    Begin
   8   2    1:3    15      Two:=One*One;
   9   2    1:3    20      Three:=Two+Two;
  10   2    1:3    25      An_Array[One]:=Chr((Two+Three) Mod 127);
  11   2    1:3    43      If An_Array [One] = Chr(One)
  12   2    1:3    52        Then Writeln ('That''s Amazing !')
  13   2    1:3    74      Else Writeln ('That''s Typical!');
  14   2    1:2    96    End
  15   2     :0     0  End.

End of Compilation.
```

The information contained in this listing is useful for debugging and analysis purposes. It is beyond the scope of this book, however.

The compiler makes two passes through the Pascal text. As the compiler does its first pass, dots are displayed on the screen for every line in the text. During the second pass dots are displayed for each procedure of your program. Also, during the second pass, the compiled listing is

---

* *IV.2 users, note:* The behavior of your p–System is different from that described in this paragraph. You will see both of the prompts described earlier, but if you respond with a simple ⟦ret⟧ to both of them, the text workfile will be compiled and the result stored in a corresponding code workfile. By editing the prompt responses before you press ⟦ret⟧ (e.g., by backspacing and typing new characters), you also have the opportunity to completely control the source and object files for the compilation, even though a workfile has been designated.

† *IV.0 users, note:* This prompt requesting the choice of a listing file does not appear during a Pascal compilation. If you want a compiled listing to be produced during a compilation, you must insert a "listing directive" in the source text file. See Appendix D for a discussion of these directives.

produced if you indicate that you want one.

If you intend to do a substantial amount of programming, we suggest that you consult Chapter 9 for further reading suggestions.

D(ebug

If you are going to develop programs with the UCSD p–System, the Debugger is a tool that can help you to diagnose errors in them.

With it, you can stop a running program at any point and look closely at what is going on. You can allow the program to continue for a while and then stop it again. Or you can step very slowly through the code. There are several other operations that the Debugger can perform which help you to determine what might be causing your program to malfunction.

When you enter the Debugger, the following two lines appear:

```
Debug [ ]
(
```

The Debugger is the only major p–System component that does not use menus or prompts. This is because any such displays could interfere with the output of the program being debugged. In order to return to the Command menu from here, you should select the invisible Q(uit activity.

It is not our intention to explain very much about the Debugger in this book although there is a section in Chapter 8 which gives a little more information about it. If you want to use the Debugger, please see Chapter 9 for further reading.

E(dit

Selecting E(dit starts the Editor. The Editor is used to work with text files. You can create a new text file or edit an existing one. When you select E(dit you are usually prompted:

```
>Edit:
No workfile is present. File? ( <ret> for no file )
```

This prompt is asking you what file you want to edit. It is covered in Chapter 5. When you have correctly answered it and entered the Editor, the Edit menu is displayed:

```
>Edit: A(djust C(opy D(el F(ind I(nsert J(ump K(ol M(argin P(age ? [ ]
```

All of the Editor activities are described in Chapter 5.

F(ile

Selecting F(ile starts the Filer. Its menu looks like this:

```
Filer: G(et, S(ave, W(hat, N(ew, L(dir, R(em, C(hng, T(rans, D(ate,? [ ]
```

The Filer is used to work with disk files, storage volumes, and communication volumes. It is described in Chapter 6.

To return to the Command menu, select Q(uit.

H(alt

H(alt terminates all p–System activity. If you want to use the p–System after you have halted it, you need to reboot.

I(nitialize

This activity causes the entire p–System to "reinitialize" itself. This resets the p–System's status to very nearly what it is when you first start it up. However, if you have changed the prefix, that change remains in effect. Also, if you have redirected any I/O, it remains redirected.

L(ink

Selecting L(ink starts the Linker. The Linker is used to combine two or more assembled code files into a single code file. It also links assembled code files to high–level language hosts.

If you need to do a substantial amount of assembly language programming, it may be very convenient to separately assemble the pieces and then link them together.

If you want to execute assembly language code within the p–System environment, it is required that you link the code to a high–level host. Only programs (which are written in high–level languages) can be X(ecuted via the Command menu.

The following display is an example of the prompts that appear when the Linker is used:

```
Host file ? MY.HOST [ret]
Opening MYDISK:MY.HOST.CODE
Lib file ? AN.ASSM [ret]
Opening MYDISK:AN.ASSM.CODE
Lib file ? 1.MORE [ret]
Opening MYDISK:1.MORE.CODE
Lib file ?  [ret]
Map name ?  [ret]
Reading MYHOST
Reading ANASSEM
Reading ONEMORE
Output file ? LINKED.UP.CODE [ret]
Linking MYHOST  #2
  Copying proc ANASSEM
  Copying proc ONEMORE
```

The first prompt asks for a host file. (This is usually the program or unit that uses an assembled routine.)

Then a recurring prompt asks you for as many assembled library files, or "lib" files, as you need. When you have entered all of them, you should type an empty [ret] in response to this prompt.

The next prompt asks for a map file name. If you enter the name of a text file, internal details of the linkage will be placed there.

The Linker then displays the names of the files that it is linking as it reads them.

Next, you are asked for an output file. You *must* include a ".CODE" suffix on the file name you enter if you want to invoke the resulting file via the X(ecute activity. It is easy to forget the suffix because it is not required in many comparable p–System situations.

Finally, you are told the names of the routines as they are linked together.

M(onitor

The M(onitor activity helps you to automate repetitive operations with the p–System. It assists you in creating script files which can serve as a source for redirected input. (For more information on redirection, see Section 4.14, page 120. Execution option strings are used to perform redirection as described under X(ecute.)

Script files contain a series of characters that you would normally enter at the keyboard. When the p–System's input, or a program's input, is redirected to a script file, that file becomes the source of the characters that you would otherwise have to type. Script files can be very convenient for long and repetitive sequences of operations. A simple script file might contain the characters "FV". If you redirect the p–System's input to this file, it would enter the Filer, "F", and select V(olumes, "V".

M(onitor can be used to place the p–System into a mode where it keeps track of what you are typing at the keyboard. All keys that you type, including special keys, are placed into a script file automatically.

When you select M(onitor, this menu appears:

```
Monitor: B(egin, E(nd, A(bort, S(uspend, R(esume
```

In order to start monitoring, you must first select B(egin. B(egin requests that you enter the name of the script file that you want to create.

The next thing that you should do is select R(esume. R(esume returns you to the Command menu. Any keys you type after that are stored in the script file.

If you are finished recording keyboard input, enter the M(onitor again and select E(nd. E(nd closes the script file so that it can now be used as a source of redirected input. After using E(nd, you should use R(esume to return to the Command menu.

If you want to temporarily halt the monitoring process, select S(uspend. After you do this, you are returned to the Command menu. However, nothing that you type is recorded. Later you can re–enter the M(onitor and use R(esume to continue monitoring from where you left off.

A(bort causes the script file that you are creating to be thrown away.

R(un

R(un is used either to execute, or to compile and execute a program. The main purpose of R(un is to assist you in using workfiles. It is convenient in this situation because it saves you from excess typing.

If you have a code workfile, selecting R(un automatically executes it. If you only have a text workfile, R(un compiles it and then executes it. There is a slight twist to this, however: if you have just created a new version of the text workfile (by using Q(uit U(pdate from the Editor), R(un compiles and executes it even if an old version of the code workfile exists.

If you do not have a workfile, R(un executes the most recently compiled code file. If you haven't compiled a file since booting the p–System, R(un asks for a text file to compile and execute.

S(et

S(et is used to check or change various characteristics that affect the operation of the p–System, including workfile designation, date and time. Select S(et and a screen something like the following appears:*

---

* *IV.0, IV.1 users, note:* This activity is only available in IV.2 p–Systems.

```
S(et: D(ate, T(ime, W(orkfile, U(serlib, C(ompiler, A(ssembler, E(ditor,?


January 3, 1985  12:00:00

Workfile:      MYFIRST
Userlib:       *USERLIB.TEXT

Compiler:      SYSTEM.COMPILER on MYVOL:
Assembler:     SYSTEM.ASSMBLER on SYSTEM:
Editor:        SYSTEM.EDITOR   on SYSTEM:

Prefix:        SYSTEM
Root:          SYSTEM

Real Size:     4 words (64 bits)
Spooler:       not available
File System:   SFS
Code Pool:     64k bytes
Stack/Heap:    64k bytes
```

One important purpose of the S(et activity is to give you an easy way to find out the current status of a number of variables that affect the p–System's behavior. The top line of status information is obviously the time and date. If your p–System has a clock facility but time has not been set, "Time not set" appears instead of the time. If your p–System doesn't have a clock, only the date appears. Remember, the time and date shown here are associated with files that you create and may be used in other situations, as well.

Select Q(uit to leave the Set menu and return to the Command menu.

Here are comments on the remaining information items on the S(et display:

- **Workfile:** The name of the currently designated workfile (without the suffix) or "none" if no workfile is designated.
- **Userlib:** The name of the current library text file.
- **Compiler:** The name of the current compiler and the volume on which it is first sought if needed to process a R(un or C(ompile activity. Note that the p–System searches for the named file (when it is needed) throughout the on–line volumes, but only if it is not found on the volume named in this status line.
- **Assembler:** The name of the current Assembler and the volume on which it is first sought during the invocation of the A(ssemble activity. The function of the volume name is the same as that described above for Compiler.
- **Editor:** The name of the current Editor and the volume on which it is first sought during the invocation of the E(dit activity. The function of the volume name is the same as that described above for the Compiler.
- **Prefix:** The current prefix, or default, volume.

- **Root:** The current root, or system, volume.
- **Real Size:** The number of words occupied by real numbers in the current configuration of your p–System.
- **Spooler:** Availability of the Print Spooler. This lines shows "available" or "not available" to indicate whether you can use the Print Spooler or not.
- **File System:** Your display almost certainly shows "SFS" for Standard File System, since the alternative, "AFS", refers to a variant of the p–System (supporting the "Advanced File System") that has not been publicly released (at least at the time of this writing).

You can change any of these fields (except the last three) using activities in the S(et menu. Those last three *can* be configured in most p–Systems, but the process is often complicated and certainly outside the scope of this book. In the remainder of this subsection, we describe the S(et menu activities.

D(ate

D(ate allows you to change the p–System's calendar date and is functionally equivalent to the Filer's D(ate activity. The p–System's date is associated with files that are created or updated so that when you do a directory listing you can tell the age of each file. Keeping the date current helps you in your housekeeping operations with files (allowing you, for instance, to know which of two versions of a file is the most recent). The date is also used for other similar functions.

When you select D(ate, the following prompt invites you to enter a new date and reminds you about the rules for doing that:

```
Correct date: (<1..31>-<Jan..Dec>-<00..99>)_
```

The day of your new date must be in the range 1 to 31, the month must be indicated by a three letter abbreviation (in which it doesn't matter whether you use capital letters or lowercase letters) and the year is designated by its last two digits.

You can enter as many elements of the date as you wish, leaving the others unchanged. So, for instance, you could enter just the day and leave the month and year unchanged or enter the day and month and leave the year unchanged.

T(ime

The T(ime activity allows you to set the p–System's internal time. Like the date, the current time is associated with files that are created or updated and for other purposes as well. If your p–System is not configured with a clock facility, you cannot set the time, and the T(ime activity does nothing.

Selecting the T(ime activity results in the following prompt:

```
Correct time? (0000..2359)_
```

In T(ime's 24–hour scale, midnight corresponds to 0000, noon to 1200, and 6:33pm to 1833. Enter the correct time in those terms. You can omit leading zeros, so 5 [ret], 05 [ret], and 005 [ret] are all valid responses that set the time to five minutes after midnight.

W(orkfile

W(orkfile enables you to choose the name of the current workfile or indicate that you don't want a workfile at all. (See the section on workfiles earlier in the chapter.)

When you select the W(orkfile activity, the following prompt appears:

```
New workfile? (<ret> clears the workfile>)_
```

An immediate [ret] clears the workfile altogether. Any other entry sets the workfile to designated file (or group of files). The file specification you enter must not have a suffix (i.e. .TEXT or .CODE), since the p–System adds the appropriate suffix when necessary. Your name can, however, include an explicit volume ID. The specified file does not have to exist when you designate it as the workfile.

U(serlib

The U(serlib activity allows you to determine the library text file used by the p–System in preparing programs for execution. The "L=" execution option can be used for the same purpose.

When the following prompt appears in response to your selection of U(serlib,

```
New userlib? (<ret> for default)_
```

respond with a complete file specification for the library text file you want to establish. Be sure to include the .TEXT suffix if the file you choose is a text file. The default library text file is "*USERLIB.TEXT". Enter an immediate [ret] in response to the prompt to re–establish this default.

C(ompiler, A(ssembler, E(ditor

These activities allow you to designate the programs that are invoked when you select the corresponding activities in the Command menu. You can change among more than one compiler, assembler or editor without having to change the names of any files. (Before the addition of these activities, changing to a new compiler involved establishing a new file with the required name "SYSTEM.COMPILER".)

When you type C, A or E, one of the following prompts is displayed:

```
Compiler file name? (<ret> for default)
Assembler file name? (<ret> for default)_
Editor file name? (<ret> for default)_
```

If you respond with an immediate [ret], the appropriate default name is established (SYSTEM.COMPILER, SYSTEM.ASSMBLER, or SYSTEM.EDITOR). Otherwise, the file name you enter is used when the p–System searches for one of these system components. Remember, you must enter a complete file name (including the suffix, if any).

Next, you are asked to specify the volume where the system component should be sought first when it is invoked:

```
On what volume? (<ret> exits)_
```

An immediate [ret] response to this prompt leaves the current volume name unchanged. Otherwise, you specify a volume ID. When the component is invoked (i.e. the Editor, Compiler or Assembler), the p–System looks first on the specified volume for the file named in the previous step. If the file is not on that volume, a search of all on–line volumes occurs. If this search is successful, a new Volume ID is established that determines the first volume to examine when the next invocation of the same component occurs.

P(refix

The P(refix activity allows you to set the prefix or default volume on which files are sought when their specifications don't include explicit Volume IDs. In response to the P(refix prompt:

```
New prefix? (<ret> exits)_
```

enter a Volume ID. An immediate [ret] leaves the prefix unchanged. A colon at the end of your Volume ID is ignored by this activity.

U(ser Restart

U(ser restart is used to restart any program that just completed execution. If, for example, you have just X(ecuted a program like this:

```
Execute what file ? MY.PROG [ret]
```

and the Command menu has reappeared, you can now run it again by simply typing "U". This is convenient when you need to run the same program several times.

There are some programs that take a relatively long time to begin running because of **associate time**. This is the time that it takes the p–System to collect information about the units that a program uses. When programs are restarted with U(ser restart, associate time is not a factor because the units are still "associated." This means that programs which use a large number of units start noticeably quicker with U(ser–restart. (The Quickstart utility, introduced in Chapter 8, provides a mechanism for reducing associate time in general.)

X(ecute

Programs that are ready to run may be started by selecting X(ecute. This activity prompts you:

```
Execute what file ? _
```

You should enter the name of an executable code file. Do not include the .CODE suffix. For example, if you want to execute a file called MY.PROG.CODE, respond to the X(ecute prompt like this:

```
Execute what file ? MY.PROG [ret]
```

It is possible to respond to this prompt with the entire name of a code file, if you add a period, ".", to the end of the file name:

```
Execute what file ? MY.PROG.CODE. [ret]
```

This can be useful since a code file's name is not required to end with .CODE. For example, you can X(ecute SYSTEM.FILER like this:

```
Execute what file ? SYSTEM.FILER. [ret]
```

If you type in the ".CODE" without a period, the file won't be found or executed. For example, if you enter "PROG.CODE", X(ecute tries to find the file "PROG.CODE.CODE" which is not what you intended.

It is possible to do several other useful things with X(ecute by using **execution option strings**. An execution option string is an optional part of your response to the "Execute what file ?" prompt. For example:

```
Execute what file ? I=SCRIPT.TEXT [ret]
```

is a valid way to use the "I" option, as described below.

Execution option strings were mentioned in the section on redirection earlier in this chapter (see Section 4.14, page 120). Using them you can redirect the p–System's input and output. You can also redirect a particular program's input and output. There are several other tasks that execution option strings can perform. Here is a summary of the six execution options:

I= This option can be followed by a quoted string or a file specification. (The file specification could indicate a script file or a communication volume such as REMIN:). The **p—System's input** is redirected to come from that input source instead of the keyboard.

O= This option is followed by a file specification (which could indicate a disk file or a communication volume such as PRINTER:). The **p—System's output** is sent to that destination instead of the screen.

PI= This option can be followed by a quoted string or a file specification. (The file specification could indicate a script file or a communication volume, such as REMIN:). The **program's input** is redirected to come from that input source instead of the keyboard.

PO= This option is followed by a file specification (which could indicate a disk file or a communication volume such as PRINTER:). The **program's output** is redirected to that destination.

P= This option is followed by a volume ID for a storage volume. It sets the **prefix** to the indicated volume ID. This is the same operation performed by the Filer's P(refix activity. *You must not include the colon after the volume ID.*

L= This option is followed by a text file specification. The .TEXT suffix is optional. The indicated text file is designated as the **library text file** (see Section 4.13, page 119).

Any execution options which you use should appear after the program's file specification. You don't have to include a program if you don't want to execute one. You can just use X(ecute to perform execution options by themselves.

If you use more than one execution option, you should separate them using space characters. The order in which you use them does not matter as long as the program name is first (if you are executing one). The prefix option, however, is always processed before anything else.

A few examples of responses to the X(ecute prompt should help to illuminate the use of these execution option strings.

The following response redirects the p—System's input to come from your file MY.SCRIPT.TEXT:

```
Execute what file ? I=MY.SCRIPT.TEXT [[ret]]
```

If this file contains the characters "FL#5:⟦ret⟧" the p–System enters the Filer, "F", selects L(ist directory, "L", and designates the volume in drive #5, "#5:⟦ret⟧". When all the characters from the input file have been read, standard input from the keyboard resumes.

In the next example, the p–System's input is redirected to a string:

```
Execute what file ? I="FL#5:," O=PRINTER: [[ret]]
```

The string causes the p–System to enter the Filer and list the directory of the disk in drive #5. The comma within the string is interpreted as ⟦ret⟧.

In addition, the p–System's output is redirected to the printer. When this is done, all prompts, menus, and other displays are printed rather than displayed on the screen. This means that the Filer's menu, the L(ist directory prompt and response, and the directory listing of the disk in drive are all printed rather than displayed on the screen. This handling of output continues until another redirection command makes a change. In the final example, the file #5:MY.PROG.CODE is executed:

```
Execute what file ? MY.PROG P=#5 L=USERLIB2 PO=PRINTER: [[ret]]
```

Before that program actually starts, however, the following actions occur:

- The prefix volume is changed to #5:.
- The library text file is changed to #5:USERLIB2.TEXT.
- The program's output is redirected to the printer. This means that everything the program normally writes to the screen is printed instead. After the program finishes, output resumes to the console screen.

5

THE EDITOR

5.1 INTRODUCTION

One area in which computers are extremely valuable is text editing. With a typewriter you can produce text on paper, but it can't be rearranged, corrected, and printed out again. An editor can save the text you create on disk. Later that text can be printed, or, if it is a program, compiled.

There are two editors available with the p–System. The first is the Screen–oriented Editor which is described in this chapter. The second is the advanced editor, EDVANCE, which is similar to the Screen–oriented Editor, but contains several more sophisticated features. EDVANCE is introduced in Chapter 8.

We introduced the Screen–oriented Editor in the first part of this book. In this chapter we cover the Editor and its activities more thoroughly and systematically.

We have laid out this chapter so that, after you read it through, you can use it as a reference guide in the future. It begins with a quick overview of the Editor. Next, the general Editor facilities are introduced. Finally, the items on the Editor menu are covered in detail.

5.2 OVERVIEW OF THE EDITOR

The Editor works with text files. Text files always have names that end with .TEXT. Here are some examples:

POEM.TEXT
PROPOSAL.TEXT
SYSTEM.WRK.TEXT

When an editing session begins, you may either create a new file from scratch, or you may edit an existing file. In either case, the copy of the file that you are editing exists in main memory and is called your **workspace**. The amount of main memory that you have determines the maximum size of your workspace. When you are finished editing the workspace, you can write it to disk. Alternatively, you can leave the Editor without saving the workspace on disk.

If you are editing an existing file and you store your workspace on disk using its original name, the old copy of the file is removed (because you can't have two files with the same name on the same volume).

During an edit session, the portion of your workspace that is displayed on the screen is said to be in the **window**. This window may be moved forward (toward the end of the workspace) or backward. In this way you can view the entire contents of your workspace, although not all at one time. (See Figure 2.1.) In order to move the window, you need to move the cursor. This is done with the cursor–moving keys and activities.

The Editor may be used in various ways to insert, delete, overwrite, copy, and locate text. It can also automatically rearrange the words in a paragraph to make the lines fit within the margins. The editing environment can be set so the Editor is especially suited for creating line–oriented text or paragraph–oriented text.

In order to use the Editor, the file SYSTEM.EDITOR must be present on an on–line volume. This file must contain the Screen–oriented Editor.

5.3 CURSOR MOVEMENT

During an editing session, the cursor may be moved to any part of your workspace by typing certain keys, or by using the appropriate Editor activities. You may examine and/or change text anywhere in your workspace by first moving the cursor to the location of that text. Before we describe these keys and activities, there are a couple of general concepts that need to be introduced. These are the **direction indicator** and the **repeat factor**.

Direction Indicator

The direction indicator determines whether the cursor is moved in the forward direction, or in the backward direction for certain keys and activities. For example, typing ⟦space⟧ normally moves the cursor one place to the right, as on a typewriter. If the direction indicator is reversed, however, typing ⟦space⟧ moves the cursor to the left (which is also what ⟦bs⟧ does).

You can tell what the direction is by looking at the character in the upper left hand corner of the screen. If it is a right angle bracket, ">", then the direction is forward. If it is a left angle bracket, "<", then the direction is backward. You can think of the angle bracket as an arrow pointing forward or backward.

In order to change the direction indicator, type the right angle bracket to make it forward or the left angle bracket to make it backward. The period, ".", and plus sign, "+", also set the direction indicator forward. Similarly, the comma, ",", and minus sign, "−", also set the direction indicator backward.

The direction indicator affects ⟦space⟧, ⟦ret⟧, ⟦tab⟧, P(age, F(ind, and R(eplace.

Repeat Factor

A repeat factor is a number that you may type just before using a cursor movement key or activity. The cursor movement is then performed that many times. For example, if you type "3" before using ⟦space⟧, the cursor moves three spaces instead of just one.

The repeat factor is always 1 unless you cause it to be otherwise. You can use repeat factors in the range 1 to 9999. You can also use a slash, "/", to indicate the infinite repeat factor. The infinite repeat factor causes the cursor movement to be repeated as many times as is possible in the workspace. For example, typing "/" followed by ⟦down⟧ moves the cursor down to the very last line in the workspace. As soon as you have used the cursor movement key or activity, the repeat factor returns to 1.

All cursor movement keys except ⟦=⟧ are affected by the repeat factor. P(age, J(ump, F(ind, and R(eplace are affected as well. In addition, when the cursor movement keys are used within A(djust, D(elete, and K(olumn, the repeat factor applies.

Another way to repeat cursor movement on some computers is to hold down ⟦repeat⟧ and the cursor movement key at the same time. As long as both keys are pressed down, the cursor movement is repeated. For example, holding down ⟦repeat⟧ and ⟦up⟧ causes the cursor to keep moving upward until the keys are released (or the first line of the workspace is reached).

On other computers, this sort of repeated cursor movement is accomplished by simply holding down the cursor movement key for a longer than normal length of time, generally over one second. For example, holding down ⟦space⟧ for less than a second moves the cursor only one space. Holding it down for more than a second causes the cursor to continue moving until the space bar is released.

Cursor Movement Keys

Here are the cursor movement keys you can use in the Editor:

⟦space⟧ The space bar moves the cursor one position to the right as on a typewriter. At the end of a line it does an automatic carriage return. A repeat factor may be used to move several spaces at a time. If the direction indicator is set backwards, the space bar moves the cursor to the left. Generally, ⟦space⟧ is used to move only a few characters from the present cursor position. If you need to move further, ⟦tab⟧ is often a better key to use.

⟦bs⟧ This key moves the cursor one position to the left. If the cursor is already occupying the first position on the line, it is moved to the last position on the line above. A repeat factor may be used with ⟦bs⟧. Like ⟦space⟧, ⟦bs⟧ is usually most effective if you are only going to move the cursor a few places.

If you are at the end of a long line and want to move quickly to the beginning, it is easier to type ⟦ret⟧ followed by ⟦up⟧ (or ⟦up⟧ followed by ⟦ret⟧) than it is to use ⟦bs⟧ several times. Several backward ⟦tab⟧s can also be used to move quickly to the left.

⟦ret⟧ This key acts like a carriage return on a typewriter. It moves the cursor to the beginning of the line below. If the direction indicator is backwards, ⟦ret⟧ moves the cursor to the beginning of the line above. Several ⟦ret⟧s can be done by using a repeat factor. However, if you need to do quite a few (say 20 or 30) it is usually better to use P(age.

⟦tab⟧ This key moves the cursor to the right until it reaches the next tab stop, again in similar fashion to a typewriter. Tab stops are normally set at every eighth space across a line. However, you can set them wherever you want by using the S(et tabstops option described under S(et E(nvironment later in this chapter.

If the direction indicator is set backwards, the cursor is moved to the next tab stop on the left. A repeat factor may be used to tab several stops beyond the current cursor position.

Arrow Keys The ⟦up⟧, ⟦down⟧, ⟦left⟧, and ⟦right⟧ keys move the cursor in the indicated directions. The arrow keys always move the cursor in the direction that they indicate; they are not affected by the direction indicator. They are, however, affected by the repeat factor.

Sometimes ⟦up⟧ or ⟦down⟧ can seem to move the cursor "off the text," that is, to a position that is really beyond the left or right margins of the current line. In this case, the cursor may seem to jump around when you use the next cursor movement key. To understand this "jumping" you should realize that the cursor is not logically located beyond the margin. (It is either at the first character or the last character of the line.)

⟦=⟧ The ⟦=⟧ key moves the cursor to the beginning of the portion of text that was just inserted with I(nsert, found with F(ind, or replaced with R(eplace. When ⟦=⟧ is typed again, the cursor returns to where it was.

The ⟦=⟧ key is often useful if you are inserting text somewhere in your workspace, and you need to look at some other part of the workspace. You can move to that other area and, when ready, return to where you last used I(nsert by simply typing ⟦=⟧.

NOTE: The special key descriptions in this subsection are summarized on the inside front cover of this book.

5.4 SPECIAL EDITOR KEYS

The Editor uses all of the p–System's special keys as described in Chapter 4. However, the meaning of ⟦esc⟧ and ⟦delete line⟧ are subtly different. The Editor also uses some additional special keys.

⟦etx⟧ This key accepts the changes that you have just made with an Editor activity. After you enter ⟦etx⟧, those changes become effective within your workspace and you are returned to the main Editor menu.

For example, when you enter text using I(nsert, you must type ⟦etx⟧ to accept the insertion.

⟦esc⟧ This key discards the changes that you have made with an Editor activity. For example, when you use I(nsert to enter text, you can use ⟦esc⟧ to discard the insertion.

⟦delete line⟧ This key allows you to erase one line at a time when you I(nsert text. It is convenient if you don't want to use ⟦bs⟧ several times.

⟦exch–ins⟧ This key inserts a blank character when you are using

X(change. It is convenient since you don't have to quit X(change and use I(nsert to place the extra blank in your workspace.

If you want to insert a single character while in X(change, you can type ⟦exch–ins⟧ followed by that character. The character is placed in the blank position opened by ⟦exch–ins⟧. You can, in fact, insert several characters in this manner.

⟦exch–del⟧ This key deletes one character when you are using X(change. It is convenient since you don't have to quit X(change and use D(elete to remove a character.

The special key descriptions in this subsection are summarized on the inside front cover of this book.

5.5 ENTERING AND REMOVING TEXT

The Editor's insertion and deletion activities usually apply at the location of the cursor. Thus, by placing the cursor appropriately, you may alter text anywhere in your workspace.

The I(nsert activity is used to place new text in your workspace. The Editor functions in one mode where, as text is being inserted, the bell beeps when you approach the end of a line (in a similar fashion to a typewriter). In this mode, you need to type ⟦ret⟧ at the end of every line to go on to the next one.

Alternatively, the Editor can function in a mode where it automatically starts a new line when the word that you are typing does not fit onto the current line.

The first mode is most often used for line–oriented editing such as creating tables or writing programs. The second mode is used to create paragraphs. In conjunction with the paragraph mode, it is possible to specify where you want the left and right margins to be, as well as how much indentation you would like for the first line of a paragraph. These two modes of inserting text are covered under I(nsert. S(et E(nvironment is used to change from one mode to another.

There are two activities that allow you to delete text: D(elete and Z(ap. With D(elete you can move the cursor around and delete text as you go. Z(ap performs an instantaneous deletion of a certain portion of text. Z(ap can be useful for deleting a very large portion of text (since it may be inconvenient to move the cursor a long distance with D(elete).

X(change is used to overwrite old text directly with new text. You can do the same thing by I(nserting the new material and then D(eleting the old material. X(change is often much easier for this sort of task, however.

C(opy can move a portion of text from one place to another within your workspace. You can duplicate that text several times if you want. You can even copy text from a disk file into your workspace using this activity.

R(eplace is able to change one sequence of characters into another. You indicate the sequence of characters to change as well as the replacement sequence. Several instances of the target sequence of characters may be replaced at once.

5.6 TEXT APPEARANCE

There are several ways in which you can affect the way your text appears. For example, you may wish to rearrange paragraphs so that each line fits within certain margins. You might want to move columns closer together or further apart. This sort of text manipulation is possible with the Editor activities introduced here.

A(djust allows you to change the indentation of one or more lines. With it you can move a single line to the right or to the left. Then, other lines (above or below) can be moved in a similar fashion.

K(olumn works like A(djust except it only affects the portion of a line which is to the right of the cursor. K(olumn is most useful for moving columns closer together or further apart.

S(et E(nvironment and M(argin work together. They enable you to automatically rearrange the words within a paragraph so that each line is as wide as possible within the margins that you specify. I(nsert is also able to rearrange text in this way.

There are several ways that you can print your text once it is in final form. These are discussed in Chapter 8 under "Editing and Printing Tools."

5.7 PARAGRAPH SEPARATION

I(nsert and M(argin, as just mentioned, are able to rearrange paragraphs. In order for this to work, however, the paragraphs must be correctly separated from each other and from any adjacent tables or columns.

I(nsert and M(argin consider a paragraph to be any single spaced text which is preceded and followed by paragraph delimiters. A paragraph delimiter is one of four items:

- A blank line.
- The beginning of the workspace.
- The end of the workspace.

- A line that starts with the **command character**.

This usually means that a blank line must exist between paragraphs if they are to be treated separately.

Alternatively, the command character may be used to indicate the beginning or ending of a paragraph by placing it as the first character on a line. The command character can be any character you choose. S(et E(nvironment allows you to change it. If, for example, the command character is carat, "^", the following two paragraphs are properly separated:

```
>Edit: A(djust C(opy D(el F(ind I(nsert J(ump K(ol M(argin P(age [ ]
  As we said in our earlier proposal, we believe
our company is best suited to perform these
tasks.

  Should you find it necessary to revise the
schedules we have included, please inform us at
the earliest possible date.
```

Although it is often easier to use blank lines between paragraphs, it is sometimes convenient to have a character such as this so that text formatting can be done in conjunction with paragraph–oriented editing.

A text formatter is a program which takes a text file and, rather than just printing it as is, formats the text before it is sent to the printer. This can mean doing proportional spacing, left and right margin justification, bold and underlined printing, and so forth.

Many text formatters use commands that start with "." (period). For example, the Print utility (which is a simple text formatting utility) can use a ".PAGE" command which means to do a page break at that point in the printing. In this case, you could set the command character to "." and create paragraphs such as:

```
>Edit: A(djust C(opy D(el F(ind I(nsert J(ump K(ol M(argin P(age [ ]
  As we said in our earlier proposal, we believe
our company is best suited to perform these
tasks.
.PAGE
  Should you find it necessary to revise the
schedules we have included, please inform us at
the earliest possible date.
```

In this way, you can use M(argin or I(nsert on either of the paragraphs above without disturbing the other paragraph. And, at the same time, you can put text formatting commands conveniently between paragraphs.

Also, the Print utility (and most text formatters) do not print lines which begin with the proper command character. This enables you to separate paragraphs (in order to edit them in paragraph mode) but print them without a blank line in between.

5.8 MARKERS

The Editor allows you to place as many as 20 invisible flags, called **markers**, at arbitrary locations within your workspace. Markers have names which you assign to them. These names may have as many as eight alphabetic or numeric characters.

The S(et M(arker activity is used to place a marker in your workspace. The markers you set remain there even after the workspace is written to disk.

Once a marker is set, you can J(ump there from any place in the workspace. You may want to set markers at locations that you frequently need to look at. They are especially useful in a large workspace.

The C(opy F(rom file activity also uses markers. This activity enables you to copy material from a disk file directly into your workspace. If you only want to copy a portion of that file, you need to indicate two markers. The text between those markers (which must already exist in the file) is copied.

5.9 THE COPY BUFFER

The copy buffer is a "scratch pad" area of memory where the Editor keeps a copy of the text that you have just inserted or deleted. Whatever is in the copy buffer may be copied back into your workspace. The copy buffer is useful for creating several copies of a piece of text, or for restoring material to your workspace that you accidentally delete.

Text inserted with the I(nsert activity is placed in the copy buffer (as well as in the workspace itself). This only happens, however, if you accept the inserted text (by typing ⟦etx⟧). If you decide to discard the insertion (by using ⟦esc⟧ instead of ⟦etx⟧) the text is not placed in the copy buffer. In this case, the copy buffer is left empty and any text it previously contained is discarded.

When you delete text using D(elete or Z(ap, it is placed in the copy buffer. This is done whether or not you accept the deletion (with ⟦etx⟧).

Once something is in the copy buffer, it may be copied into the workspace if you wish. This is done by placing the cursor where you would like the copying to occur and selecting C(opy B(uffer.

Using C(opy B(uffer does not change the contents of the copy buffer. This means that you can use it to place the same piece of text into your workspace several times. However, the next time that you do an insertion or deletion, the newly inserted or deleted material replaces what was previously in the copy buffer. As we mentioned, if you use I(nsert followed by ⟦esc⟧, the copy buffer is left empty. Using the M(argin activity also leaves the copy buffer empty.

If you want to have another copy of some text which already exists in your workspace, you can place it into the copy buffer by deleting it with D(elete, and then typing ⟦esc⟧. This leaves the original copy of the text unaltered. You can then move the cursor, if desired, and duplicate the text someplace in your workspace by selecting C(opy B(uffer. In this way, you end up with two copies of the original text.

If you D(elete text and then use ⟦etx⟧ (instead of ⟦esc⟧), the original text is removed from the workspace and placed in the copy buffer. You can then place the text back into the workspace somewhere else, leaving only one copy of the original text. This can also be done using Z(ap.

With both D(elete and Z(ap, you may receive an error message which indicates there is no room to copy the deletion. This means that if you proceed, the deleted text will not be placed in the copy buffer because of memory space limitations. That text will then be lost. (This error message is covered in Appendix A, "Error Messages for Major Activities.")

5.10 TOKENS AND LITERAL STRINGS

The F(ind and R(eplace activities locate or replace sequences of characters such as "Hi" or "Section 12". These character sequences are either viewed as **tokens** or as **literal strings**. The difference has to do with the context in which a given character sequence can be identified by F(ind or R(eplace.

A token must not be directly adjacent to a letter or digit. A literal string, on the other hand, may be placed in any context. For example, these sequences contain the token "Hi":

Hi
Hi there
Like Hi?

All of the above also contain the literal string "Hi". Each of these next four sequences contain the literal string (but not the token) "Hi":

8Hi9
Hithere
Hit parade
WATCHit

F(ind, for example, is able to locate only the first four of these sequences when it is searching for tokens. However, it can locate all eight of them as literal strings.

There is another difference between tokens and literal strings. Blank spaces and carriage returns are not significant parts of a token. However, they are significant within literal strings. For example, if you try to F(ind the token "Hi there", you could conceivably locate: "Hithere". However, if you search for it as a literal string, you won't find "Hithere" because the space is missing.

In either literal strings or tokens, upper and lower case distinctions are made. For instance, each of these is considered to be a different sequence:

Hi

HI
hi

S(et E(nvironment is used to determine whether F(ind and R(eplace search for tokens or literal strings by default. F(ind and R(eplace can override this default, however.

5.11 ENTERING THE EDITOR

To begin an edit session, select E(dit from the Command menu. If you have a workfile (see Chapter 4) then it is read into your workspace and displayed automatically.* Otherwise, the following prompt asks you what file you would like to edit:

```
>Edit:
No workfile is present. File? (<ret> for no file ) FILE-SPEC [ret]
```

Type the file specification for the desired text file but do not include the .TEXT suffix. For example:

```
>Edit:
No workfile is present. File? (<ret> for no file ) #5:MY.FILE [ret]
```

reads in MY.FILE.TEXT from the disk in drive #5. If the Editor cannot find the file that you indicated, you are asked to type in a file name once again:

```
>Edit:
No workfile is present. File? (<ret> for no file ) FILE-SPEC [ret]
Not present. File? FILE-SPEC [ret]
```

You may keep trying until you correctly indicate an existing text file which is on the correct disk.

If, instead of editing an existing file, you want to create a new file, respond to the prompt by simply typing ⟦ret⟧:

```
>Edit:
No workfile is present. File? (<ret> for no file ) [ret]
```

If you change your mind and would rather not enter the Editor at all, respond to the prompt by typing ⟦esc⟧.

When the Editor is entered, its main menu appears on the top line of the screen:

```
>Edit: A(djust C(opy D(el F(ind I(nsert J(ump K(ol M(argin P(age ? [ ]
```

---

* *IV.2 users, note:* The workfile is not read into the workspace automatically. The workfile's name is displayed and you need to press ⟦ret⟧ to confirm that choice. Then the workfile is read in.

Below this menu, the first portion of the text within your workspace (if any) is displayed.

5.12 LEAVING THE EDITOR

In order to leave the Editor, select Q(uit. When you do this, the following options are displayed:

```
>Quit:
     U(pdate the workfile and leave
     E(xit without updating
     R(eturn to the editor without updating
     W(rite to a file name and return
```

Here are the results of selecting each of these options:

- **U(pdate the workfile and leave:** Your workspace is placed on the system disk and called SYSTEM.WRK.TEXT. The Editor is then exited and the Command menu returns. SYSTEM.WRK.TEXT is now your workfile.* If you receive the message "ERROR writing out the file," several problems may have occurred. These are covered below.
- **E(xit without updating:** Your workspace is not saved on disk. Instead, the Editor is simply exited. Any changes that you may have made are not saved.†
- **R(eturn to the editor without updating:** You do not leave the Editor at all. Nothing is saved on disk. The material that was previously on the screen is redisplayed just as it was before you selected Q(uit.
- **W(rite to a file name and return:** You can write your workspace to disk and give it a name other than SYSTEM.WRK.TEXT. If your workspace was read in from a disk file, you can write it out to the same file by entering $ ⟦ret⟧, or you can enter a full file specification to write the workspace out to some other file. Alternatively, if your workspace was created from scratch, your only choice in Q(uit W(rite is to enter the file specification indicating where the workspace should be written. The Q(uit W(rite prompt appears below. The second line only appears, and the second response is only allowed, when your

---

* *IV.2 users, note:* Q(uit U(pdate does not produce SYSTEM.WRK.TEXT. It either gives the output file the same name as it had originally, or, if you created the workspace from scratch, the Editor asks you to name the output file.

† *IV.2 users, note:* If you select this alternative after making changes to the workspace, you are asked to confirm that you wish to discard those changes.

workspace was read in from a disk file.

```
Quit:
'$'<ret> writes to OLD-FILE-NAME
Name of output file (<cr> to return)  --> FILE-SPEC [ret]
                                           $ [ret]
```

There are two possible responses. You can enter a file specification. However, you may, if you wish, enter dollar sign, "$", followed by ⟦ret⟧. This writes the workspace to disk and gives it the same name that it originally had.

You can simply type ⟦ret⟧ in answer to either version of the W(rite prompt. This returns you to the Editor without saving anything on disk.

If the name that you give to your file is the same as some other file currently on the disk, the old file is removed. The Editor assumes you realize what you are doing and does not warn you about this.*

As your workspace is written to disk, the word "Writing" is displayed, usually followed by several dots. If there is some problem in saving the workspace, you receive the message:†

```
Writing......
ERROR writing out the file.  Please press <spacebar> to continue.
```

This indicates one of several problems:

- There is not enough room on the disk for the file that the Editor is trying to create there. When you type ⟦space⟧, you are returned to your workspace. You can then Q(uit W(rite it to some other disk. Later you can try to fit it on the disk where you wanted to save it originally.

  When the Editor saves a workspace on disk, it removes the old file with the same name if one exists (as we already mentioned). However, the old file isn't removed until after the workspace is saved. This means that there must be enough room for two copies of the file in order for the Editor to save it.

  If you have to resort to writing it to another disk, you may be able to use the Filer's T(ransfer activity to move it back to the original disk. T(ransfer removes the existing file before it places the new file on disk.

---

* *IV.2 users, note:* The Editor requests confirmation before removing an existing file, unless you use the "$" option.

† *IV.2 users, note:* The generalized error message shown does not appear. Instead, a specific input/output error message appears. See Appendix B for explanations of these errors and possible recovery actions.

Sometimes, even this may not work because the newest version of your file has grown larger than the older version. In this case, even though the old version is removed, there is still not enough room for the new one. You may be able to explicitly R(emove unnecessary files and/or K(runch the disk to make more room. R(emove and K(runch are both Filer activities and are described, along with T(ransfer, in Chapter 6.

- The volume where you are saving the file isn't on–line. If you didn't indicate a volume, this could still be the problem (when the prefixed volume isn't on–line). The solution is to place the appropriate disk back in the drive. When you type ⟦space⟧, you can try again to save the workspace on that volume. Alternatively, you can save it on another volume.
- The file name that you specified was syntactically incorrect. For example, you may have entered a name that is longer than the 15 character limit. (Remember that ".TEXT" is appended to the name you enter.) In this case, you should type ⟦space⟧ and try again with a valid file name.

When your workspace is successfully written to disk using W(rite, you are notified in this fashion:

```
>Quit:
Writing...............
Your file is 15297 bytes long.
Do you want to E(xit from or R(eturn to the editor?
```

The dots after "Writing" appear as your workspace is saved on disk. The third line tells you the length of your file in bytes (or characters). The last line prompts you to select E(xit to leave the Editor or R(eturn to re–enter it and continue editing from where you left off. You might use R(eturn if you are simply writing your workspace to disk for safety, and you want to continue editing.

5.13 THE EDITOR MENU

In this section, the Editor's menu items are covered individually in alphabetical order. Most of these items display error messages under certain circumstances. These error messages are covered in Appendix A, "Error Messages for Major Activities."

A(djust

A(djust changes the horizontal position of one or more lines of text.

How to use it:

Place the cursor on the line you wish to adjust. Select A(djust and this line is displayed:

```
>Adjust: L(just R(just C(enter <left,right,up,down-arrows> {<etx> to leave}
```

Pressing ⟦right⟧ moves the line one place to the right. Pressing ⟦left⟧ moves it to the left. Pressing ⟦up⟧ or ⟦down⟧ causes the adjustment that was done to the current line to be repeated on the line just above or below.

Selecting L(just moves the line to be flush against the left margin. Selecting R(just moves the line to the right margin. And selecting C(enter causes the line to be centered between the margins. (These margins are not necessarily the left and right screen boundaries; they are the L(eft and R(ight margins which can be set to any column using S(et E(nvironment.)

A line can only be moved to the left until it is flush against the left screen boundary. When moving to the right, however, the line may be moved beyond the edge of the screen. Text may seem to disappear off the screen to the right but it is still present. An exclamation mark, "!", is displayed in the right–most column as an indicator whenever text lies beyond it.

When you move vertically in A(djust, you can accumulate horizontal movement by using ⟦left⟧ or ⟦right⟧ on any given line. The accumulated horizontal adjustment is then applied to succeeding lines, above or below, if you continue moving vertically.

When you have finished with A(djust, you must use ⟦etx⟧ to accept the changes that you have made. It is not possible to use ⟦esc⟧ to leave A(djust.

Example:

If you want to indent your entire workspace 2 columns, place the cursor at the beginning and select A(djust. Type ⟦right⟧ twice to adjust the first line:

```
This is the first line.   <-- BEFORE ADJUST
  This is the first line. <-- AFTER ADJUST
```

Then type the infinite repeat factor, "/", followed by ⟦down⟧. Every line in your workspace is moved two places to the right.

As an example of accumulated horizontal movement, you could A(djust a line three places to the right:

```
>Adjust: L(just R(just C(enter <left,right,up,down-arrows> {<etx> to leave}
Monthly Report:
1. The Good News ....... Page 3
2. The Bad News ........ Page 4
```

```
>Adjust: L(just R(just C(enter <left,right,up,down-arrows> {<etx> to leave}
   Monthly Report:
1. The Good News ....... Page 3
2. The Bad News ........ Page 4
```

type [down] once, adjusting the line below:

```
>Adjust: L(just R(just C(enter <left,right,up,down-arrows> {<etx> to leave}
   Monthly Report:
   1. The Good News ....... Page 3
2. The Bad News ........ Page 4
```

and then adjust that line three more places to the right:

```
>Adjust: L(just R(just C(enter <left,right,up,down-arrows> {<etx> to leave}
   Monthly Report:
      1. The Good News ....... Page 3
2. The Bad News ........ Page 4
```

and finally type [down] once more:

```
>Adjust: L(just R(just C(enter <left,right,up,down-arrows> {<etx> to leave}
   Monthly Report:
      1. The Good News ....... Page 3
      2. The Bad News ........ Page 4
```

The last line is indented 6 places which corresponds to the accumulated horizontal movement up to that point.

C(opy

C(opy inserts text from the copy buffer, or from a text file on disk, into your workspace.

How to use it:

Select C(opy and this menu is displayed:

```
>Copy: B(uffer  F(rom file  <esc>
```

Typing [esc] exits the C(opy activity.

Selecting B(uffer causes the contents of the copy buffer to be inserted into the workspace where the cursor is. The cursor is then left at the end of the inserted text. (As covered earlier in this chapter, the copy buffer contains whatever you last inserted with I(nsert, or deleted with D(elete or Z(ap.)

Selecting F(rom file allows you to copy material from a text file stored on disk into your workspace:

```
>Copy: From what file [marker,marker] ?  FILE-SPEC [ret]
                                          FILE-SPEC [MARKER1,MARKER2] [ret]
                                          FILE-SPEC [,MARKER] [ret]
                                          FILE-SPEC [MARKER,] [ret]
```

The .TEXT suffix should not be included in your response to this prompt.

The first response copies all of the specified file into your workspace.

The second response only copies that portion of the file which lies between the two indicated markers.

The third response copies from the beginning of the file to the indicated marker.

And the fourth response copies from the marker to the end of the specified file.

Example:

If you insert:

```
>Insert: Text {<bs> a char,<del> a line} [<etx> accepts, <esc> escapes]
The quick brown fox jumps over the lazy dog.
_
```

with a final carriage return as shown, and accept it with ⟦etx⟧, that line is placed in the copy buffer. Now, if you type "CB", for C(opy B(uffer, the line is duplicated:

```
>Edit: A(djust C(opy D(el F(ind I(nsert J(ump K(ol M(argin P(age ?
The quick brown fox jumps over the lazy dog.
The quick brown fox jumps over the lazy dog.
_
```

D(elete

D(elete removes text from your workspace.

How to use it:

Select D(elete and this line is displayed:

```
>Delete: < > <Moving commands> {<etx> to delete, <esc> to abort}
```

You can now delete text by moving the cursor with any cursor movement key. The original cursor position is called the anchor. When you move the cursor away from the anchor, text is deleted. When you move the cursor toward the anchor, the deleted text is restored.

When you are satisfied, type ⟦etx⟧ to accept the deletion or ⟦esc⟧ to exit D(elete and leave the workspace unaltered.

If you accidentally delete something valuable, you can restore it by using C(opy B(uffer.

Example:

In order to remove "John" from the line below, place the cursor as indicated:

```
>Edit: A(djust C(opy D(el F(ind I(nsert J(ump K(ol M(argin P(age ?
Mr. John Smythe,
```

Select D(elete and type ⟦space⟧ five times:

```
>Delete: < > <Moving commands> {<etx> to delete, <esc> to abort}
Mr.      Smythe,
```

Now type ⟦etx⟧, and the deletion is accepted:

```
>Edit: A(djust C(opy D(el F(ind I(nsert J(ump K(ol M(argin P(age ?
Mr. Smythe,
```

In order to remove the end of the second line below, place the cursor immediately after "Cash" and select D(elete:

```
>Delete: < > <Moving commands> {<etx> to delete, <esc> to abort}
Check No. 972     $  43.22      Food
Check No. 973     $ 100.00      Cash_    VERIFY THIS AMOUNT
Check No. 974     $  21.74      Misc
```

Type ⟦ret⟧:

```
>Delete: < > <Moving commands> {<etx> to delete, <esc> to abort}
Check No. 972     $  43.22      Food
Check No. 973     $ 100.00      Cash
Check No. 974     $  21.74      Misc
```

Now you must type ⟦bs⟧ to get the cursor back up to the second line:

```
>Delete: < > <Moving commands> {<etx> to delete, <esc> to abort}
Check No. 972     $  43.22      Food
Check No. 973     $ 100.00      Cash                        _
Check No. 974     $  21.74      Misc
```

At this point you can use ⟦etx⟧. (If you don't use ⟦bs⟧ first, the "Check 974" line is pulled up immediately after "Cash". If you ever do this accidentally, you can select I(nsert and type ⟦ret⟧ to correct the situation.)

F(ind

Find attempts to locate a sequence of characters that you specify.

How to use it:

Select F(ind and one of the following prompts is displayed:*

---

* *IV.2 users, note:* F(ind has two additional items on its prompt: C(ase and I(d. See the R(eplace description for details.

```
>Find[n]: L(it <target> => _
```

```
>Find[n]: T(ok <target> => _
```

First enter a **delimiter** (which is any special character such as ".", ",", or "/"). Next, enter the sequence of characters that you want to locate (the **target**). Finally enter a matching delimiter.

F(ind can search forward or backward depending upon the direction indicator. If no repeat factor is used, F(ind searches for the first occurrence of the target. If a repeat factor is used, F(ind attempts to locate that occurrence of the target. (The [n] in the prompt indicates the repeat factor. The "n" will be a number or a slash.)

F(ind can search for either tokens or literal strings (see Section 5.10, page 147). F(ind assumes that you are looking for a token if T(oken default (within S(et E(nvironment) is true. Likewise, it assumes that you are searching for a literal string if T(oken default is set to false. If the assumed mode is token, the prompt displays "L(it". If the assumed mode is literal, the prompt displays "T(ok". You can override the default and specifically search for a literal string or a token by selecting L(it or T(ok before entering the target string.

Once you have used F(ind to locate a target, you can find another instance of the same target without retyping the delimiters and the sequence of characters. Instead, you can simply type "FS", for F(ind "same".

Example:

This use of F(ind:

```
>Find[1]: L(it <target> => .Section 3.
```

searches for the first occurrence of the token "Section 3" in the forward direction. In order to find "Section 3.2" you would need to use a delimiter other than a period:

```
>Find[1]: L(it <target> =>/Section 3.2/
```

If you then change the direction indicator, enter a repeat factor of 10, select F(ind, and respond:

```
<Find[10]: L(it <target> =>LS
```

F(ind attempts to locate the tenth occurrence of the "same" literal string ("Section 3.2") in the backward direction. It is possible that "Section 3.21" could be found because you are searching for a literal string.

I(nsert

I(nsert places new text into your workspace.

How to use it:

Select I(nsert and this line is displayed:

```
>Insert: Text {<bs> a char,<del> a line} [<etx> accepts, <esc> escapes]
```

You can now enter whatever text you want. The ⟦bs⟧ key erases characters that you have inserted. The ⟦ret⟧ key moves the cursor to the next line, as on a typewriter. The ⟦delete line⟧ key erases one entire line of inserted text. The ⟦etx⟧ key leaves I(nsert after accepting the new material into your workspace. The ⟦esc⟧ key leaves I(nsert after discarding everything that you have entered.

When you I(nsert in the middle of existing text, the new material is inserted between the character just to the left of the cursor, and the character that the cursor is directly over. (See Figure 2.3.) The line of text on which the cursor is located is split to indicate where the new text will go. When you leave I(nsert, the gap is closed.

Only the line where you are inserting is split; any text on lines above or below remains unchanged on the screen. As you proceed with the insertion, however, you may overflow the current line or you may specifically type ⟦ret⟧. In either case, the text below the current line disappears from the screen. When you leave I(nsert, the text below is redisplayed.

Within S(et E(nvironment there are options which allow you to I(nsert text in two different modes. One of these modes is best for creating line–oriented text (such as programs, tables, or columns). The other is more suitable for paragraphs. In the line–oriented mode, you must explicitly type ⟦ret⟧ at the end of every line. The bell sounds a warning as you approach the end of a line (as on a typewriter).

When you are using line–oriented mode, you can also use automatic indentation if you wish. Automatic indentation means that when you type ⟦ret⟧, the next line begins at the same level of indentation as the current line. (You can move the cursor left or right if you don't want the line to start there.) If you are not using automatic indentation, the cursor always moves to the left margin when you type ⟦ret⟧.

In the paragraph–oriented mode, a carriage return is done automatically whenever the word you are entering doesn't fit onto the current line. That word is moved down to the next line. This is convenient since you don't have to concern yourself about typing ⟦ret⟧.

Also, in the paragraph–oriented mode, when you accept the insertion, the rest of the paragraph (below what you have just entered) is rearranged to fit within the left and right margins. This rearrangement is convenient because it automatically keeps a paragraph within the proper margins even if you I(nsert something in the middle of it.

The default I(nsert mode is line–oriented with automatic indentation. The S(et E(nvironment options which determine the I(nsert mode are called A(uto indent and F(illing.

NOTE: You should be careful not to I(nsert in the middle of line–structured text while using the paragraph–oriented mode. If you do this to a table or set of columns, for example, they will be turned into one large paragraph!

NOTE: You should be sure your paragraphs are properly separated from each other and from any other text (see Section 5.7, page 144).

Example:

In order to insert "John" into "Mr. Smythe", place the cursor as follows:

```
>Insert: Text {<bs> a char,<del> a line} [<etx> accepts, <esc> escapes]
Mr. Smythe
```

Select I(nsert and the line is split:

```
>Insert: Text {<bs> a char,<del> a line} [<etx> accepts, <esc> escapes]
Mr. _                                                            Smythe
```

Type in "John" followed by a space to separate it from "Smythe":

```
>Insert: Text {<bs> a char,<del> a line} [<etx> accepts, <esc> escapes]
Mr. John _                                                       Smythe
```

And type ⟦etx⟧:

```
>Insert: Text {<bs> a char,<del> a line} [<etx> accepts, <esc> escapes]
Mr. John Smythe
```

As an example of automatic indentation, you might start an outline by inserting this line followed by ⟦ret⟧:

```
>Insert: Text {<bs> a char,<del> a line} [<etx> accepts, <esc> escapes]
Chapter 1: Insects
_
```

You can now type ⟦space⟧ twice (for indentation) and enter the next line:

```
>Insert: Text {<bs> a char,<del> a line} [<etx> accepts, <esc> escapes]
Chapter 1: Insects
  Section 1.1 Butterflies_
```

When you type ⟦ret⟧ again, the cursor is moved to the same indentation as the current line:

```
>Insert: Text {<bs> a char,<del> a line} [<etx> accepts, <esc> escapes]
Chapter 1: Insects
  Section 1.1 Butterflies

  _
```

This makes it easy to continue at that level of indentation:

```
>Insert: Text {<bs> a char,<del> a line} [<etx> accepts, <esc> escapes]
Chapter 1: Insects
  Section 1.1 Butterflies
  Section 1.2 Beetles_
```

In paragraph mode, you might I(nsert this quote from Thoreau:

```
>Insert: Text {<bs> a char,<del> a line} [<etx> accepts, <esc> escapes]
"If one advances confidently in the direction of his dreams, and
endeavors to live the life which he has imagined, he will meet with
a success unexpected in common hours."_
```

In this example the right margin is set at column 70. Now if you I(nsert " Thoreau writes, " after "dreams," and press ⟦etx⟧, the paragraph is rearranged to fit within 70–character lines:

```
>Insert: Text {<bs> a char,<del> a line} [<etx> accepts, <esc> escapes]
"If one advances confidently in the direction of his dreams,"
Thoreau writes, "_and endeavors to live the life which he has
imagined, he will meet with a success unexpected in common hours."
```

Note that it wasn't necessary to type ⟦ret⟧ while inserting this.

J(ump

J(ump moves the cursor to the beginning of your workspace, to the end of your workspace, or to a marker.

How to use it:

Select J(ump and this menu is displayed:

```
> JUMP: B(eginning E(nd M(arker <esc>
```

Selecting B(eginning moves the cursor to the beginning of your workspace. Selecting E(nd moves the cursor to the end of your workspace. Typing ⟦esc⟧ exits J(ump. If you select M(arker, you are asked which marker to jump to:

```
Jump to what marker? _
```

You should enter the name of a marker; the cursor is relocated there. If you simply type ⟦ret⟧, J(ump is exited.

Example:

When you are editing in the middle of your workspace, you may need to look briefly at some material near the beginning and then return to where you were working. You can use J(ump to get to the beginning:

```
> JUMP: B(eginning E(nd M(arker <esc> B
```

When you want to return you may be able to use J(ump again if you are editing near a marker or near the end of the file. Otherwise, you could return using ⟦=⟧, P(age, or F(ind. (You may want to set a marker before you leave.)

K(olumn

K(olumn, abbreviated K(ol, changes the horizontal position of the text which lies to the right of the cursor on one or more lines.

How to use it:

Select K(olumn and this line is displayed:

```
>Kolumn: <vector keys> {<etx>,<esc> CURRENT line}
```

Typing ⟦right⟧ moves the text to the right of the cursor one position to the right. Typing ⟦left⟧ moves the text to the right of the cursor one position to the left. Typing ⟦up⟧ or ⟦down⟧ cause the lines above or below, respectively, to be affected in the same manner as the current line.

You can move text beyond the right margin of the screen without losing it. However, any text moved in the left direction which disappears "into" the cursor is removed from the workspace. This text isn't placed in the copy buffer and can't be recovered (except on the current line when you type ⟦esc⟧).

When you move the cursor vertically within K(olumn, you can accumulate horizontal movement by using ⟦left⟧ or ⟦right⟧ on the current line. The accumulated horizontal movement will be applied to succeeding lines above or below.

You should use ⟦etx⟧ to accept any changes that you have made. You can use ⟦esc⟧ to exit K(olumn, but only the most recent changes on the current line are ignored; any other changes made while using K(olumn are accepted.

NOTE: When K(olumn deletes text, that text is irrecoverable. You should be especially careful when ⟦left⟧ is used followed by vertical movement. The use of repeat factors in this situation is even more risky.

Example:

One of the most useful ways to use K(olumn is to align or manipulate columns. For example, if you place the cursor, as shown, between two columns:

```
>Kolumn: <vector keys> {<etx>,<esc> CURRENT line}
     Hear          _    Music
     Taste              Food
     Touch              People
     See                Sky
     Smell              Flower
```

and use K(olumn with ⟦right⟧ to move "Music" to the right:

```
>Kolumn: <vector keys> {<etx>,<esc> CURRENT line}
     Hear          _       Music
     Taste              Food
     Touch              People
     See                Sky
     Smell              Flower
```

you can then use ⟦down⟧ to change succeeding lines below in the same manner:

```
>Kolumn: <vector keys> {<etx>,<esc> CURRENT line}
     Hear                  Music
     Taste                 Food
     Touch         _       People
     See                Sky
     Smell              Flower
```

M(argin

M(argin rearranges the text in a paragraph so that it conforms as closely as possible to the margins defined within S(et E(nvironment.

How to use it:

Place the cursor within a paragraph and select M(argin. Your text briefly disappears from the screen. It is then redisplayed and the paragraph is appropriately rearranged.

To use M(argin, several options within S(et E(nvironment must be appropriately set. A(uto indent must be false. F(illing must be true. And the L(eft, R(ight, and P(aragraph margins must be set sensibly. These margins should correspond to the columns that you wish to use as margins for your paragraphs.

M(argin removes all extra spaces from a paragraph. Only one space is left between words. A maximum of two spaces is left after a period.

NOTE: Text which is not separated from a paragraph by a blank line or a line which starts with the command character is considered to be part of that paragraph (see Section 5.7, page 144). You should be sure that your *paragraphs are correctly separated from each other and from other text.*

NOTE: Single–spaced line–structured text (such as columns or tables) will be rearranged into a paragraph by M(argin. Since it is easy to accidentally type "M", you should be sure F(illing is set to false within S(et E(nvironment when you are editing line–structured text.

Example:

If you have created a paragraph that looks like this:

```
>Edit: A(djust C(opy D(el F(ind I(nsert J(ump K(ol M(argin P(age [ ]
  I was walking along that same tree-lined road one Autumn afternoon.
The breeze was pleasant
and everything
brought back fresh memories of long past days.  It felt good to
visit this place once again.
```

and the margins are set as follows:

L(eft margin	5
R(ight margin	55
P(ara margin	7

you could use the M(argin activity and obtain the following rearranged paragraph:

```
>Edit: A(djust C(opy D(el F(ind I(nsert J(ump K(ol M(argin P(age [ ]
       I was walking along that same tree-lined road
     one Autumn afternoon. The breeze was pleasant and
     everything brought back fresh memories of long
     past days.  It felt good to visit this place once
     again.
```

P(age

P(age causes the next screen full of text to replace what is currently displayed in the window (see Figure 2.1).

How to use it:

Select P(age from the main Editor menu and the next screen full of text appears in the window.

A repeat factor may be used to indicate how many pages the window is to be moved. The direction indicator determines whether the paging proceeds forward or backward.

Example:

P(age is useful for browsing through the text in your workspace. If you are trying to locate a particular area, you can page through the entire workspace in a short length of time.

If you happen to know that the area you are looking for is a certain number of pages from the beginning of the workspace, you can J(ump B(eginning, enter the appropriate repeat factor, and select P(age. This same technique can be used from the end of the workspace with a reversed direction indicator.

R(eplace

R(eplace locates occurrences of a sequence of characters that you select (called the target) and replaces them with another sequence of characters (called the substitution string).

How to use it:

Select R(eplace and one of these two prompts is displayed:*

```
>Replace [n]: L(it V(fy <targ> <sub> => _
```

```
>Replace [n]: T(ok V(fy <targ> <sub> => _
```

Enter a delimiter (which is a special character such as ".", "/", or "$"); then enter the target string followed by a matching delimiter. After that, enter another delimiter followed by the substitution string and a matching delimiter.

The delimiters for the target string may be the same as the delimiters for the substitution string. However, you should be sure that a delimiter does not appear within the string being delimited. For example, if the target contains a comma, you should not use a comma as the delimiter.

If you have used R(eplace at least once since entering the Editor, you can indicate the most recently used target and/or substitution string by simply typing "S" for "same." In fact, if you have used F(ind during the current editing session, you can type "S" to indicate the most recent target that has been used by F(ind or R(eplace.

A repeat factor may be used to replace several occurrences of the target. It is shown within the square brackets where the "n" appears in the prompts above. (Note that the repeat factor does not mean to replace the n'th occurrence of the target; it means to replace n occurrences of it.) The direction indicator determines whether targets in the forward or backward

---

* *IV.2 users, note:* R(eplace has two additional items on its prompt: C(ase and I(d. Choose C(ase to make the search process independent of the **case** of a letter (e.g. 'a' or 'A'). Choose I(d to have the search use the matching rules that apply to UCSD Pascal identifiers.

direction will be replaced.

Target and substitution strings are treated as either tokens or as literal strings (see Section 5.10, page 147). R(eplace works with tokens when T(oken default within S(et E(nvironment is true. It works with literal strings when T(oken default is false. You may override the default by selecting L(it or T(ok from the R(eplace prompt. (The prompt displays the opposite of the default.) L(it or T(ok must be selected before entering the target or between entering the target and substitution.

The V(erify option, abbreviated V(fy, allows you to select the occurrences of the target which are to be replaced. If you use a repeat factor without V(erify, all occurrences of the target that are found are replaced automatically. If you would rather watch the progress and determine whether or not a given occurrence of the target should be replaced, select V(erify before entering the target or substitution string. When you do this, each time the R(eplace activity encounters an occurrence of the target, it prompts you:

```
>Replace: <esc> aborts, 'R' replaces, ' ' doesn't
```

When this occurs, the cursor indicates which instance of the target has just been found. Type "R" to replace it, ⟦space⟧ to leave it unchanged, or ⟦esc⟧ to leave it unchanged and cancel the R(eplace operation.

When the V(fy option is used, this prompt is redisplayed until you have replaced as many occurrences of the target as you indicated with the repeat factor, or until the last occurrence of the target is found, or until you use ⟦esc⟧.

Example:

You might want to replace all occurrences of the word "January" with "February". From the beginning of your workspace, type slash, "/", to indicate the infinite repeat factor. Then select R(eplace and respond:

```
>Replace [/]: L(it V(fy <targ> <sub> => /January/ /February/
```

The replacements are done and the cursor is left at the end of the last "February" placed in the workspace.

If you want to replace the string "2000.00 / 2" with "1,000" you could do it like this:

```
>Replace [1]: L(it V(fy <targ> <sub> => ,2000.00 / 2, /1,000/
```

Since a period and a slash occur in the target, neither of them can serve as the delimiter; comma is a good choice. In the substitution string, however, a comma occurs; slash is chosen as the delimiter.

If you want to change most occurrences of "Section 3" with "Section 2", you could type "/", and use R(eplace with L(iteral and V(erify in this manner:

```
>Replace [/]: L(it V(fy <targ> <sub> => LV /Section 3/ /Section 2/
```

For each literal string "Section 3", you are asked to verify if you want to make the replacement. You might decide to replace it in the case of "Section 3" or "Section 3a". However, you might decide not to replace it if "Section 30" is found.

S(et E(nvironment

S(et E(nvironment displays useful information about the status of your workspace. It also enables you to set several options which determine how the Editor behaves.

How to use it:

Select S(et and this prompt is displayed:

```
>Set: E(nvironment M(arker <esc>
```

then select E(nvironment and a display similar to this appears:

```
>Environment: {Options} <spacebar> to leave _
    A(uto indent  True
    F(illing      False
    L(eft margin  1
    R(ight margin 80
    P(ara margin  6
    C(ommand ch   ^
    S(et tabstops
    T(oken def    True

    1987 bytes used, 16445 available.

    Patterns:
      <target>= 'Your target' <subst>= 'Your substitution string'

    Markers:
      MARKER1   MARKER2   SO_FORTH

Editing: YOUR.FILE
Created January 1, 1985; Last updated January 1, 1985 (Revision 1)
Editor Version [ ]
```

Several options are shown: A(uto indent, F(illing, and so forth. Most of these options have a value associated with them. (The values shown above are typical of what you might see.) In most cases, these values are a number or a true/false indication. Below the options and their values is additional information that reflects the state of your workspace. (Not all of this information is present every time you enter S(et E(nvironment.)

To alter the value associated with an option, select the option by typing the corresponding letter. The cursor is moved to the line where the old value is displayed. To enter a numeric value, type the number followed by [ret]. To enter a true/false indication, type "T" or "F". To enter a character value, type the character.

A(uto indent

A(uto indent stands for "automatic indentation." Its default value is true.

When A(uto indent is true, typing [[ret]] in I(nsert causes the next line to start at the indentation of the current line. When A(uto indent is false, typing [[ret]] in I(nsert starts the next line at the left margin.

F(illing

F(illing stands for "line filling." Its default value is false.

When F(illing is false, you are editing in the line–oriented mode (as described under I(nsert). M(argin cannot do anything in this mode.

When F(illing is true and A(uto indent is false, you are editing in the paragraph–oriented mode (again, described under I(nsert). M(argin does function in this mode.

L(eft, R(ight, and P(ara Margins

The L(eft margin, R(ight margin, and P(ara margin options allow you to define the Editor's margins. These margins affect I(nsert and M(argin when you are editing in paragraph mode.

The left margin's initial value is 1 (which is the first column on the screen). The right margin's initial value is 80 (which is the last column on most screens.) The paragraph margin indicates the indentation that you want the first line of a paragraph to have; it has an initial value of 6.

C(ommand ch

C(ommand ch stands for command character. Its initial value is carat, "^".

The command character (see Section 5.7, page 144) may be used to indicate the beginning or ending of a paragraph by placing it as the first character on a line. It is recognized by M(argin and I(nsert when you are editing in paragraph–oriented mode.

S(et tabstops

S(et tabstops allows you to change the positions of the tab stops. By default, tab stops are placed at every eighth position across the screen.

Select S(et tabstops and the following display appears:*

---

* *IV.0 users, note:* The S(et tabstops menu is more elaborate, containing several types of tabs. We recommend you use only L(eft tabstops.

```
Set tabs: <right, left vectors> C(ol# T(oggle tab <etx>
T-------T-------T-------T-------T-------T-------T-------T-------T-------T-------T------
    Column # 1
```

The dashed line represents the 80 columns on the screen. Each "T" indicates a tab stop.

In order to add or delete a tab stop, you must first place the cursor at the desired location along the dashed line. To move the cursor, use the [left] or [right] keys. Alternatively, you can select C(ol # and enter a column number followed by [ret]. The cursor is moved there.

Once you have positioned the cursor, you may select T(oggle tab. This creates a tab stop there if one does not currently exist. It removes a tab stop if one does currently exist.

When you have the tab stops set up to your satisfaction, type [etx] to return to the S(et E(nvironment display. When you continue editing, the new tab stops are in effect.

T(oken def

T(oken def stands for token default. Its default value is true.

You can specify to F(ind and R(eplace whether a token or a literal string search should be used. When you do not specify, however, a token search is used if T(oken default is true and a literal string search is used if T(oken default is false.

The Rest of S(et E(nvironment

Below all of the options on the S(et E(nvironment display, there is some more information. It looks similar to this:

```
                .
                .
                .
   1987 bytes used, 16445 available.

   Patterns:
     <target>= 'Your target' <subst>= 'Your substitution string'

   Markers:
     MARKER1   MARKER2   SO_FORTH

Editing: YOUR.FILE
Created January 1, 1985; Last updated January 1, 1985 (Revision 1).
Editor Version [ ].
```

Not all of this information is present all the time. The "Patterns" and "Markers" are displayed only when applicable.

The first line indicates how many bytes (or characters) are used and how many are still available within your workspace. The sum of these two numbers is the maximum size your workspace can be. This maximum size varies among computers and depends upon the amount of main memory that your particular computer has.

The next line shows the target string and substitution string patterns (if they exist). If you used either F(ind or R(eplace in the current editing session, you introduced a target string. If you used R(eplace, you introduced a substitution string.

Next, the names of any markers that you have set are displayed. The markers are displayed by S(et E(nvironment so that you can easily check to see what markers exist.

Next, the name of the file from which the workspace was copied is shown. If the workspace was created from scratch, "unnamed" appears.*

The next line shows the date the workspace was first created, the date it was last updated to disk, and the number of times it has been revised on the disk.

The final line shows the version number of the p—System Editor that you are using.

S(et M(arker

S(et M(arker places markers in your workspace.

How to use it:

Position the cursor where you want the marker to be located and select S(et M(arker. You are prompted for a marker name:

```
Set what marker ? MARKER [ret]
```

The name should consist of eight or fewer characters. You may set as many as 20 markers. (If you attempt to set more, you are asked if you want to remove one of the existing markers in order to set another one.)

Example:

There may be a section of text within your workspace, called "Section 3", that you need to J(ump to frequently. You could place the cursor there and use S(et M(arker:

```
Set what marker ? SECT3 [ret]
```

Later, you can find this location by using J(ump M(arker like this:

```
Jump to what marker ? SECT3 [ret]
```

---

* *IV.0 users, note:* This line does not appear.

V(erify

V(erify assures that the screen reflects the actual contents of your workspace.

How to use it:

There are some rare circumstances under which text can be inappropriately left on the screen. It is usually obvious when this happens.

Selecting V(erify causes the text on the screen to briefly disappear and then be redisplayed. If there was anything extraneous on the screen, it is no longer present after the V(erify.

V(erify also tends to move the window so that the cursor is near the middle of the screen.

W(rite

W(rite causes the Editor to write your workspace out to disk and return you immediately for further editing.*

How to use it:

This activity makes it easy for you to periodically store your workspace on disk (so that an unexpected power outage or other catastrophe does not cause you to lose too much work). If, in the current Editor session, your workspace was read in from a disk file, invoking W(rite causes it to be written to that same file (removing the old version of it). If your workspace was created from scratch, the first W(rite requires you to enter a file specification indicating where on disk the workspace should be written.

As your workspace is written to disk, "Writing...." is displayed. If an error occurs during the operation, a message appears identifying the error. Check Appendix B, "Execution Errors," for an explanation of the error and possible recovery steps.

---

* *IV.0, IV.1 users, note:* This activity is available only in IV.2 p–Systems.

X(change

X(change enters new text by overwriting existing text within your workspace.

How to use it:

Select X(change and the following line is displayed:

```
>eXchange: Text <vector keys> {<etx>,<esc> CURRENT line}
```

Type in the text you want. The original text at the location of the cursor is replaced by what you enter.

It is possible to move the cursor without affecting the existing text. In order to do this, you can use any cursor movement key except ⟦space⟧. If you use ⟦space⟧, a blank character replaces what was originally there.

To accept the changes that you have made, use ⟦etx⟧. You can use ⟦esc⟧ to exit X(change, but if you have moved to more than one line, only the most recent changes to the current line are discarded.

While in X(change, you can insert an extra blank character by typing ⟦exch–ins⟧. And, you can delete a character by typing ⟦exch–del⟧. These keys are convenient since you do not have to exit X(change and use I(nsert or D(elete; you can remain in X(change and simply type a key.

Example:

If you want to change:

```
>Edit: A(djust C(opy D(el F(ind I(nsert J(ump K(ol M(argin P(age [ ]
One for the money
```

to "Two for the show", select X(change and enter the new line:

```
>eXchange: Text <vector keys> {<etx>,<esc> CURRENT line}
Two for the showy
```

Now, you need to delete the last "y". One way to do this is to accept the changes you have made with X(change, and to use D(elete. However, it is easier to simply type ⟦exch–del⟧ once:

```
>eXchange: Text <vector keys> {<etx>,<esc> CURRENT line}
Two for the show_
```

Now use ⟦etx⟧ and the changes are accepted.

Z(ap

Z(ap deletes all text between the current cursor position and the first character associated with the most recent F(ind, R(eplace, or I(nsert.

How to use it:

Before using Z(ap, you should be sure you know the location of the first character associated with the most recent F(ind, R(eplace, or I(nsert. Place the cursor at some other location and select Z(ap to remove the material that lies between those two positions.

If you are removing more than 80 characters, this prompt appears:

```
WARNING: You are about to zap more than 80 chars, do you wish to zap? (y/n)
```

Type "Y" if you wish to proceed and "N" otherwise.

Example:

If you insert and accept a sentence which you then want to delete, you can remove it by simply typing "Z" (since the cursor is already at the end of the sentence).

If you F(ind or R(eplace a sequence of characters, the cursor ends up at the end of the sequence. You can, if you want, remove the sequence by selecting Z(ap.

You can also use Z(ap to remove a large section of text. The first step is to move the cursor to the beginning of the section as shown in the example screen that follows.

```
>Edit: A(djust C(opy D(el F(ind I(nsert J(ump K(ol M(argin P(age [ ]
This is the beginning of a large portion of
text to be discarded ...
```

Select I(nsert and then immediately exit it with ⟦esc⟧ or ⟦etx⟧. Next, move the cursor to the end of the text to be deleted:

```
>Edit: A(djust C(opy D(el F(ind I(nsert J(ump K(ol M(argin P(age [ ]
... Here is the end of the large portion of
text to be discarded._
```

Now, select Z(ap and you receive the warning:

```
WARNING! You are about to zap more than 80 chars, do you wish to zap? (y/n) Y
```

If you type "Y" as shown, the text is deleted. This is often easier than using D(elete to remove the text.

When you perform Z(ap on a large portion of text, you may also receive a message indicating that there is "no room to copy the deletion." This is described in Appendix A, "Error Messages for Major Activities."

6

THE FILER

6.1 INTRODUCTION

The Filer is responsible for managing files on your disks. It allows you to see what files are there, move them around, change their names, and so forth. It also allows you to change the name of a storage volume, initialize its directory, and check its magnetic recording surface for physical problems.

In addition, the Filer allows you to interact with communication volumes. For example, files may be printed or displayed on the console.

Chapter 4, "The Operating System," covers files and volumes in some detail. The Filer is principally concerned with them and so most of that material is especially relevant to this chapter.

The next few sections summarize what the Filer can do. Next, the activities on the Filer menu are described in alphabetical order. At the end of this chapter, there are sections covering some more advanced topics: subsidiary volumes, wild cards, and utility programs for recovering lost files or directories.

6.2 VIEWING FILES AND VOLUMES

As we just mentioned, files and volumes are covered in Chapter 4. Briefly, storage volumes (which are usually disks) contain information in the form of files. Several files may reside on a disk. At the beginning of a storage volume, the p–System maintains a file directory. The name of every file on the volume is kept there. Other information, such as the location of each file, its size, and the date it was created, is also stored in the directory.

When you want to view the files on a disk, you can either use the L(ist directory or E(xtended list directory activities.

L(ist directory informs you what files are on a disk and gives you their sizes and dates of creation.

E(xtended list directory works just like L(ist directory except that more information is displayed. This extra information includes the location of each file and its type (such as code or text file). Also, the unused areas on the disk are shown.*

If you want to see what volumes are accessible to the p–System, you should use V(olumes. V(olumes displays the names of all storage volumes and communication volumes which are on–line.

6.3 CREATING AND REMOVING FILES

The editors and compilers can create files. An editor creates text files and a compiler creates code files. The Filer can be used to create files, as well. It also has the ability to remove files (no matter how they were created).

M(ake creates a disk file. The content of the new file is whatever happened to be on the disk in the area where the file was created.

R(emove deletes a file (or several files) from a disk.

Z(ero can also be used to remove files. If there are files on a disk to begin with, Z(ero removes all of them.

6.4 MOVING FILES AROUND

Often, you may need to move a file from one disk to another. Perhaps you will want to move all of the files on a master disk to a back up disk. Or you may want to move a file from one place on a disk to another location on that same disk.

T(ransfer can do all of these things. If you use T(ransfer to move a file to the same volume that it was originally on, and you give it the same name, the old copy of the file is removed. However, if you give the file a new name, or if you transfer it to a different disk, the original copy of the file remains.

You may find it convenient to use wild cards in conjunction with T(ransfer. Wild cards allow you to transfer several files at a time very easily. (They are described in the "Wild Cards" section later in this chapter.)

---

* *IV.2 users, note:* The time of creation for each file is shown, also.

K(runch is a special tool for "crunching" a disk. It moves all the files together so that the free space on a disk is consolidated into one large area. K(runch is especially useful when a disk has become "fragmented," that is, when its files are spread out. In this situation, disk space may only be available in relatively small portions. For example, a fragmented disk might have enough free space to store a large file. However, if no single unused area is big enough to hold that file, it can't be stored on the disk. After you use K(runch in this situation, the large file can fit onto the disk.

6.5 PRINTING AND DISPLAYING FILES

You can also use the Filer's T(ransfer activity to print or display files. When a file is transferred to PRINTER:, it is printed. Similarly, when a file is transferred to CONSOLE:, it is displayed on the screen. In either case, if it is a text file, it appears exactly as it does in the Editor.

You can T(ransfer other kinds of files to the printer or the console. However, some files are not intended for this. Code files, for example, contain material that is not meant to be viewed directly. If you try to print or display a code file, you receive "garbage" as your output. On the other hand, some kinds of data files consist of readable material that can be printed or displayed using T(ransfer without any difficulties.

6.6 THE DISK SURFACE

The recording surface of a magnetic disk can be damaged in several ways. Physical damage may occur from long or rough use. A surge of voltage when the disk is in the drive can hurt the recording surface. A poorly functioning disk drive can also damage a disk.

Sometimes the damage caused by these problems is permanent, but often it is not. The Filer has facilities for finding any problems that might exist on a disk's surface and correcting them if possible.

The B(ad blocks activity discovers these kinds of problems. B(ad blocks informs you which blocks, if any, on a particular disk are having problems.

X(amine allows you to test the blocks that you suspect are bad to see if they are permanently bad, or if they can be fixed. If the troublesome areas on your disk's surface can be returned to normal, X(amine does this for you. Otherwise, you can mark the bad blocks so that valuable material is not written, and perhaps lost, there. You might choose to discard disks with bad blocks, however.

There are three utility programs that may assist you in recovering from disk problems. They are Recover, Copydupdir, and Markdupdir. These utilities are covered at the end of this chapter.

6.7 ENTERING AND EXITING THE FILER

To use the Filer, SYSTEM.FILER must reside on a volume which is on–line.

In order to enter the Filer, select F(ile from the Command menu. The Filer menu is displayed and looks like this:

```
Filer: G(et, S(ave, W(hat, N(ew, L(dir, R(em, C(hng, T(rans, D(ate,?  [ ]
```

If you type "?" twice, the remaining portions of this menu are displayed:

```
Filer: Q(uit, B(ad-blks, E(xt-dir, K(rnch, M(ake, P(refix, V(ols,? [ ]
```

```
Filer: X(amine, Z(ero, O(n/off-line, F(lip-swap/lock [ ]
```

To exit the Filer, select Q(uit and you are returned to the main p–System menu.

6.8 DISK SWAPPING

When you enter the Filer, code is read into main memory from the disk file SYSTEM.FILER. Some of the code may remain on disk, however. Each time you select an activity, it is possible that a disk access will be required to read a portion of SYSTEM.FILER into main memory. If you have removed the disk which contains SYSTEM.FILER from its drive, you are prompted to replace it and type ⟦space⟧ to continue. This can be an inconvenience if you only have two disk drives (since the Filer performs many disk–to–disk operations and removing the disk containing SYSTEM.FILER is often required).

The F(lip–Swap/Lock activity addresses this problem. If your computer has enough main memory, the entire Filer can be "locked" into memory. This means that no further disk accesses will be required to read the Filer's code. (If your computer doesn't have enough memory, you will not be able to take advantage of F(lip–Swap/Lock.)*

6.9 THE FILER MENU

In this section, the activities on the Filer's menu are covered alphabetically. Most of these activities display error messages under certain circumstances. The errors are covered in Appendix A, "Error Messages for Major

---

* *IV.0 users, note:* The F(lip–Swap/Lock activity is not available. Therefore, you need to make sure that the volume containing SYSTEM.FILER is on–line when you select a new activity in the Filer.

Activities." The file and volume notational conventions (see Section 4.16, page 122) are especially applicable to these descriptions.

B(ad Blocks

B(ad blocks, abbreviated B(ad–blks, scans a disk's surface for physical problems which can cause I/O errors.

How to use it:

Select B(ad blocks and one or more of the following prompts appear:

```
Bad block scan of what vol ? VOLUME-ID [ret]
Scan for ### blocks ? (Y/N) Y or N
Scan for how many blocks ? ### [ret]
```

The first prompt asks for the volume that you want to check.

The second prompt only appears if there is a valid directory on the volume. This prompt displays the total number of blocks on that volume and asks if you want to check all of them.

If you indicate that you don't want to check the entire volume, or if no valid directory exists, the third prompt asks how many blocks you want to check.

After this, the checking proceeds. The bad block scan can take several seconds to a minute (or more) depending upon the speed and storage capacity of your disk hardware. If no problems are found, you are simply informed:

```
0 bad blocks
```

If errors are found, they are reported like this:

```
Block ## is bad
Block ## is bad
Block ## is bad
3 bad blocks
File(s) endangered:
FILE-NAME-1      ##  ##
FILE-NAME-2      ##  ##
```

The block numbers for any bad blocks are given. (You can use the X(amine activity to attempt to fix them.) The endangered files (in which those blocks occur) are listed. The numbers which follow an endangered file indicate the first and last block of that file.

Example:

If you are encountering I/O errors with a disk, it is reasonable to suspect that there are bad blocks on it. To check the disk surface, you would use B(ad blocks in a fashion similar to this:

```
Bad block scan of what vol ? MYDISK: [ret]
Scan for 320 blocks ? (Y/N) Y
Block 32 is bad
1 bad block
File(s) endangered:
MY.FILE.TEXT     30  38
```

The next step is to use the X(amine activity to attempt to fix block 32.

C(hange

C(hange, abbreviated C(hng, alters the name of a file or storage volume.

How to use it:

Select C(hange and one or more of the following prompts appear:

```
Change what file ? FILE-SPEC [ret]
Change to what ? NEW-FILE-NAME [ret]
Remove old VOLUME-NAME:NEW-FILE-NAME ? Y or N
VOLUME-NAME:FILE-NAME   -->   NEW-FILE-NAME
```

The first prompt asks you to indicate the file that is to have its name changed.

The second prompt asks for the new name to be given to that file.

If there is already a file on the disk with the new name, the third prompt asks if you want to remove it. (You can't have two files with the same name on the same disk.)

If you type "Y", or if there wasn't already a file with that name, the change takes place and the final line is displayed.

In order to change a volume name, the process is similar:

```
Change what file ? VOLUME-ID [ret]
Change to what ? NEW-VOLUME-NAME: [ret]
VOLUME-NAME:   -->   NEW-VOLUME-NAME:
```

The first two prompts ask for the volume name to change and for the new volume name. The third line indicates that the change was made successfully. If an existing volume with the new name is on–line, the change operation will not go through.

It is possible to specify the old name and the new name in response to C(hange's first prompt by using a comma, like this:

```
Change what file ? FILE-SPEC , NEW-FILE-NAME [ret]
```

This is convenient since it is usually easier to type.

Wild cards may be used with C(hange. They allow you to change the names of several files at once. See the "Wild Cards" section at the end of this chapter for more information about this.

Example:

To change the name of a file on MYDISK: from FILE.TEXT to OLD.FILE.TEXT, use C(hange like this:

```
Change what file ? MYDISK:FILE.TEXT [ret]
Change to what ? OLD.FILE.TEXT [ret]
MYDISK:FILE.TEXT  -->  OLD.FILE.TEXT
```

To change the name of a disk from SYSTEM2: to MYDISK: you can use C(hange like this:

```
Change what file ? SYSTEM2: [ret]
Change to what ? MYDISK: [ret]
SYSTEM2:  -->  MYDISK:
```

D(ate

D(ate displays the p–System's current date and allows you to alter that date if you wish.*

How to use it:

Select D(ate and the p–System's current date is displayed along with a prompt asking for the new date:

```
Date set: <1..31>-<Jan..Dec>-00..99
Today is 1-Jan-85
New date ? _
```

You can respond to the prompt by entering a new date. In order to do this, type the number of the day, hyphen, the first three letters of the month, hyphen, and the last two numbers of the year. For example:

```
New date ? 2-JAN-85 [ret]
```

You don't always have to type all of this. If you only want to change the day, you can simply type that number followed by [ret]. In this case, the month and the year remain the same. You can also change just the day and the month if you wish. Given that the date is currently set to 1–Jan–85, all of the following responses change it to 2–Jan–85:

```
New date ? 2 [ret]
New date ? 2-JAN [ret]
New date ? 2-JAN-85 [ret]
```

If you simply type [ret] in response to the D(ate prompt, the date remains the same.

---

* *IV.2 users, note:* You can use the Command menu's S(et D(ate activity for this same purpose.

E(xtended List

E(xtended list directory, abbreviated E(xt–dir, displays a disk directory in the same way that L(ist directory does, except that more information about the files is provided.

How to use it:

Select E(xt–dir and this prompt is displayed:

```
Dir listing of what vol? VOLUME-ID [ret]
                         FILE-SPEC [ret]
                         VOLUME-ID , FILE-SPEC [ret]
```

The first response lists the directory of the specified volume on the console.

The second response only lists the directory entry for the particular file indicated. If that file is specified using wild cards, a subset of the directory (such as all the text files) can be listed. (See "Wild Cards" later in this chapter.)

The third response creates a listing of the volume and sends that listing to the file specified. If that file is a disk file, the listing is saved on disk. (Normally, you would specify a text file to do this.) If the file specification indicates a communication volume, the listing is sent there. For example, if the file specification is PRINTER:, the directory listing is printed.

Example:

Select E(xt–dir and respond as follows:

```
Dir listing of what vol? #4: [ret]
```

The directory listing of the disk in drive #4: then appears on the console and looks similar to this:

```
MY_VOL:
SYSTEM.PASCAL     113  1-Jan-85     6    512    Codefile
SYSTEM.MISCINFO     2  1-Jan-85   119    512    Datafile
SYSTEM.FILER       32  1-Jan-85   121    512    Codefile
SYSTEM.EDITOR      49  1-Jan-85   153    512    Codefile
SYSTEM.LIBRARY     21  1-Jan-85   202    512    Codefile
SYSTEM.INTERP      30  1-Jan-85   223    512    Datafile
< UNUSED >          9             253
TEST.TEXT           4  1-Jan-85   262    512    Textfile
TEST.CODE           9  1-Jan-85   266    512    Codefile
< UNUSED >          4             275
SCRIPT.TEXT         4  1-Jan-85   279    512    Textfile
< UNUSED >         37             283
9/9 files<listed/in-dir>, 270 blocks used, 50 unused, 37 in largest
```

Each file name is followed by the length of the file in blocks. The next column contains the date the file was created or last modified.* The fourth column shows the starting block of each file. The fifth column indicates the number of bytes in the last block of the file. The last column shows the file type. The unused areas can be clearly seen.

The last line indicates: 9 files have been listed out of 9 total; there are 270 blocks in use on the volume; there are 50 blocks still available; and the largest single unused area is 37 blocks long.

F(lip Swap/Lock

F(lip Swap/Lock determines whether or not portions of the Filer's code are allowed to be swapped between main memory and disk (see Section 6.8, page 175).†

How to use it:

Select F(lip Swap/Lock and this message is displayed indicating that the Filer's segments are locked into main memory:

```
Filer segments memlocked. [#### words]
```

If you type "F" again, the situation is reversed:

```
Filer segments swappable. [#### words]
```

The number of 16–bit words available in main memory is displayed in both cases. Often there is less memory space available when the Filer is locked into memory. If the amount of remaining main memory is too small, some of the Filer's activities will work more slowly. (On some computers, there isn't even enough main memory to lock the entire Filer into memory.)

Example:

You may have a computer with only two disk drives. If you need to use the Filer to do several disk–to–disk operations, it is likely that you will need to remove the disk containing SYSTEM.FILER (which is probably the system disk). Before doing this, you should lock the Filer into memory by selecting F(lip swap/lock.

---

* *IV.2 users, note:* An extra column appears before the date column. It shows the time the file was last modified.

† *IV.0 users, note:* This activity is not available. Therefore you need to make sure that the volume containing SYSTEM.FILER is on–line when you select a new activity in the Filer.

G(et

G(et designates a text file and/or code file as the workfile.*

How to use it:

Select G(et and one or more of the following lines appear:

```
Get what file ? FILE-SPEC [ret]
Throw away current workfile ? Y or N
Text file loaded
Code file loaded
Text & Code file loaded
No file loaded
```

Respond to the first prompt by indicating the file to be designated as your workfile. The suffixes .TEXT and .CODE are automatically appended to the name you enter.

The second prompt only appears if SYSTEM.WRK.TEXT or SYSTEM.WRK.CODE (the temporary workfiles) are on your system disk. If you respond with "Y", the SYSTEM.WRK files are removed from the disk. If you type "N", G(et is cancelled. If you want to use G(et but do not want to lose the existing temporary workfiles, you should use S(ave first.

One of the last four messages is displayed when G(et is finished. The first message indicates that a text file was found which has the name you entered. That text file is now your work file. If the second message appears, a code file was found. The third message indicates that a text file and a code file match the name you gave. And the final message indicates that no file was found with that name. In the last case, you do not have a workfile after using G(et.

Example:

If you have the file PROGRAM.TEXT on your disk, you can select G(et and respond:

```
Get what file ? PROGRAM [ret]
Text file loaded
```

If you now Q(uit the Filer and select E(dit, PROGRAM.TEXT is automatically loaded into the workspace. If you select C(omp, PROGRAM.TEXT is automatically compiled.

---

* *IV.2 users, note:* This activity is not available. Use the Command menu's S(et activity instead.

K(runch

K(runch consolidates all of the unused space on a disk into one contiguous area. It does this by moving the files as far forward (or backward) as possible.

How to use it:

Select K(runch and one or more of the following lines are displayed:

```
Crunch what vol ? VOLUME-ID [ret]
From end of disk, block ### ? (Y/N) Y or N
Starting at block # ? ### [ret]
Moving forward FILE-NAME-1
Moving forward FILE-NAME-2
Moving backward FILE-NAME-3
VOLUME-NAME: crunched
```

The first prompt asks for the volume that you want to K(runch.

The second prompt asks if you want K(runch to start from the end of the disk and move all of the files forward. If you type "Y", the crunching proceeds. If you type "N", the third prompt appears and asks where you would like the crunching to begin.

In response to the third prompt, enter the number of the block where you want K(runch to start. Files in front of that block are moved toward the beginning of the disk; files behind it are moved toward the end. The effect is to collect all unused space on the disk into a single area containing the indicated block.

As the crunching proceeds, a "Moving forward" or "Moving backward" message is displayed for each file which is moved.

The final message indicates that K(runch has successfully completed its operation.

If SYSTEM.FILER or SYSTEM.PASCAL are moved during the K(runch operation, you are prompted to reboot (because the p–System cannot gracefully recover under these circumstances).

NOTE: K(runch is dangerous to use on a disk that has bad blocks which are not marked as .BAD files. K(runch can move good files on top of these areas, destroying valuable data. It is a good habit to do a B(ad block scan before you K(runch a disk.

Example:

Consider the volume described by this extended listing:

```
MY_VOL:
SYSTEM.PASCAL     113  1-Jan-85     6    512    Codefile
SYSTEM.MISCINFO     2  1-Jan-85   119    512    Datafile
SYSTEM.FILER       32  1-Jan-85   121    512    Codefile
SYSTEM.EDITOR      49  1-Jan-85   153    512    Codefile
SYSTEM.LIBRARY     21  1-Jan-85   202    512    Codefile
SYSTEM.INTERP      30  1-Jan-85   223    512    Datafile
< UNUSED   >        9             253
TEST.TEXT           4  1-Jan-85   262    512    Textfile
TEST.CODE           9  1-Jan-85   266    512    Codefile
< UNUSED >          4             275
SCRIPT.TEXT         4  1-Jan-85   279    512    Textfile
< UNUSED >         37             283
9/9 files<listed/in-dir>, 270 blocks used, 50 unused, 37 in largest
```

If you want to place a forty block file on this disk, it won't fit. The reason is that this disk doesn't contain 40 blocks in one unused area. However, there are more than 40 available blocks throughout the disk. In order to consolidate that unused disk space, you can select K(runch and respond:

```
Crunch what vol ? MY_VOL: [ret]
From end of disk, block 320 ? (Y/N) Y
Moving forward TEST.TEXT
Moving forward TEST.CODE
Moving forward SCRIPT.TEXT
MYVOL: crunched
```

If you do another extended listing, you can see that the unused disk space has been consolidated at the end of MY_VOL:

```
MY_VOL:
SYSTEM.PASCAL     113  1-Jan-85     6    512    Codefile
SYSTEM.MISCINFO     2  1-Jan-85   119    512    Datafile
SYSTEM.FILER       32  1-Jan-85   121    512    Codefile
SYSTEM.EDITOR      49  1-Jan-85   153    512    Codefile
SYSTEM.LIBRARY     21  1-Jan-85   202    512    Codefile
SYSTEM.INTERP      30  1-Jan-85   223    512    Datafile
TEST.TEXT           4  1-Jan-85   253    512    Textfile
TEST.CODE           9  1-Jan-85   257    512    Codefile
SCRIPT.TEXT         4  1-Jan-85   266    512    Textfile
< UNUSED >         50             270
9/9 files<listed/in-dir>, 270 blocks used, 50 unused, 50 in largest
```

Now there is enough room to place the forty block file on MY_VOL:.

L(ist Directory

L(ist directory, abbreviated L(dir, displays the names (and other pertinent information) of all the files on a disk.

How to use it:

Select L(ist directory and this prompt is displayed:

```
Dir listing of what vol? VOLUME-ID [ret]
                         FILE-SPEC [ret]
                         VOLUME-ID , FILE-SPEC [ret]
```

The first response lists the directory of the specified volume on the console.

The second response lists the directory entry only for the indicated file. If that file is specified using wild cards, a subset of the directory (such as all of the code files) can be listed. (See the "Wild Cards" section later in this chapter.)

The third response creates a listing of the indicated volume and sends that listing to the file specified. If the file specification indicates a disk file, the listing is placed in that file. However, the file specification might be a communication volume such as PRINTER:. In this case, the directory listing is printed.

Example:

In order to view the directory of the disk in #4:, use L(ist directory like this:

```
Dir listing of what vol? #4: [ret]
```

The directory listing then appears on the console and looks similar to the following example:*

```
MY VOL:
SYSTEM.PASCAL    113  1-Jan-83
SYSTEM.MISCINFO    2  1-Jan-83
SYSTEM.FILER      32  1-Jan-83
SYSTEM.EDITOR     49  1-Jan-83
SYSTEM.LIBRARY    21  1-Jan-83
SYSTEM.INTERP     30  1-Jan-83
TEST.TEXT          4  1-Jan-83
TEST.CODE          9  1-Jan-83
SCRIPT.TEXT        4  1-Jan-83
9/9 files<listed/in-dir>, 270 blocks used, 50 unused, 37 in largest
```

Each file name is followed by the length, in blocks, of the file, and the date it was created or last modified. The final line indicates that there are 9 files listed out of 9 files total; there are 270 blocks of disk space used and 50 available; and out of those 50, the largest contiguous area is 37 blocks long.

If you want to print this listing for future reference, you could do it like this:

```
Dir listing of what vol? #4: , PRINTER: [ret]
```

Alternatively you could send the listing to a disk file:

```
Dir listing of what vol? #4: , LIST.TEXT [ret]
```

Later, you could use T(ransfer to send LIST.TEXT to PRINTER:. This prints the directory listing in the same way that the first response did. It may be useful to have a copy of the directory saved in a disk file, however.

---

* *IV.2 users, note:* Two columns are used for the directory listing.

M(ake

M(ake creates a disk file. The initial information in such a file is whatever happens to be on the disk in the area where the file is created.

How to use it:

Select M(ake and this prompt is displayed:

```
Make what file ? FILE-NAME [ret]
                 FILE-NAME SIZE-SPEC [ret]
                 VOLUME-ID:FILE-NAME [ret]
                 VOLUME-ID:FILE-NAME SIZE-SPEC [ret]
```

You should enter the name of the file you want to make. As these four responses indicate, you may include a size specification and/or a volume ID.

If your file name ends with .TEXT, a text file is created. Similarly, if it ends with .CODE, .FOTO, .BACK, .BAD, or .SVOL, the corresponding type of file is created. (The .BACK and .FOTO files aren't covered in this book.) If none of these suffixes are used, a data file is created.

You can choose the size of a file you make by using a size specification (see Section 4.5, page 108). For instance, the following response makes a 10 block file:

```
Make what file ? FILE-NAME[10] [ret]
```

When a file length is given like this, the file is created in the first unused area on the disk that is large enough to hold it. In this example, the file occupies the first available area that is at least 10 blocks long.

If you do not specify a length, the file is made as large as it can be and occupies the largest available area on the volume.

M(ake can be used to create .SVOL files (which contain subsidiary volumes). When you use M(ake to create an .SVOL file, it displays some extra prompts which are covered in the "Subsidiary Volumes" section, later in this chapter.

Example:

Select M(ake and respond:

```
Make what file ? #5:MY.FILE.TEXT[22] [ret]
```

A 22–block text file is created on the volume in drive #5. It is created in the first unused area which is at least 22 blocks long.

N(ew

N(ew cancels the workfile status of the current workfile. Temporary (unsaved) workfiles are removed by N(ew.*

How to use it:

Select N(ew and, if your workfile is saved, you are informed:

```
Workfile cleared
```

The file still exists on the disk but is no longer the workfile. This is essentially the opposite of the action that G(et performs. If you have a temporary workfile, you are prompted:

```
Throw away current workfile ? Y or N
```

If you type "N", N(ew is cancelled and nothing changes. If you type "Y", the temporary workfile(s) are removed.

Example:

You may have been using a workfile for a while and are now ready to use a new one. Enter the Filer and, if you want to save the work that you have been doing, use S(ave. Then select N(ew and you are informed:

```
Workfile cleared
```

At this point you can G(et another workfile if you want.

O(n/Off–Line

O(n/Off–line **mounts** and **dismounts** subsidiary volumes (which are covered in Section 6.10).†

How to use it:

Select O(n/Off–line and the following menu is displayed:

```
Subsidiary Volume: M(ount, D(ismount, C(lear
```

---

* *IV.2 users, note:* This activity is not available. Use the Command menu's S(et activity instead.

† *IV.0 users, note:* This activity is not available. Since the subsidiary volumes it deals with are also not supported, it isn't needed.

If you select M(ount, these lines are displayed:

```
Mount what vol ? FILE-SPEC [ret]
VOLUME-ID: FILE-NAME  --> Mounted
```

The response must indicate an .SVOL file. If you select D(ismount, these lines are displayed:

```
Dismount what vol ? VOLUME-ID [ret]
VOLUME-NAME:   --> Dismounted
```

The response must indicate a volume ID for a subsidiary volume. That volume is dismounted.

Notice the difference between the response that is expected for mounting and the one that is expected for dismounting. In the first case you specify the .SVOL file, and in the second case you specify the subsidiary volume ID.

If you select C(lear, all mounted subsidiary volumes are dismounted.

Example:

If you have a disk on which you have 5 subsidiary volumes, you can mount all of them using the equal sign wild card:

```
Subsidiary Volume: M(ount, D(ismount, C(lear M
Mount what vol ? HARDSK:=.SVOL
HARDSK:DOCS1.SVOL      --> Mounted
HARDSK:DOCS2.SVOL      --> Mounted
HARDSK:UTILS.SVOL      --> Mounted
HARDSK:D_BASE.SVOL     --> Mounted
HARDSK:PLAY.SVOL       --> Mounted
```

After this operation DOCS1:, DOCS2:, UTILS:, D_BASE:, and PLAY: are all on–line. The V(olumes activity can be used to see which device numbers these volumes are assigned. (The equal wild card is discussed in the "Wild Cards" section later in this chapter.)

P(refix

P(refix designates a given storage volume as the default disk (see Section 4.7, page 110).

How to use it:

Select P(refix and these lines are displayed:

```
Prefix titles by what vol ? VOLUME-ID [ret]
Prefix is VOLUME-ID
```

The response to the prompt indicates the volume you wish to designate as the default disk.

If you P(refix to a device number, the disk in the drive (if one is present) becomes the prefixed volume. If there is no disk in the drive, the device itself (e.g. #5:) is used as the prefix. This means that whatever disk you place in the prefixed drive is the prefixed volume.

Example:

If you are doing a lot of work with files on a disk called DISK2:, you can respond to p–System prompts in this fashion:

```
Transfer what file ? DISK2:MY.FILE , DISK2:MY.FILE.BACK [ret]
Remove what file ? DISK2:ANOTHER.FILE [ret]
```

However, if you use P(refix like this:

```
Prefix titles by what vol ? DISK2: [ret]
```

you can then answer these prompts with less thought and effort:

```
Transfer what file ? MY.FILE , MY.FILE.BACK [ret]
Remove what file ? ANOTHER.FILE [ret]
```

R(emove

R(emove deletes one or more files from the directory of a storage volume.

How to use it:

Select R(emove and these lines are displayed:

```
Remove what file ? FILE-SPEC [ret]
VOLUME-NAME: FILE-NAME   -->  removed
Update directory ? Y or N
```

The response to the first prompt should indicate the file that you want removed.

The second line indicates the action that is taking place.

The third line asks if you are certain that you want to remove the indicated file. (This is a double check.) If you type "Y", the file is removed; otherwise it is not.

You should not use R(emove to delete temporary workfiles. Always use N(ew for this.

Wild cards may be used with R(emove. They allow you to remove several files at once. See the "Wild Cards" section, later in this chapter, for more information about this.

Example:

To remove OLD.FILE.TEXT from the volume in #5:, use R(emove as follows:

```
Remove what file ? #5:OLD.FILE.TEXT [ret]
MYDISK:OLD.FILE.TEXT  -->  removed
Update directory ? Y
```

S(ave

S(ave changes the temporary workfiles (SYSTEM.WRK.TEXT and SYSTEM.WRK.CODE) into permanent workfiles (sometimes called named work files).*

How to use it:

Select S(ave and, if you have any temporary workfiles, one or more of the following lines are displayed:

```
Save as VOLUME-NAME:OLD-FILE-NAME ? Y or N
Save as what file ? FILE-SPEC [ret]
Text file saved
Code file saved
Text & Code file saved
```

The first prompt is only displayed if you initially used G(et to designate the workfile. This prompt is asking you if you want to save the workfile under its original name. If you do, the original workfile is removed.

If you type "N" for the first prompt, or if you didn't designate the workfile with G(et, the second prompt is displayed. It asks you for the name to give the saved workfile. Respond with any proper file name that you want, but do not include a suffix (.TEXT or .CODE).

One of the last three lines is then displayed. This indicates that a text file, a code file, or both have been saved as the permanent workfile.

If you don't have any temporary workfiles when you select S(ave, you are simply notified:

```
Workfile is already saved
```

If you don't have any workfile at all, you are informed:

```
No workfile to save
```

---

* *IV.2 users, note:* This activity is not available. The Q(uit U(pdate activity in the Editor always produces permanent workfiles rather than temporary workfiles.

After a file is saved, it remains your workfile. In order to cancel its workfile status, you should use N(ew.

You can save your workfiles on the system disk (where the temporary versions reside) or on some other disk. If you save them on the system disk, the names of the SYSTEM.WRK files are actually changed to the names that you want. If you save your temporary workfiles on another disk, the SYSTEM.WRK files still remain as they were (although permanent versions of them now exist elsewhere).

Example:

You may be developing a program using workfiles. If your program is working well so far, you might want to save it in its current state before adding more material that could cause it to fail. To do this, enter the Filer, select S(ave, and indicate the program's file name:

```
Save as what file ? PROGRAM [ret]
Text & Code file saved
```

The files PROGRAM.TEXT and PROGRAM.CODE are now your permanent workfiles. If you enter the Editor, PROGRAM.TEXT is loaded into the workspace. You can then use Q(uit U(pdate and a new SYSTEM.WRK.TEXT is created. You can use the compiler to create a new SYSTEM.WRK.CODE. However, the old text and code versions remain unaltered as PROGRAM.TEXT and PROGRAM.CODE.

T(ransfer

T(ransfer moves files from one place to another. It can also move a volume onto another volume. In addition, T(ransfer can print or display files by sending them to the printer or to the console.

How to use it:

To transfer a file, select T(ransfer and one or more of these prompts are displayed:

```
Transfer what file ? FILE-SPEC [ret]
To where ? NEW-FILE-SPEC [ret]
Remove NEW-VOLUME-NAME:NEW-FILE-NAME ? Y or N
VOLUME-NAME:FILE-NAME   -->   NEW-VOLUME-NAME:NEW-FILE-NAME
```

The first prompt requests a file to be transferred.

The second prompt asks where to transfer that file.

If you indicate a destination file which already exists, the third prompt appears and asks if you want to remove the existing file. If you type "Y", the Filer removes it before placing the new copy on the disk. If you type

"N", the T(ransfer activity is cancelled because two files with the same name can't exist on the same volume.

The fourth line indicates that the transfer was successful.

Usually, the source file remains undisturbed. It is only removed when the destination file is placed on the same disk as the source file and given the same name. Even then, you are asked if you want to remove the source file (since it conflicts with the destination file name).

Wild cards can be used in conjunction with T(ransfer. With wild cards, you can easily transfer several files from one disk to another. This is a very convenient method of maintaining back up disks. (See the "Wild Cards" section later in this chapter.)

T(ransfer can also copy an entire storage volume onto another storage volume. To do this, respond to the T(ransfer prompts with volume ID's instead of file names. When you do volume–to–volume (or disk–to–disk) transfers, one or more of these prompts are displayed:

```
Transfer what file ? VOLUME-ID [ret]
To where ? NEW-VOLUME-ID [ret]
Transfer ### blocks ? Y or N
# of blocks to transfer ? ###  [ret]
Destroy EXISTING-VOLUME-NAME: ? Y or N
```

The first and second prompts ask for the source and destination volumes.

The third prompt asks if you want to transfer the total number of blocks on the source volume. (This prompt only appears if a valid directory exists on the source volume.)

If you don't elect to transfer the entire source volume, the fourth prompt asks how many blocks you do want to transfer.

The final prompt verifies that you want to go through with the transfer. If you do, any existing information on the destination volume is overwritten. (This prompt only appears if a valid directory already exists on the destination volume.)

NOTE: When doing a volume–to–volume T(ransfer, make sure that the two volumes do not have the same name. The p–System cannot distinguish between them if they do. When you T(ransfer a master disk onto a backup disk, the backup disk ends up with the same name as the master. You should C(hange the backup disk's name before performing this operation again.

NOTE: You should only do a volume–to–volume T(ransfer between disks of the same storage capacity. This is because the disk directory (which indicates the storage capacity of the volume and the locations of the files) is directly copied from the source disk to the destination disk. If the destination disk does not have enough storage capacity to contain the rest of the disk image, the directory will be incorrect.

It is possible to indicate the source and destination files in response to the first T(ransfer prompt by using a comma, like this:

```
Transfer what file ? FILE-SPEC , NEW-FILE-SPEC [ret]
```

This can be convenient because it is easier to type. Also, you can use ⟦bs⟧ to erase any mistake that you make while typing the source file (because you haven't typed ⟦ret⟧ yet).

In order to print a file, you can T(ransfer it to PRINTER: or #6:. In order to display a file on your computer's screen, T(ransfer it to CONSOLE: or #1:. In general, only text files should be transferred to the printer or console. Most other types of files are not intended to be viewed in this way.

It is possible to T(ransfer your input at the keyboard to a communication device or to a disk file. To do this, T(ransfer CONSOLE:, or #1:, to the desired destination. When you have finished typing your input, type ⟦eof⟧. If, for example, you T(ransfer CONSOLE: to PRINTER:, the p–System waits for you to enter something at the keyboard. When you have finished and you type ⟦eof⟧, your input is printed.

Example:

To T(ransfer a file called MY.FILE.CODE from your system disk to the disk in drive #5:, use T(ransfer like this:

```
Transfer what file ? *MY.FILE.CODE ⟦ret⟧
To where ? #5:MY.FILE.CODE ⟦ret⟧
SYSDISK:MY.FILE.CODE    -->  DISK2:MY.FILE.CODE
```

In order to print a file called LISTING.TEXT, use T(ransfer like this:

```
Transfer what file ? LISTING.TEXT ⟦ret⟧
To where ? PRINTER: ⟦ret⟧
```

If you want to test your printer to see that it is correctly interfacing with your computer, you can use T(ransfer like this:

```
Transfer what file ? CONSOLE: ⟦ret⟧
To where ? PRINTER: ⟦ret⟧
THIS IS A TEST ⟦ret⟧ ⟦eof⟧
```

If all goes well, "THIS IS A TEST" is printed.

V(olumes

V(olumes, abbreviated V(ols, displays the volumes that are on–line. A storage volume is on–line if the disk is correctly placed in a drive. A communication volume is on–line if it is properly connected and the p–System is able to access it.

How to use it:

Select V(olumes and this display appears:

```
Vols on-line
  1      CONSOLE:
  2      SYSTERM:
  4 #    VOLNAME:             [###]
  5 #    VOLNAME:             [###]
  6      PRINTER:
  7      REMIN:
  8      REMOUT:
Root vol is - VOLNAME:
Prefix is   - VOLNAME:
```

The first column shows the device numbers of the on–line volumes. In the next column, the volume names are listed. Storage volumes show a number sign ("#") between the device number and the volume name. In this example display, devices #4: and #5: are the only storage volumes on–line. Following a storage volume name, its maximum storage capacity in blocks is displayed between square brackets, "[" and "]".* The other devices shown are the standard communication volumes (see Section 4.11, page 117).

The "root vol" is the system disk (the disk that you booted with). The prefix volume is the default volume (see Section 4.7, page 110).

Example:

If you select V(olumes, this display might appear:

```
Vols on-line
  1      CONSOLE:
  2      SYSTERM:
  4 #    MYDISK:              [  320]
  5 #    DISK2:               [  640]
  6      PRINTER:
  7      REMIN:
  8      REMOUT:
  9 #    BIG:                 [10000]
 10 #    RAMDISK:             [  240]
Root vol is - MYDISK:
Prefix is   - BIG:
```

This shows all of the standard communication devices on–line. It also shows four storage devices. There are two floppy disks: a 320 block disk in #4 and a 640 block disk in #5. Device #9 contains a hard disk, called BIG:, which has a 10,000 block storage capacity. And, #10 is a RAM disk (a virtual disk which exists in main memory). The system disk (called "root vol" here) is MYDISK:. The default disk (called "prefix" here) is BIG:.

---

* *IV.0 users, note:* The storage capacity numbers within square brackets do not appear.

W(hat

W(hat tells you the status of your workfile, if you have one.*

How to use it:

Select W(hat, and one of these messages appears:

```
Workfile is VOLUME-NAME:FILE-NAME
Workfile is VOLUME-NAME:FILE-NAME (not saved)
Not named (not saved)
No workfile
```

The first and second messages indicate your current workfile. There may be a text and/or code version of this file. In the second case, the phrase "not saved" indicates that there is a temporary version of the workfile.

The third message indicates that your workfile is a temporary workfile (SYSTEM.WRK.TEXT and/or SYSTEM.WRK.CODE).

The fourth message simply indicates that you do not currently have a workfile.

Example:

If you G(et a file called MY.PROG.TEXT and then select W(hat, you are informed:

```
Workfile is VOLNAME:MY.PROG
```

If you edit that file and use Q(uit U(pdate to leave the Editor, the temporary version of MY.PROG.TEXT is created. Now, if you enter the Filer and select W(hat, you are informed:

```
Workfile is VOLNAME:MY.PROG (not saved)
```

This reminds you that the most current version of MY.PROG is not S(aved under an explicit name.

---

* *IV.2 users, note:* This activity is not available. Use the Command menu's S(et activity instead.

X(amine

X(amine attempts to fix bad blocks on a disk.

How to use it:

Select X(amine, and one or more of the following prompts appear:

```
Examine blocks on what vol ? VOLUME-ID [ret]
Block-range ? ###-### [ret]
File(s) endangered:
FILE-NAME-1    ##  ##
FILE-NAME-2    ##  ##
          .
          .
          .
Fix them ? Y or N
Block ## may be ok
Block ## is bad
          .
          .
          .
Mark bad blocks ? (Y/N) Y or N
```

The first prompt asks you to designate the volume that you want to examine.

The second prompt asks which blocks on that volume are to be checked. In response to this prompt you can enter a single number or two numbers separated by a hyphen. If you enter a single number, that block is examined. If you enter two numbers with a hyphen, those two blocks and all blocks between them are examined.

If any files overlap the block range, they are listed as "File(s) endangered." In this case you are asked if you want to "Fix them." These files are endangered because X(amine may destroy information contained in any of the blocks that are examined. (Because of this danger, you should only examine blocks that are apparently bad, according to the B(ad blocks activity.)

If you elect to proceed (or if no files were endangered) X(amine attempts to fix any problems by reading and writing to each block in the block range several times. The block numbers are displayed followed by "may be ok" or "is bad." If the message "may be ok" is displayed, it is likely that the block is fine. You should check to be sure by using B(ad blocks again.

If any blocks are bad, the final prompt, above, asks if you want to mark them. If you do, the bad blocks are marked by placing a .BAD file over them. (You are warned if existing files must be removed in order to mark the bad blocks.) A bad file created by X(amine has the name:

BAD.#####.BAD

where "#####" is the block number. The p–System does not move such a file when K(runch is used. This means that it is safe to K(runch a disk with bad blocks as long as they are marked. You may decide to discard disks with bad blocks just to be safe, however. You might also try formatting the disk again in an attempt to fix the bad blocks.

Example:

If the B(ad blocks activity indicates that blocks 25 and 27 are bad, you could use X(amine like this:

```
Examine blocks on what vol ? MY_DISK: [ret]
Block-range ? 25-27 [ret]
File(s) endangered:
PROGRAM.CODE  24  32
Fix them ? Y
Block 25 may be ok
Block 26 may be ok
Block 27 is bad
Mark bad blocks (files will be removed!) ? (Y/N) Y
```

In this example, PROGRAM.CODE (which occupies blocks 24 through 32) overlaps the bad blocks. Even though X(amine was able to fix block 25, block 27 was beyond repair. In order to mark block 27, PROGRAM.CODE must be removed. (Hopefully, there is a back up copy of PROGRAM.CODE on another disk!)

Z(ero

Z(ero places a new directory on a storage volume. This new directory is empty, indicating that no files currently exist on the disk.

How to use it:

Select Z(ero and one or more of these prompts are displayed:

```
Zero dir of what vol ? VOLUME-ID [ret]
Destroy VOLUME-NAME: ? Y or N
Duplicate dir ? Y or N
Are there ### blks on the disk ? (Y/N) Y or N
# of blocks on the disk ? ### [ret]
New vol name ? NEW-VOLUME-NAME: [ret]
NEW-VOLUME-NAME: correct ? Y or N
NEW-VOLUME-NAME: zeroed
```

The first prompt asks which volume is to be Z(eroed.

The second prompt only appears if the volume already has a directory (that is, if it is not blank). This prompt asks if you want to overwrite the current directory. If you do, the old files on that disk are no longer going to appear in the directory and are essentially lost. It is usually possible to recover them, but this can be a tedious task.

The third prompt asks if you want a duplicate directory (see Section 4.8, page 111) to be maintained on the Z(eroed volume. If you do, two copies of the disk directory are kept on the new volume for safety.

The fourth prompt only appears if the volume already has a directory. It displays the current size of the volume, in blocks, and asks if you want the new directory to indicate the same size.

If you don't want the disk to show that number of blocks (or if there is no current directory) the fifth prompt asks for the size that you would like. Usually, you should respond to this prompt with the maximum capacity of your disks. (Refer to the inside front cover of this book.)

The sixth prompt asks for the new volume name.

The second–to–last prompt verifies that you want the name you entered. This is your last chance to cancel the Z(ero activity without actually affecting the disk in question.

The final message indicates that the volume has been successfully Z(eroed.

NOTE: Most computers require that a blank diskette be "formatted" by a disk formatting utility before it can be Z(eroed by the Filer (and subsequently used by the p–System in general). In some cases, the disk formatting utility performs the initial Z(ero operation on the disk for you.

Example:

If you are initializing a blank disk, you might use Z(ero like this:

```
Zero dir of what vol ? #5: [ret]
Duplicate dir ? N
# of blocks on the disk ? 320
New vol name ? MYDISK: [ret]
MYDISK: correct ? Y
MYDISK: zeroed
```

6.10 SUBSIDIARY VOLUMES

This section covers a more advanced topic: **subsidiary volumes**. A subsidiary volume is a file that can be used as if it were a separate disk altogether. It has its own directory and may contain its own files. The disk that contains the subsidiary volume is called the **principal volume**.*

Subsidiary volumes are especially useful when dealing with large capacity disks. Using subsidiary volumes, you can divide such disks into logical portions. For example, you can have one subsidiary volume for personal programs, one for professional use, and so forth.

Also, the p–System is able to store many more files than it otherwise could. A volume is able to hold, at most, 77 files with the current p–System. This is far too few files for a large capacity disk. However, each subsidiary volume is able to hold 77 files of its own. This means that you could conceivably have as many as 77 subsidiary volumes with as many as

---

* *IV.0 users, note:* This facility is not supported at all, so this section is not relevant to you.

77 files on each.

The files that contain subsidiary volumes use the .SVOL suffix. The part of the file name that precedes .SVOL is usually the name of the subsidiary volume and must contain 7 or fewer characters. Here are some valid file names and corresponding subsidiary volume names:

File Name	Subsidiary Volume It Contains
WORK.SVOL	WORK:
PLAY.SVOL	PLAY:
MEMOS_1.SVOL	MEMOS_1:
THESIS.SVOL	THESIS:

Figure 6.1 gives you an idea of the structure of subsidiary volumes. It shows a directory on the principal volume which includes an .SVOL file. The directory within the .SVOL file is shown along with the files contained within the subsidiary volume.

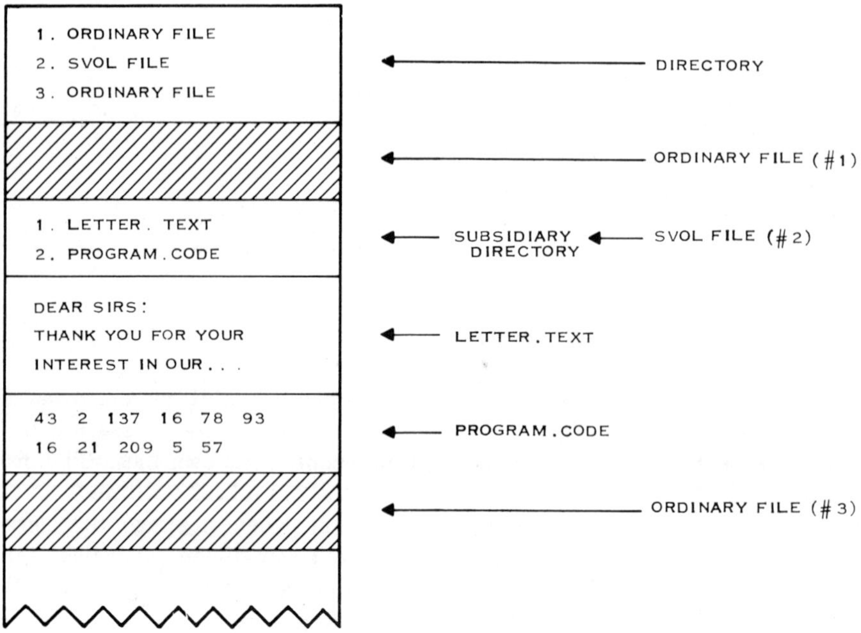

Figure 6.1

In order for a subsidiary volume to be used, it must be **mounted**. Mounting a subsidiary volume is similar to bringing an ordinary disk volume on–line. A subsidiary volume is not necessarily mounted just because the corresponding .SVOL file resides on an on–line volume.

There are two ways that you can mount a subsidiary volume. The first way is to simply have the principal volume on–line when the p–System is booted or reinitialized. The initialization process mounts, as far as it is able to, all of the subsidiary volumes that are found on all of the on–line principal volumes.*

You can use the O(n/Off–Line activity (described with the other Filer activities) to manually mount subsidiary volumes. You can also use this activity to dismount subsidiary volumes.

In addition, when you use the M(ake activity to create a subsidiary volume, it is mounted automatically.

NOTE: There is a limit to the number of subsidiary volumes that you can have mounted at one time. This limit can be set by you and is subject to memory constraints and tradeoffs. It is beyond the scope of this book to go into this, however. See Chapter 9 for further reading about subsidiary volumes and the Setup utility.

You should attempt to keep a principal volume on–line as long as you are using a subsidiary volume that resides on it. This is a safety precaution since, under certain circumstances, it is possible to confuse the p–System about a subsidiary volume if you remove the principal volume and replace it with some other disk.

The V(olumes activity (described with the other Filer activities) has some special provisions for subsidiary volumes. It displays additional information for subsidiary volumes. The name of the principal volume is given. Also, the location of the subsidiary volume is shown. The following is an example:

```
Vols on-line
   1        CONSOLE:
   2        SYSTERM:
   4 #      SYSTEM:[  320]
   5 #      PASCAL:[  320]
   6        PRINTER:
   7        REMIN:
   8        REMOUT:
  12 #      HARDISK:[20000]
  13 #      MY_SVOL:[ 3000]on volume HARDISK:   starting at block 2000
  14 #      ANOTHER:[ 2500]on volume HARDISK:   starting at block 5000
Root vol is - SYSTEM:
Prefix is   - SYSTEM:
```

In this example, a 20,000 block disk, called HARDISK:, is on–line as device #12. The two subsidiary volumes, MY_SVOL: and ANOTHER:, are located on HARDISK: at the indicated starting blocks. The size of each subsidiary volume, in blocks, is shown (e.g., 3000 for MY_SVOL) just as it is for any other storage volume. The device numbers are also shown as they are for the rest of the volumes; in this example, MY_SVOL: is device #13.

In order to create an .SVOL file, you should use M(ake (which is described with the other Filer menu items). Whenever you M(ake an .SVOL

---

* *IV.2 users, note:* Only the subsidiary volumes on the system disk are automatically mounted during initialization.

file, the Filer realizes that you want to create a subsidiary volume. In order to do this, it asks you one or two extra questions:

```
Make what file ? VOLNAME.SVOL [###] [ret]
Zero subsidiary volume directory ? Y or N
Duplicate dir ? Y or N
```

The response to the first prompt should be the name of the subsidiary volume and may include the size specification.

If a subsidiary volume directory previously existed where you are now creating the .SVOL file, you are asked if you want to Z(ero the old directory. If you do, the new subsidiary volume will contain no files. If you don't, the new subsidiary volume will contain the same files that the old subsidiary volume did.

The third prompt asks if you want a duplicate directory to be maintained on the subsidiary volume. Duplicate directories are a safety precaution that you may use if you wish.

When a subsidiary volume is created with M(ake, it is mounted automatically unless you have already mounted as many subsidiary volumes as your system configuration allows.

6.11 WILD CARDS

Wild cards allow you to refer to more than one file in a shorthand fashion. They are convenient to use in conjunction with many of the Filer activities. Wild cards can help you to avoid excessive typing and the errors that may result.

There are three wild card symbols: equal sign (=), question mark (?), and dollar sign ($). They can be used as part of a file name when you are responding to Filer prompts.

The equal sign matches any sequence of characters. For instance:

A.PROG=

matches all of the following:

A.PROG.TEXT
A.PROG.CODE
A.PROGRAM
A.PROG

The R(emove activity, for example, removes all of those files (if they exist to begin with) if you enter this response:

```
Remove what file ? A.PROG= [ret]
```

The equal sign, by itself, designates all of the files on a disk. For instance, if you respond to the R(emove prompt like this:

```
Remove what file ? = [ret]
```

or

```
Remove what file ? MYDISK:= [ret]
```

all files are removed from the prefix disk or from MYDISK:, respectively.

The question mark behaves just like the equal sign except that you are asked, for each matching file, whether you want that file included in the operation. For example, you can use R(emove like this:

```
Remove what file ? A.PROG? [ret]
Remove A.PROG.TEXT ? Y, N, or [esc]
Remove A.PROG.CODE ? Y, N, or [esc]
Remove A.PROGRAM ? Y, N, or [esc]
Remove A.PROG ? Y, N, or [esc]
Update directory ? Y or N
```

For each match, you are asked if you want to remove that particular file. You should respond to each prompt with "Y" for yes, "N" for no, or [esc] to discontinue this series of prompts at any point. Typing [esc] exits the R(emove activity altogether if you have not indicated that you want to remove any files so far. If you have indicated that one or more files are to be removed, typing [esc] skips to the "Update directory?" prompt. If you don't update the directory, none of the files are removed.

The dollar sign wild card indicates "the same file name as before." It is only used with T(ransfer (although the compilers and assemblers can use this wild card as well). T(ransfer prompts you for a source file and a destination for that file. If you indicate dollar sign as the destination, the original file name is given to the transferred file. It is not necessarily transferred to the same volume as the source file, however. The volume ID is independent of the dollar sign wild card. As an example, you might use T(ransfer like this:

```
Transfer what file ? VOL1:FILE.NAME [ret]
To what file ? VOL2:$ [ret]
VOL1:FILE.NAME  -->  VOL2:FILE.NAME
```

This saves you from having to retype the destination file name. You could also use T(ransfer like this:

```
Transfer what file ? VOL1:A.PROG= [ret]
To what file ? VOL2:$ [ret]
VOL1:A.PROG.TEXT   -->  VOL2:A.PROG.TEXT
VOL1:A.PROG.CODE   -->  VOL2:A.PROG.CODE
VOL1:A.PROGRAM     -->  VOL2:A.PROGRAM
```

This transfers all files on VOL2: that match A.PROG= to VOL2:. It gives them the same name that they originally had.

If there is a source and destination, as in the case with T(ransfer and C(hange, wild cards must be used on both sides, or not at all. The following T(ransfer operation is not correct because several files cannot be transferred to one file:

```
Transfer what file ? A.PROG= [ret]
To what file ? MYDISK:A.PROG.TEXT [ret]
```

The single exception to this rule is that a dollar sign may be used as the destination in T(ransfer for a file which is specified without wild cards (as shown above).

The Filer activities that can use wild cards are:

C(hange
E(xtended list directory
L(ist directory
O(n/off line
R(emove
T(ransfer

The next two sections demonstrate useful operations that can be performed by using wild cards in conjunction with R(emove and T(ransfer.

Removing Several Files from a Volume

If you want to remove every file from a volume, you can use R(emove like this:

```
Remove what file ? VOLNAME:= [ret]
VOLNAME:A.FILE.TEXT--> removed
VOLNAME:A.FILE.CODE--> removed
VOLNAME:ANOTHER.FILE--> removed
VOLNAME:YET.ANOTHER--> removed
VOLNAME:LAST.FILE.TEXT--> removed
Update directory ? Y or N
```

The prompt at the end is a double check. If you type "Y", all of the files are removed. If you type "N", nothing is removed.

You can remove all of the text files, or all of the code files on a disk like this:

```
Remove what file ? VOLNAME:=.TEXT [ret]
```

```
Remove what file ? =.CODE [ret]
```

The first response removes all text files on VOLNAME:. The second response removes all code files on the prefix disk.

You can also use the question mark wild card so that you are prompted, for each file, whether or not it should be removed. This is demonstrated in the discussion about the question mark wild card above.

Backing Up Disks Using T(ransfer

There are two convenient ways to use T(ransfer to back up the files on a disk. The first is to do a disk–to–disk transfer. This amounts to transferring one volume to another and is described under T(ransfer.

The other way is to do a file–by–file T(ransfer using wild cards. For example, you could use T(ransfer like this:

```
Transfer what file ? MASTER:= [ret]
To where ? BACKUP:$ [ret]
MASTER:FILE.NAME.1  --> BACKUP:FILE.NAME.1
MASTER:FILE.NAME.2  --> BACKUP:FILE.NAME.2
MASTER:FILE.NAME.3  --> BACKUP:FILE.NAME.3
                   etc.
```

If an existing file on the destination disk has the same name as a file being transferred, you are asked if you want to remove the existing file. If you decide not to remove it, the corresponding file from the source disk is not transferred. Otherwise, the transfer goes through. In either case, the Filer then goes on to the next file on the source disk. (This practice of asking you if you want to remove a file that has the same name is a standard safety precaution used by T(ransfer. In order to save time and effort, you may want to remove any matching files on the backup disk before you do this sort of T(ransfer operation.)

6.12 FILE AND DIRECTORY RECOVERING

There are several ways that files and directories can be lost. Files can be lost, for example, if you accidentally remove them. A directory can be lost if you unintentionally Z(ero a disk, or if you somehow overwrite the directory.

There are three utility programs which can assist you in recovering lost files or directories. They are the Copydupdir, Markdupdir, and Recover utilities. This section describes how to use these utilities.

The Copydupdir and Markdupdir Utilities

Copydupdir and Markdupdir are used in conjunction with duplicate directories (see Section 4.8, page 111). If you are maintaining a duplicate directory on a disk, Copydupdir can copy it into the main directory if necessary. If you aren't maintaining a duplicate directory, Markdupdir can create one for you.

When you X(ecute Copydupdir, the following prompts are displayed:

```
Duplicate Directory Copier [ ]
Enter drive # of user's disk (4,5,9,10,11) ? DEVICE NUMBER [ret]
Are you sure you want to zap directory of VOLNAME: {blocks 2-5} ? Y or N
Directory copy is complete.  Type <ret> to exit.
```

The first line identifies the Copydupdir utility.

The second prompt asks for the disk's device number. This is the disk that will have the duplicate directory copied into the main directory. Do not include the number sign or colon when you enter the device number.

The third prompt asks you to verify that you want to "zap" that volume's directory. You should be aware that when the duplicate directory is copied, the current main directory will be destroyed.

The final line indicates that the copying is complete. When you type [ret], Copydupdir is exited.

If a duplicate directory is not currently being maintained on the disk, you are warned that this is the case. If you go ahead with the copying, the contents of blocks 6 through 9 are written into the main directory. It is important that a correct duplicate directory exists in that location because, otherwise, the newly copied directory will be invalid.

When you X(ecute Markdupdir, the following prompts are displayed:

```
Duplicate Directory Marker [ ]
Enter drive # of user's disk (4,5,9,10,11) ? DEVICE NUMBER [ret]
A duplicate directory is not being maintained on VOLNAME:
WARNING! It appears that blocks 6-9 are not free for use.
  Are you sure they are free ? Y or N
Do you want the directories to be marked ? Y or N
Directories are now marked as duplicate.  Type <ret> to exit. _
```

The first line identifies the Markdupdir utility.

The second prompt asks for the disk's device number. This is the disk that will be marked as having a duplicate directory.

The third line indicates that a duplicate directory is not currently being maintained on the disk. (If one is, you are notified of that, and the Markdupdir utility is exited.)

The next two lines are a warning. They indicate that an existing file may be overlapping blocks 6 through 9. If this is the case, that file will be overwritten when you create a duplicate directory. If the disk does contain a file there, you should move it before marking the directory. This warning always appears, even if there is no file in that area.

The second to last prompt verifies that you want to mark the directory as duplicate.

The final prompt notifies you that a duplicate directory will now be maintained.

The Recover Utility

Recover is useful for recovering files that have been lost. This utility looks at the directory and informs you of the files that currently appear there. It then looks through the disk and locates areas that resemble text files or code files. (Other sorts of files cannot be recovered since they do not have a distinguishable format.) The files that are found are entered into the directory, if you want.

When you execute Recover, these prompts appear:

```
Recover [ ]
USER'S DISK IN DRIVE # (0 exits): DEVICE NUMBER [ret]
USER'S VOLUME ID: VOLUME NAME [ret]
FILE.NAME.1 found
FILE.NAME.2 found
       .
       .
       .
Are there still IMPORTANT files missing (Y/N) ? Y or N
File DUMMY01X.TEXT inserted at blocks ###-###
File DUMMY02X.TEXT inserted at blocks ###-###
File FILE.NAME.CODE inserted at blocks ###-###
       .
       .
       .
GO AHEAD AND UPDATE DIRECTORY (Y/N) ? Y or N
```

The first line identifies the Recover utility.

The second line asks for the device number of the disk to be recovered.

The third line requests a volume name. This name will be recorded on the disk when its directory is updated.

Next, the names of all files currently listed in the directory are displayed.

Following these names is a prompt asking you if there are still some important files missing. If you indicate that there are, Recover begins to look for lost files. The file names are displayed followed by a block range indicating where the files are located. Text files are named DUMMY01X, DUMMY02X, and so forth. This is because there is no way to tell what name they originally had. You need to examine the contents of these files (perhaps using the Editor) to identify them. You will also have to determine which copy of a particular file is the most recent version. Code files are given names that correspond to the program contained within them.

The final prompt asks if you want to update the directory. If you elect to do so, the recovered files are entered into the directory. If you don't, the directory remains as it was before Recover was executed.

7

MODULES:
A THEME OF THE p-SYSTEM

7.1 INTRODUCTION

The old saying, "divide and conquer," is just as true for modern software engineering as it was for the ancient battles fought by the man who is said to have first used the phrase (Julius Caesar). In software work, instead of dividing enemy armies, we divide large programs into **modules**. But "conquering" of one sort or another is still the intended result.

This chapter discusses the ways in which this well–known principle is applicable to the p–System. We aren't trying to provide a "cookbook" for using modules in the p–System. Instead, we concentrate on strategies––the strategies that guided the original design of the p–System and the strategies that you can take advantage of in your use of it.

This chapter should be most valuable if you intend to make serious use of the p–System, particularly in developing programs. No matter how you intend to use your p–System, we hope you find this discussion interesting and valuable.

Since you're probably not much interested in "conquering" in the military sense, here are some more directly useful restatements of the principle:

- "Divide and isolate." The p–System is divided into modules. One result is the isolation of the small portion of the System that must be changed when it is moved among dissimilar computers. This means that most of the components of the p–System, and most p–System application programs, can be run without change on almost any kind of personal computer.

- "Divide and understand." The p–System makes it easy for you to break large programs into smaller modules. Understanding all the modules individually is generally easier than dealing with the single large program.
- "Divide and reuse." The modules of a program are not only easier to understand; if they are carefully designed, they may even be usable in other programs! This leads to a pleasant prospect for you as a p–System programmer: major parts of a large program may already exist (as previously written modules) before you start work!
- "Divide and manage." Ready–to–run p–System programs are composed of modules called **segments**. When a program is executed, only segments that are actively directing the computer need to be in main memory. Thus the p–System can handle programs that are bigger than the available main memory space.

In the remainder of this chapter, we explore these four variations of "conquer" in each of three general areas of the use of modules in the p–System. The first topic is the p–System portability strategy.

7.2 USING MODULES TO ACHIEVE PORTABILITY

We must first address some basic questions: "Why is portability hard to achieve?" "Why can't all software run on any computer?" The reason is that most brands of computers are quite different in the details of their construction and operation, even though they may look similar and serve similar functions.

For instance, two personal computers may contain different kinds of **microprocessors** ——the tiny silicon chips that direct a small computer's activities. Each kind of microprocessor has a distinct vocabulary of instructions that it obeys. These **instruction sets** may be as different as French is from English. It shouldn't be surprising, therefore, that you have to choose the right set of instructions in order to communicate properly with a microprocessor.

Even when two computers contain the same kind of microprocessor, there can still be portability barriers, because their style of interaction with input/output peripherals (such as diskette drives or the console display and keyboard) may be different. In other words, the "languages" of input/output interaction may differ, even if the central processor languages are compatible.

Examples of these two kinds of differences among personal computers are shown in Figure 7.1, in which several computers made by one company

(Texas Instruments) are shown. The two computers on the left use the same kind of microprocessor instruction set, but different kinds of peripherals, so their edge patterns are different. The third computer, the TI Professional Computer, is different from the other two in the processor language it uses, as well as in the peripheral conventions it expects.

The figure also shows the p–System with an application program for each computer. Since the same p–System can be used in all three configurations, the edge patterns on the System are the same. The figure is not complete, however, since no direct connection exists between the p–System and the host computer hardware.

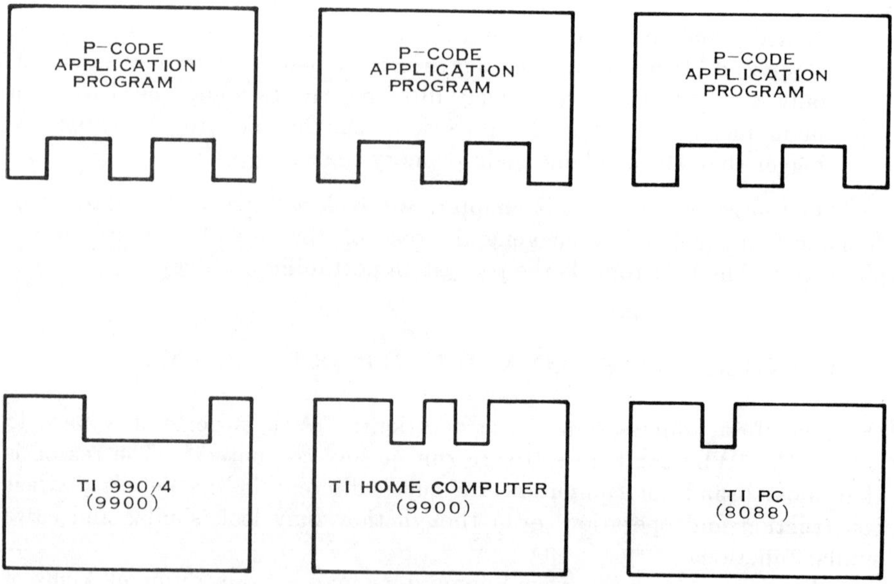

Figure 7.1

The secret of the portability of the p–System is the use of a foundation software module which deals with the host computer microprocessor and its peripherals, while isolating the rest of the p–System from the details of this hardware. Figure 7.2 shows this module in place. Notice that it adapts to the various peculiar interface patterns, while presenting the same edge pattern to the p–System.

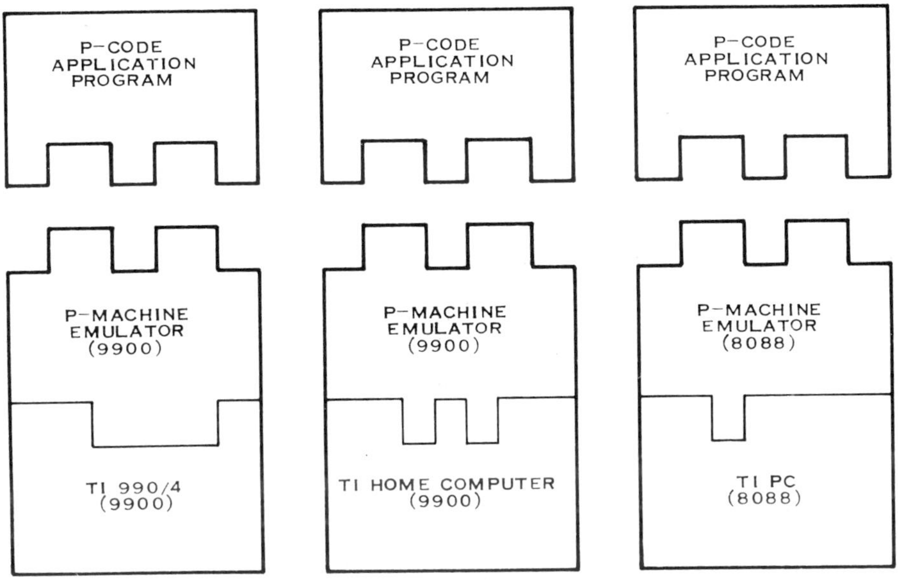

Figure 7.2

This foundation module is the **p—machine emulator** (PME). This emulator turns the host computer into a **p—machine**. All p—machines work alike, regardless of differences in the host computers on which they run.

The p—machine is an idealized computer architecture that was designed as a foundation for the p—System. Instructions for the p—machine are called **p—code**. The compilation process that we dealt with in Chapter 3 translates high level language source statements (written in UCSD Pascal or FORTRAN—77) into p—code. The resulting p—code program can then be executed to accomplish some useful task such as producing a series of payroll checks ("p—checks?").

The p—machine contains a smaller module, called the Basic I/O Subsystem (BIOS). This module handles the peripherals of the host computer and serves to isolate the bulk of the PME from dependence on those peripherals.

When the p—System in installed on a particular type of computer, an appropriate PME and BIOS must be configured. This task involves some sophisticated programming. Fortunately, it has already been done for most of the popular personal computers. If you are interested in an adaptation for a particular model of computer, but don't know a source, you could check with SofTech Microsystems.

Because the PME and BIOS modules hide the peculiarities of the various personal computer types, an application program represented in p–code can be used on a wide variety of computers. Figure 7.3 shows this wide range. Microprocessor types are listed along the left (in "8–bit" and "16–bit" groups). Next to each processor name is one or two personal computers that incorporate that microprocessor. The p–System has been implemented on all the personal computers shown.

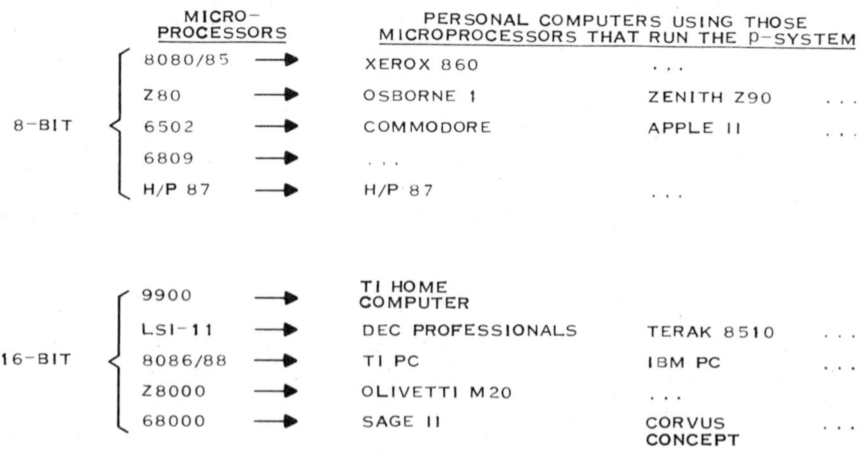

Figure 7.3

What are the implications of the p–System's wide portability for you? One implication is that the number of p–System applications for your computer is not nearly so dependent on the kind of computer you have, as it would be if you weren't using the p–System. You should benefit from the fact that application suppliers don't have to invest a lot of effort customizing their applications to your particular model of computer. You may even become an applications supplier yourself!

You also gain freedom of hardware choice with the p–System. If you replace your current computer or add additional computers in your organization, they can be selected on the basis of hardware capabilities and cost–effectiveness, with confidence that the p–System can (almost certainly) be installed on the equipment you finally select.

Furthermore, your investment in acquiring or building p–System software for your current environment is conserved, when you use the same software in new hardware environments.

Finally, there is a subtle but important benefit from the fact that tens of thousands of personal computer users are pounding on the same software you're using. In the world of software, "used" goods are often more valuable than "new" goods, because the feedback from thousands of users can be crucial to making software more reliable.

The use of modules to achieve portability is primarily an example of the "divide and isolate" principle. In the next section, we discuss the use of modules during p–System program development, where all four senses of "conquer" (isolation, understanding, reuse, and management) can be important objectives.

7.3 USING MODULES IN PROGRAM DEVELOPMENT

Some psychologists believe that there are fundamental limits on the number of distinct ideas that a human mind can productively deal with at one time. They claim that the magic number is seven (plus or minus two). For example, consider the task of memorizing the following list of numbers:

5 7 4 2 2 7 8 3 2 8 0 0 5 5 5 1 6 8 9

Unless you have special gifts of memory, you're probably intimidated by the thought of juggling all those digits in your head. What if, however, we group them like this:

574–22–7832 (800) 555–1689

Now the task is much less intimidating, because the numbers can be recognized as Social Security and telephone numbers. The stream of digits can be considered in **groups** (six of them). The first two groups in the phone number are particularly easy to remember, because they have special meanings. This is "divide and comprehend" in action!

One way you can divide a program is to use a **procedure**, a named group of language statements that usually serves a coherent purpose. (The formal name of the "procedure" construct in a particular language may be something else. The name "subroutine" is used in FORTRAN–77, for example.)

A procedure could, for instance, have responsibility for requesting and accepting a calendar date from a user at the console keyboard. A program containing this procedure could invoke it (in many places, if necessary) by using the procedure's name.

Consider the program that follows, which produces verses of a well–known song. The program is written in Pascal, but its operation should be clear, even if your expertise is in some other language. The comments (enclosed in braces "{}") should help.

```
program NinetyNineBottlesofBeer;

{This "variable" maintains a record of the bottle count.}
 var Count: integer;

 Procedure OneVerse;
  begin

   {Write lines of a verse, inserting appropriate bottle count.}
   writeln(Count,' bottles of beer on the wall,');
   writeln(Count,' bottles of beer;');
   writeln('If one of those bottles should happen to fall:');

   {Reduce the bottle count by one, and write the last line.}
   Count := Count - 1;
   writeln('There'd be ',Count,' bottles of beer on the wall.');
   writeln;

  end;

begin

 {Start with 99 bottles.}
 Count := 99;

 {Produce verses by invoking the procedure once for each verse.}
 OneVerse;
 OneVerse;
 OneVerse;
 OneVerse;
end.
```

Using procedure modules can contribute to program development in all of the ways identified in our introduction. For example, OneVerse captures, in one place, the structure of a verse. This makes it easy, for instance, to make different choices for the punctuation of each line, while maintaining consistency over the entire song.

OneVerse is also easy to reuse. If we hadn't used procedures in this program, it would have been very long, because each of the occurrences of "OneVerse" would have been replaced by the details of a particular verse. Getting those details right (over and over again!) would not have been easy.

In spite of all their benefits, procedures do have some drawbacks. One of these is that it is not very convenient to reuse a procedure in several different programs. First, you must copy the text of the procedure into each program that needs it. If you want to change the procedure, you have to find all the copies and fix them individually.

Another difficulty is that in many situations the author of a procedure may not want you to know its internal details. The details may be a trade secret!

Enter the UCSD Pascal **unit** construct. It addresses these difficulties with procedures, and has other benefits, as well. (The other two p–System languages, BASIC and FORTRAN–77, have comparable, though somewhat less powerful, constructs. We describe the UCSD Pascal version, here.)

A unit is a group of procedures and data structures, usually related to a common task area. A program or another unit can access these facilities by naming the unit in a simple **uses** statement. The using program or unit is called the **client**.

A unit has two parts. The first is the **interface part**, which describes the procedures and data items that are "public" (that is, made available to clients). The second part of a unit is the **implementation part**, which contains the detailed definitions of the public procedures, plus any other "private" procedures or data that are needed in the unit.

A unit can be compiled by itself, with no knowledge of potential clients. This means that when you work on a program containing many units, you can save a significant amount of program development time by recompiling only the modified units when the program is changed. Units that are not changed, do not generally have to be recompiled. The exception is that when the interface section of a unit is changed, all clients of that unit must be recompiled.

In its compiled (p–code) form, a unit still includes textual source definitions for the interface section. These definitions become available to clients. Note, however, that no details on the implementation section are available to clients.

A sample unit, called SimpleGraphics, is shown below. It provides three public services: putting a dot at a particular (x,y) coordinate on the graphics screen of a host computer; choosing the color for subsequent dots; and clearing the entire graphics screen. Here is the unit:

```
Unit SimpleGraphics;
  Interface

    Procedure PutDot (xCoordinate, yCoordinate: integer);
    Procedure ChangeColor (NewColor: integer);
    Procedure ClearScreen;

  Implementation
    Var CurrentColor: integer;

    Procedure PutDot; begin ... end;
    Procedure ChangeColor; begin CurrentColor := NewColor end;
    Procedure Clearscreen; begin ... end;

end.
```

Only one of the procedure definitions is shown (ChangeColor). The variable CurrentColor stores the color selected most recently by the client. CurrentColor is updated whenever ChangeColor is called.

A program or another unit that needs the facilities offered by SimpleGraphics need only include the statement "USES SIMPLEGRAPHICS".

SimpleGraphics is a good example of the way in which units can contribute to useful isolation in programs. As a user of SimpleGraphics, you need only know the functional effects of the three interface procedures, so the implementation can be changed to cater to different kinds of graphic devices (screens, plotters, or a graphics printer, for example) without impacting your programs.

The full–fledged graphics package called Turtlegraphics (which is described in the next chapter) is another example of the isolation benefits of units. It has been implemented on several different computers that have different display hardware details, but Turtlegraphics' interface to client programs is preserved in each of these adaptations.

Units don't just "divide and isolate." They address all four of the variations on "divide and conquer" that we listed in the introduction. Here are brief comments on the others:

- "Divide and understand." Since you only need to understand the services a unit provides, and not how it implements those services, it is easier to deal with a large program that is composed of many units than it would be if you had to wade through all that implementation detail.
- "Divide and reuse." A carefully designed unit can often be used in many different programs, not just in the original context that justified its creation. As you work in the p–System environment, you can accumulate a growing arsenal of program building blocks that can be applied to new projects. Reusability of units can result in enormous savings of your program development energy.
- "Divide and manage." Splitting a large program into units can make it easier for a group of programmers to work cooperatively on the program. Once the group decides on interface definitions for the units of the program, individual programmers can proceed on their own with the writing and testing of the implementation sections.

In this section, we have stressed the aspects of units that affect program development. In the next section we turn our emphasis to the execution of programs; we first examine the handling of units during program execution.

7.4 USING MODULES DURING PROGRAM EXECUTION

The independence that characterizes units during program development also applies during program execution. The compiled p–code for the units that a program needs can be spread across several code files. When you execute a program, the operating system searches in these files for all the needed units.

In most other operating systems, the modules of a program must be stitched together by a link editor utility and stored in a single file before the program can be executed. In the p–System, this "stitching" step is unnecessary. This results in two important benefits.

The first benefit occurs when you make a change to a unit of a program and want to re–execute it to test the impact of the change. Because the p–System doesn't require a link editing step, you can immediately re–execute the modified program after recompiling the unit or units that you changed. The result: fast progress in the program development process.

The second benefit is that a collection of related programs can share a single copy of a unit. This sharing can produce dramatic savings in disk storage space, which is often a scarce resource when large application programs are used on small personal computers.

For very large programs with many units, the dynamic "stitching" that takes place when a p—System program is executed can take some time. This is not ideal when your only interest is in routine execution of a previously developed program. The most recent versions of the p—System include a way (called the Quickstart utility) to do most of the stitching once, when a program is readied for production use. Sharing of units among related programs can still occur under this scheme.

While the p—code of a program is being executed, it must be in main memory. Large programs frequently require more space than is available in main memory, so the p—System allows p—code to be broken into **segments**. Each segment only needs to be in main memory when p—code within it is being executed; otherwise, the segment can wait on disk until it is called upon.

These segment modules in the p—System allow you to run very large programs. If you want to develop such a program, all you need to do is designate the segment boundaries in your source program and recompile it. The compiler produces a code file that contains the segments you indicated. The details of marking segments vary with the language. In UCSD Pascal, for instance, the main program and every unit are independent segments by default. You can divide any of these modules into more than one segment by declaring **segment procedures**.

The strategies for deciding how a large program should be segmented are beyond the scope of this book. We can, however, mention one excellent candidate for segment treatment: the parts of a program that are used only when the program is starting or completing execution. When these "initialization" or "termination" parts of a program are independent segments, they are out of the way when not being used. Therefore, the main part of the program has more space for its work.

When a segment is in memory, it is stored in a **code pool**, along with other segments that have been used recently. When the amount of available main memory is 64k bytes or less, the code pool is maintained between two dynamically changing data areas called the "stack" and the "heap." This arrangement is shown in Figure 7.4 (A). These data areas are used for variables that you declare in your program or for other storage it needs. The p—System operating system also uses some of this data space.

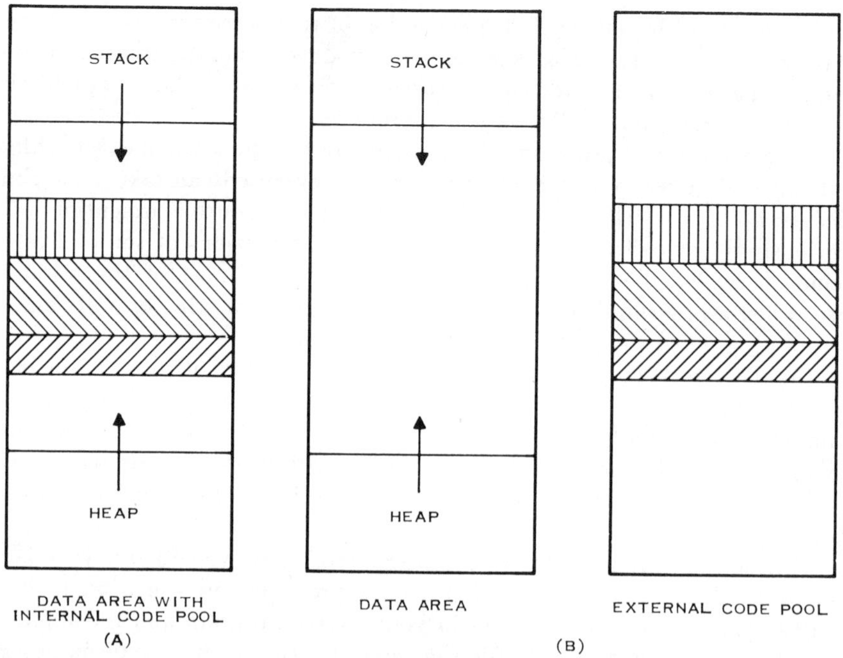

Figure 7.4

As the need for data space varies, the code pool can expand, contract, or shift to accommodate these changes.

As we mentioned above, a segment that is being actively executed must be in main memory. In addition, when one segment turns over control to another segment, both must be resident. Usually there is much more space available within the code pool than is required to meet these minimums. In this case, the p–System retains in the code pool as many of the most recently used segments as possible.

When more than 64k bytes of main memory are available, another arrangement for code and data storage is possible. In this **extended memory** configuration, shown in Figure 7.4 (B), the code pool is stored outside the data area. This eliminates competition between code and data for memory space, and allows more room for both.

What are the implications of these code pool approaches to managing code segments? They are primarily of the "divide and manage" variety.

First, a program that runs on a computer with a small memory (say 64k bytes) can also run, without change, when the available main memory is doubled. When more memory is available, the program will probably run faster, because the segments needed by the program are frequently already in the code pool when required. This adjustment for different memory sizes is managed automatically by the p–System, without special programmer planning.

Second, and perhaps more important, this sophisticated handling of code segments allows much larger programs to be run in the p–System than would otherwise be possible on a given size of memory. No other microcomputer operating system that we know of provides as much assistance for running programs that are larger than the available main memory.

In Version IV.2, these facilities are enhanced to allow many external code pools, so the amount of memory available for storing program segments is essentially unlimited (within the constraints of available physical memory, of course). Furthermore, through the use of special operating system services, programmers can even store data in these dynamically managed pools.

8

p–SYSTEM TOOLS AND PROGRAM BUILDING BLOCKS

The p–System was created to provide an excellent software environment for the development and execution of applications programs. The portability and modularity of this environment, as discussed in the previous chapter, make the p–System powerful and flexible toward this end. That chapter gave you some insight into the conceptual structure of the p–System. Here, we are more concerned with its components. These components fall into two general categories: tools and program building blocks.

A software tool is like a carpenter's tool; it allows you to build something——better and more easily——than you could without it. The Editor is an example of such a tool. With it you can create textual end products such as letters or books. A compiler is another tool. It allows you to create executable programs.

A program building block is a prefabricated module that you can use as an integral part of your programs. The p–System offers several general–purpose program building blocks that may greatly assist you in writing applications programs. They perform functions in such areas as screen control and file management.

In the remaining sections of this chapter we consider:

- Text Manipulation Tools.
- Program Development Tools.
- Applications Building Blocks.

8.1 TEXT MANIPULATION TOOLS

Text editing is an important type of text manipulation. The need for text editing is widespread and has many facets. You may want to write letters, memos, manuscripts, computer programs, poems, books, or other sorts of material. Within such text there may be paragraphs, columns, double–spaced lines, tables, or even special "pictures" made of ordinary characters placed all over the screen. You may want to save your text on disk so that it can be printed. Later you might want to change what you have created.

Once you have prepared your text, you may want to print it. Perhaps you would like it to appear on paper exactly as it does on the screen. Or, you might want to do some more elaborate things. For example, you may want to do page breaks at arbitrary places, use special form lengths, add running heads or page numbers, and so forth. Perhaps you will want to go beyond this and include proportional spacing, right margin justification, bold face printing, and so forth.

There are tools available with the p–System to perform all of these tasks. The first job, editing, is done with one of the p–System's editors: the Screen–oriented Editor or the advanced editor (EDVANCE).

Editing Text

The **Screen–oriented Editor** provides the standard facilities for creating, altering, and examining text files. All of the various kinds of line–oriented and paragraph–oriented material can be created with it. It is described in Chapter 5 so we won't go into any detail about it here.

EDVANCE is similar in many ways to the Screen–oriented Editor. It includes all of the standard Editor's activities and is used in about the same way. However, EDVANCE has additional capabilities which provide you with some more sophisticated editing techniques.

Perhaps the most important feature of EDVANCE is that it can work with much larger text files than the standard editor. This is because EDVANCE does not necessarily read an entire text file into main memory as the standard editor does. Part of the file being edited can remain on disk while the portion you are working on is in main memory. The memory buffer may "slide" forward or backward allowing you to move to any location within the file.

Another important feature of EDVANCE is that it allows you to give special "macro" definitions to as many as eight function keys. If your computer has keys that you can use for this, you may find this very convenient. You are able to assign a string of characters to any function key. Whenever a function key is typed, it reproduces those characters. If you are using I(nsert, for example, pressing a function key inserts the characters into your workspace. This might be convenient if you need to insert the same thing several times. The characters produced by a function key may also invoke editor activities. You can use this facility to perform all sorts of repetitive operations.

EDVANCE also has several additional activities. Many of these help to move the cursor easily. For example, you can, by pressing a single key, move the cursor from word to word, to the end of a line, to the top left corner of the screen, and so forth.

Both editors store your text on disk in the form of text files. There are a variety of ways that these files may be printed, as we describe next.

Printing Files

The simplest way to print a text file is to use T(ransfer (as described in Chapter 6). When you T(ransfer a file to the printer, it is printed exactly as it appears on the screen when you edit it. In most situations, this is not the best way to produce a final copy of your text because no special form lengths or page breaks are taken into consideration. However, when you want to quickly and easily print something, T(ransfer is a good mechanism. (Files containing compiled or assembled listings can be printed quite well using T(ransfer since they have their own pagination.)

The **Print** utility, provided with the p–System, is a very useful tool for producing many sorts of final copy output. It allows you to control page breaks, form length, headings (which can include the date, page number, and text file name), and more. You can even connect several text files together so that they are printed consecutively (and without a page break between them, if you want).

Print is especially good for items that need a professional appearance but don't require the same level of sophistication as large documents and books. Print works very well with letters, memos, small contracts, and so forth.

At the upper end of the printing spectrum are **text formatters**. Text formatters allow much more control over the printing process then the other methods we have mentioned. The printed page that you are now reading was, in fact, taken from the output of the ScenicWriter text formatter.

With text formatters you can underline text or cause it to appear in **bold face** on many printers. Several printers are able to do proportional spacing and many text formatters are able to handle this. Proportional spacing means that thinner letters, like "i," take up less horizontal space than wider ones, like "W." This causes the output to look as though it were typeset. If proportional spacing is not used, the output looks similar to what most typewriters produce.

Text formatters are also able to do right (as well as left) margin justification. Paragraphs that are right–justified line up exactly with the right–hand margin. This, of course, is how most books are printed.

There are many other things that text formatters can do. Pages can be numbered. Special headings and footings can be used. Some text formatters are able to automatically generate an index and table of contents. ScenicWriter even has an associated spelling checker which can help you to eliminate spelling errors in your text.

In order to use a text formatter you need to place special directives in your text files. These directives may indicate that you want to turn bold face on, indent the next line, do a page break if the next three lines don't fit on the current page, and so forth. The exact directives that are used depend upon the particular formatter.

When you have mastered the use of a good text formatter (along with the p–System's editing and file managing facilities), you are in a good position to do very powerful word processing!

Several text formatters are available to run with the p–System. See the *p–System Applications Catalog* or the USUS *Software Source Directory* (described in Chapter 9) for further information.

There is another p–System tool that falls into the printing category: the **Print Spooler**. The Print Spooler is a facility that allows you to print text files at the same time that you are using the p–System for other activities. You can, for example, print a file while you are using the Screen–oriented Editor or the Filer.

It is possible to print a document using the Print Spooler with the level of sophistication that the Print utility offers. This is done by running the text through the print utility first, and sending the output to a disk file (instead of directly to the printer). Later, the Print Spooler can send that file (or several such files) to the printer.

To use the Print Spooler, you need to execute SPOOLER.CODE. This utility allows you to place the names of the text files to be printed in a first–in–first–out queue (called SYSTEM.SPOOLER). The utility also allows you to suspend, restart, or quit the printing at any point.

The printing process is performed by the operating system. A unit called Spoolops must be installed in the operating system in order for spooling to work. (Standard p–System configurations provided by some vendors do not have this unit already installed in SYSTEM.PASCAL. You may need to install it before you can use the Print Spooler.) The Spoolops unit scans the file SYSTEM.SPOOLER for text file names and prints those files in the order listed.

For many p–System activities, such as editing with the Screen–oriented Editor, the printing process goes on at a very reasonable rate and p–System response is normal. (At this writing, however, editing with EDVANCE should not be done in conjunction with print spooling.)

8.2 PROGRAM DEVELOPMENT

The p–System provides a wide array of tools to assist you in developing programs. This development process includes editing, compiling, debugging, and optimizing.

The editing phase involves using one of the p–System's editors to produce the program text. The compilers translate the program text into code which can be executed by the computer. The problem of debugging comes in when a program doesn't do what you intended. Optimization involves making correct programs run better (i.e., more quickly, consuming less memory space, and so forth). The next three sections discuss compiling, debugging, and optimizing programs with the p–System.

Compiling Programs

The p–System currently offers three compilers: UCSD Pascal, BASIC, and FORTRAN–77. Each compiler translates program text into p–code which can be executed within the p–System environment.

The **UCSD Pascal** language (the most popular with the p–System) is a somewhat extended version of standard Pascal. It is modularly structured for clarity and has many powerful features. These include programmer–defined variable types, powerful string and array operations, random access to files, 36 decimal digit arithmetic, 32 and 64 bit real arithmetic, separate compilation, and more.

The p–System's **FORTRAN–77** language is a subset of the full ANSI (American National Standards Institute) FORTRAN–77 language. Known for its scientific and arithmetic capabilities, the p–System's FORTRAN–77 language includes the If–Then–Else construct, a built–in character type, and all FORTRAN numeric intrinsic functions.

The **BASIC** available with the p–System is a compiled (rather than interpreted) language with an expanded syntax. It includes the If–Then–Else construct, optional line numbers, and virtual disk arrays.

These compilers can create programs or program modules. The **Library** utility can combine two or more compiled modules together. As we pointed out in Chapter 7, compiled modules, called units, can reside in separate code files known as libraries. When the host program is executed, the necessary units are found in the libraries. This provides a useful way of sharing the separately compiled modules among several programs.

The Library utility offers another approach. With it you can place the units directly into a host program's code file. Although this uses up more disk space if two or more program code files on a disk contain the same unit, it is convenient in many circumstances. For example, if all of the code for a particular program is in one file, that program can be easily moved from disk to disk, or from computer to computer. If, on the other hand, some of a program's code resides in libraries, you need to be certain that the correct libraries are always around when you move the program to another environment. Beyond this, the library utility is useful for placing several units into one file which can then be designated as a library.

Another p–System tool that you can use to create executable code is an **assembler**. Assembly language programming, while more tedious than higher–level programming, may be attractive to you in certain situations. The assembled machine code is directly executed by your computer's microprocessor. This means it is faster (although usually more bulky) than the p–code which the compilers produce. Also, low–level machine–specific programming can be done in assembly language. This is not possible from the higher–level languages. The p–System currently offers assemblers for all of these processors: 8080, Z80, LSI–11/PDP–11, 6502, 6809, 9900, 8086/8088/8087, and 68000.

Assembly language routines can be called from Pascal, BASIC, or FORTRAN. The **Linker** (introduced in Chapter 4) is used to bind the assembled routines into the host (which may be a compiled module or another assembled module).

So, the compilers and assemblers, along with the Library utility and the Linker, allow you to create and combine executable programs and program modules.

Debugging Programs

To help you determine what might be going wrong with a program, the p–System provides several tools.

The **Debugger** is a very useful tool for interactively finding errors in programs written in UCSD Pascal, FORTRAN, or BASIC. In order to use the Debugger effectively, however, you need to have a good understanding of the internal details of the p–System.

Interactive debugging means that while your program is running, you can "interact" with it. You can stop it, look at what values are being assigned to variables, step through the code very slowly, and so forth. These kinds of things are often helpful in determining what might be going wrong with a program that you are developing.

With Pascal, the debugger can be used symbolically. This means that variables can be accessed by name (rather than by a numerical offset as they otherwise are). And break points can be specified by procedure name and line number (rather than by procedure number and p–code offset).

It is often essential to have a compiled listing of the code being debugged. This helps you keep track of where you are when you use the Debugger. A compiled listing also shows p–code offsets, procedure numbers, and other useful information that you need to successfully take advantage of the Debugger's capabilities.

Sometimes it is useful to have detailed information about the internal contents of a code file. However, to ordinary humans, the raw content of a code file is practically incomprehensible. Fortunately, the **Decode** utility can be used to "decode" this content so that it is quite a bit easier to understand. Probably, you will only want to view a code file at this level of detail if you are debugging a very complex piece of code and are very knowledgeable about the internal details of the p–System.

One thing the Decoder can show you is the executable p–code within a file. If you look directly at p–code with the Patch utility (which is described next), it appears to be a very strange collection of hexadecimal (base 16) digits. The Decoder displays the p–code in a more meaningful way called mnemonic form. In this form you can see the name of each individual p–code. The following two columns show the same piece of code in both formats:

Mnemonic Form		Hexadecimal Form
LDCB	50	8032
SRO	1	A501
CXG	3 1	940301
SLDO	1	30
LDCI	400	819001
EQUI		B0
FJP	4	D4F6
CXG	4 2	940402
RPU	0	9600

At first glance, mnemonic form may seem almost as difficult to comprehend as plain hexadecimal digits. Admittedly, it is not a trivial task to understand p–code in either format. However, when you know what each p–code operator does, mnemonic form is certainly easier to understand. (See Chapter 9 for further reading about the p–code operators.)

The Debugger has a simple decoder built into it for your convenience. It can display p–code in mnemonic form. But the Decoder utility, besides giving you a more informative listing, can print the mnemonic output so that you can easily reference it while you are debugging.

There is more to a code file than just the p–code itself. Sometimes there is an **interface section** which contains text. Also, since code files may be divided up into one or more **code segments**, the code segment names, sizes, and so forth, are stored in the code file. Sometimes a code file requires additional code from another file in order to run. In this case, very specific information about that separately compiled (or assembled) code is stored in the code file. All of this information may be of value to you and the Decoder can display it in an easily readable format.

The **Patch** utility offers another view of the internal structure of files. Although Patch can be used for purposes other than program development (for example, recovering lost files) it is often as useful here as the Debugger or Decoder. For example, if your program creates some sort of data file, and you suspect that something is incorrect within that file, Patch can be used to view its internal details.

Patch reads a block from the file and displays it on the console. This display can either be in hexadecimal notation (base 16, 0 through F), or in printable characters. You can move the cursor around this display and alter any values if you want. And, you can write the (presumably altered) block back out to disk. This sort of "patch" accounts for the utility's name.

Optimizing Programs

The p–System offers several tools and facilities to assist you in making programs efficient with respect to both execution speed and memory space requirements.

The modular design of the p–System is an important factor in memory space management. As discussed in the previous chapter, you can divide programs into segments. Large programs, which might not otherwise fit into a small computer's main memory, can be run if they are segmented. Also, the unit feature can be used for effectively managing disk space, since sharable code doesn't have to be duplicated.

The time/space tradeoffs between p–code and machine–level code can also be optimized. P–code (the compilers' output) is generally more compact than machine code. However, it is also slower.

A common rule of thumb is that 20% of the code is executed 80% of the time. In many programs, it is the case that some small portion of a program is significantly more time–critical then the rest. It makes sense, therefore, to translate that portion to machine–level code, sacrificing some memory space in favor of noticeable execution speed improvements.

There are two ways that you can do this with the p–System. One is to write the time–critical code by hand in assembly language. The other, much easier approach, is to use the **Native Code Generator**.

The code generator is a very powerful tool that translates portions of the p–code within a code file into machine–level code, more commonly called **native code**. It is easy to experiment with the code generator (translating different routines into native code and so forth) to determine the optimal way to use it on a particular application.

The code generator's output always contains a hybrid mixture of p–code and native code. This means that the resulting code file can only be executed within the p–System environment. (The assemblers can be used to create code that runs outside of the p–System environment, if that is desired.)

The **Quickstart** utility can be useful for making programs start more quickly. If a program is divided into a fairly large number of units, it may take several seconds, or tens of seconds, for it to start running. This is because of the **associate time** requirements. During associate time, tables of information concerning the program's units are set up. This information is needed so that the various pieces of code can be located when they are needed during the program's execution. With the Quickstart utility, these tables can be created for a program and stored in the code file so that association time is no longer a significant factor. As long as the libraries that contain the program's units remain unaltered and on the same disks, the tables are valid.

Another utility, called **Real Convert**, is useful for increasing the execution speed of certain programs which use floating point constants. Real Convert is helpful when a program contains code segments which are frequently swapped into and out of memory and which also have a large number of real constants. Normally, every time a code segment is read into memory, any real constants it contains must be converted from the machine–portable **canonical form** to the machine–specific **native form**. If there is a large number of real constants, this conversion process can slow down the program's execution speed. Real Convert changes the real constants in the code file to the native form for the processor in use when the utility is run. The resulting code file can only be run on that processor. For example, if you execute Real Convert while using a four word 8086 system, the real constants in the program's code file are converted from canonical form to four word 8086 form. This means that the code file will now only run on a four word 8086 system. (It should run more quickly, however.)

Another useful tool for helping to optimize (or even debug) Pascal programs is the cross referencer, **Xref**. Xref takes as input the text for a Pascal program. It produces a listing which contains several tables that may be an aid in program analysis. These tables give you information about which procedures call which other procedures, where variables are referenced, and so forth.

8.3 APPLICATION BUILDING BLOCKS

Although you could write your applications programs entirely from scratch, it is likely that you would be duplicating existing and available code in some areas. Furthermore, as the p–System continues to evolve, it is possible that you would have to upgrade some of that code whereas the standard applications building blocks are maintained by the p–System developers. So, it may be greatly to your advantage to use some of the applications building blocks that are covered here.

These building blocks are available in the form of pre–compiled units. They provide such services as controlling the screen in a portable fashion, managing disk files from programs, manipulating color graphics images, and more.

A few of these units reside within the operating system. The others must be placed in a library or your program code file (using the Library utility).

Operating System Units

The operating system, SYSTEM.PASCAL, has been discussed throughout this book. It is, of course, the core of the p–System and it contains a lot of code to perform its various tasks. Some of this code can be useful to applications programs and so it has been made generally accessible. In particular, there are portions of the operating system which facilitate screen handling, allow you to chain programs together, and help you to intercept certain kinds of p–System error messages and change them to fit your particular application.

One important thing that most applications programs must do is display information on the screen and retrieve user responses. When you write applications using the p–System, you will probably want to take this a step further and insure that your user interface is portable (as well as clean). This issue of portability could be a problem since there are so many types of computer terminals and displays, most of which have their own way of doing things.

Fortunately, the operating system's screen handling unit, **Screenops**, provides some very useful routines which are independent of the particular brand of hardware that an end user might have. Screenops includes routines which blank out a single line or clear the entire screen. There are routines to move the cursor in any direction or to place it at a specific location on the screen. If you intend to use the kind of menus and prompts that the p–System uses, there are routines that display them and help you to read the user's input (including the special control keys which vary from computer to computer). There is also some miscellaneous information which you can get at using Screenops (for example, the current date).

Another thing that you may want to do, as an applications developer, is create your own user–friendly environment. If you do this, it is convenient to be able to start up one or more programs from a central menu and later return. (SYSTEM.MENU, which is briefly introduced in Chapter 4, can be very useful in this context.) The **Commandio** unit within the operating system has some facilities that allow you to chain programs together. Chaining means that when one program finishes executing, another is started automatically (without the user having to enter something at the keyboard). For example, from a simple menu program, you can chain to other programs which the user selects. The routine that does this is called CHAIN.

Another routine within Commandio, called REDIRECT, allows you to redirect input and output in the same manner as execution option strings (see Section 4.17, page 135). This may come in handy in various situations. For example, you may want to save the user from needless troubles by automating a series of tasks. This might be done by redirecting your program's input (or the p–System's input) to a script file.

When you are creating your own user–friendly environment like this, there is another operating system unit which may be of some value. It is called **Errorhandler**. It allows your application programs to intercept execution errors and errors that can occur when a necessary disk has been removed from a drive. For example, if the user accidentally removes a needed disk from its drive, normally a message like this is displayed:

```
Need segment SEGNAME: Put volume VOLNAME in unit U then type <space>
```

But, your particular application could arrange for a more specific message to be used, for instance:

```
Please place the DB Manager disk back in its drive.  Then type space.
```

In Version IV.2, the Errorhandler unit is significantly augmented to allow you to handle runtime errors in your program and otherwise make your programs more robust.

Also in Version IV.2, an additional unit called **DataSegManager** allows you to store data in the dynamically managed pool area that in earlier p–Systems is reserved for code. These **data segments** are under program control and are not removed from memory without program direction. This facility can allow you to make better use of large main memories, without foreclosing the possibility that your applications can also run in small main memories.

In order to compile a program which uses any of these units, you need to have available the code files SCREENOPS.CODE, COMMANDIO.CODE, ERRORHANDL.CODE, or DATASEGS.CODE. This is because those files have the interface sections which are needed by the compiler. When you run such a program, however, only SYSTEM.PASCAL needs to be available if the code for these units (without the interface sections) resides there. This is normally the case for SCREENOPS and COMMANDIO, but the other two units must be explicitly placed in SYSTEM.PASCAL if you want them to be used from there.

File Management Units

You have seen how the Filer handles disk files in this book. You may want to do the same sort of file managing directly from your applications programs. The Filer is an ordinary program, and your programs can do the same things that it does. However, it is not a trivial programming task to implement the Filer activities. So, there are four units that have been made available and are known as the **File Management Units.**

One of these units, called DIR.INFO, helps your programs to access disk directories. It allows you to list directories, change file names, change the date of a file or volume, remove a file, and several other tasks.

Another unit, FILE.INFO, can be used to gain information about particular files. With it you can see if a file is open or not, find its length, determine what volume it is on, and so forth.

The third unit, SYS.INFO, allows you to access information which is stored globally in the p–System. For example, you can determine what the name of the work file is, find out the name of the system disk, change the internal p–System date, and more.

A fourth unit called WILD provides some wild card facilities that can be used with the other File Management Units. These wild cards are similar to those used by the Filer. For example, using DIR.INFO and the equal wild card like this: "=.TEXT", you can get a list of all text files on a certain volume.

In Version IV.2, two additional file management units are available. TRANSFER allows your programs to do essentially the operations supported by the Filer's T(ransfer activity. With ATTRIBUTES, your programs can query and set the attributes of a file. For instance, you can find out the name of a file.

Liaison Network Services

In connection with Liaison, the local networked version of the p–System, a number of communication facilities are available to applications. Your Liaison application running on several computers joined by a local network can locate network "servers" operating on the network and establish connections with them. You can even build server programs yourself! For instance, a data base server running on one computer might cater to the needs of a distributed data entry application running on several other computers in a network.

We refer you to the references in Chapter 9 for further reading on Liaison.

Insight Window Designer

Insight is a powerful collection of facilities that can provide your applications with sophisticated and lively user interfaces supporting colorful, dynamically managed windows of text and an easy to use menu structure. In addition, Insight extends the p–System's portability benefits to applications that make extensive use of display screen facilities (i.e. color, reverse video, flashing, etc.) and printer capabilities (i.e. bold and compressed print). Finally, Insight allows you to build applications that are easily adapted for use in many countries, even those with different languages or cultural conventions such as the order in which the elements of a date are written. (This is yet another form of portability!)

Insight's facilities are too numerous to detail here. We refer you to further reading on the topic described in Chapter 9.

Xenofile

Xenofile is a facility which allows users of the p–System to access CP/M disk files. It consists of three units (one for Pascal, BASIC, and FORTRAN). Each unit provides several CP/M functions to p–System programs.

For example, your p–System programs can open, close, delete, create, and rename CP/M files. They can read and write records to and from such files. They can handle the CP/M file control blocks. They can write–protect CP/M disks. And, there are several other such functions which you can use from your p–System programs.

Xenofile also includes a utility program which acts as a simple CP/M "filer." With it you can display a CP/M directory and transfer text files between a p–System disk and a CP/M disk.

Xenofile for DOS

A similar facility provides access from your programs to PC–DOS or MS–DOS disks. Its functional capabilities are similar to those described above for the original Xenofile product.

KSAM

KSAM is a file management system which allows programs to store and retrieve data in a keyed or sequential fashion. It is especially useful for developing such applications as data base managers, reservation systems, inventory control programs, and so forth.

For example, using KSAM, you can create a file of names, addresses, and zip codes. This file can be maintained so that all of the entries are in alphabetical order according to last name. You can then access individual entries sequentially (going from the names that start with "A" to the ones that start with "Z"). Or you can access any entry randomly by using a specific key (in this case, a particular last name).

Furthermore, you could sort this same example file in zip code order. You might do both if you want to insert and delete random entries according to last name, and then print out all entries on mailing labels according to zip code.

KSAM is designed to access files efficiently so that it is practical for you to maintain large files if necessary.

The main part of KSAM consists of two units. The main unit performs various functions with respect to a primary key. The second unit allows you to have as many alternate keys as you need. There are two additional units which allow KSAM to interface with BASIC or FORTRAN. These last two units are not necessary if you are using Pascal.

Turtlegraphics

Many computers are able to display graphic images on their screens. This means that all sorts of figures, charts and graphs can be created. The Turtlegraphics unit can help your programs to display these sorts of things if your computer hardware supports graphics.

Turtlegraphics is so named because it uses the concept of a turtle which moves across your screen leaving a trail as it goes. You can tell the turtle to move a given distance in a given direction. Or, you can tell it to move to some specific location. In either case, as it moves, it leaves its trail if you want it to. The trail may be in various colors if your hardware allows. The trail can appear to be over, under, or on the same level as other portions of the figure being created. Although the trail is always a straight line, circles and other curves can be "drawn" by programmatically moving the turtle very short distances and slightly changing the direction each time.

Once a figure has been created, the turtle can rest. The resulting work of art may be stored in a .FOTO file on disk. It can be loaded and displayed again at any time. Several figures may be displayed on the screen at the same time. They can be placed in various locations and can appear to be over, under, or on the same level as each other when they intersect.

On some computers, Turtlegraphics is already configured and ready to use. In other cases, you must install the Turtlegraphics package in order to use it. This involves writing some assembly language routines that are specific to your hardware. These routines perform the basic tasks of setting a point to a particular color, drawing a line segment, and so forth. Turtlegraphics builds upon them to provide higher level services to your p–System programs.

9

FURTHER READING

This book is not a complete description of the p–System since that would have required thousands of pages of text. In this short chapter we indicate some of the other sources of p–System information that are available. One important source is SofTech Microsystems (SMS). Another source is the UCSD p–System User's Society (USUS)—–see Appendix H. Here's how to contact SMS:

SofTech Microsystems, Inc.
16875 West Bernardo Drive
San Diego, California 92127
(619) 451–1230

9.1 p–SYSTEM REFERENCE MANUALS

SofTech Microsystems publishes a series of reference manuals which serve as the formal descriptions of the p–System. Many p–System suppliers simply provide these manuals with the p–System software. Some suppliers, however, choose to rework these manuals into their own formats. In this section, we describe the manuals as distributed by SMS.

Operating System Reference Manual: This document describes the aspects of the p–System that are of interest to all p–System users (non–programmers as well as programmers). It covers the following topics:

Operating System
 Menus and prompts

- Command menu items
- Execution option strings
- Redirection

File Management
- File names and types
- Devices and volumes
- Recovering files
- Workfiles
- Subsidiary volumes
- User–defined serial devices
- Filer menu items

Screen–oriented Editor

Utilities
- Print
- Print Spooler
- Quickstart
- Real Convert
- Setup
- Copydupdir
- Markdupdir
- Recover
- Library
- Disksize

Program Development Reference Manual: This document covers tools and general principles of p–System program development. The various programming languages are not described here. The following topics are covered:

Pascal Compiler
- Using the compiler
- Compiler options
- Selective USES

User Interfacing from Programs
- SYSTEM.MENU and SYSTEM.STARTUP
- Program chaining and redirection
- Screen handling unit
- Error handling unit

File Management Units

Debugger

Utilities
- Decode
- Patch
- Xref

Application Development Guide: This book supplements the p–System reference manuals by bringing together a wide variety of advice on developing p–System–based applications. If you're doing serious application development, this book could be crucial to you. Prior to the availability of this guide, information of this type was learned only by long experience with the p–System. The following topics are addressed:

- Program Design Philosophy
  - Program development steps
  - Example of program development
- Program Development Tools
  - Filer
  - Editors
  - Compilers
  - Assemblers
  - Debugger
  - Utilities
- Program Building Blocks
  - Segment routines
  - Units
  - Client–unit communication
  - Libraries
- p–System Facilities
  - I/O redirection
  - Application units
  - Turnkey facilities
  - Memory configuration
- Multi–Lingual Facilities
  - Choosing a language
  - Inter–lingual facilities
  - Inter–lingual examples
- Portability
  - Byte sex
  - Disk format
  - Other portability problems
  - Universal Medium
- Performance
  - Segments and units
  - Quickstart utility
  - Memlock and Memswap
  - Usage of OS units
  - Real constants
  - Disk space
- Programming Techniques
  - Listing unit interface sections

- Determining Nil
- Converting ASCII to decimal
- Converting decimal to hex
- Comparing files
- Check sum of a file
- Setting printer options
- Quick readln and writeln
- I/O checking
- Range checking
- Error handling
- Controlling segment residency
- Screen/keyboard usage
- Using TurtleGraphics
- Chaining to script files

Debugging Programs
- Debugger commands
- Debugging techniques
- Allocation of variable offsets
- Symbolic debugging

Assemblers Reference Manual: This book addresses the p–System assemblers, the Linker, and the COMPRESS utility. These specific topics are covered:

- Assembler Directives
- Macros
- Linking and Relocation
- The Compress Utility
- Using the Assembler
- Assembler Listings
- Processor Specific Information

8086 Assembler Reference Manual: This book is equivalent to the assembler manual, above, except it concentrates on the 8086/8088/8087 processors. It contains additional information concerning the 8086 family opcodes, registers, and flags.

Internal Architecture Reference Manual: This book describes various aspects of the internal workings of the p–System. The following topics are addressed:

P–machine Architecture
- Stack / heap
- Code pool
- Code segments
- Task environments

- P–code operators
- Low–Level I/O
  - Runtime Support Package (RSP)
  - Basic I/O Subsystem (BIOS)
- Operating System Internal Details
- Program Execution Internal Details

Adaptable System Installation Manual: Detailed directions for installing the Adaptable System are presented in this book. The Adaptable System packaging of the p–System allows you to adapt the p–System to the input/output conventions of your computer. Sophisticated assembly language programming is required. (It is usually preferable to acquire a p–System that has already been adapted to your computer. Contact SofTech Microsystems for references if you can't locate one yourself.) The following topics are addressed:

- Bootstrapping
- Terminal Handling
- Simplified BIOS (SBIOS)
- Utilities
  - Booter
  - Diskchange
  - Screentest

FORTRAN–77 Reference Manual: This book is the reference for the the p–System implementation of FORTRAN–77.

BASIC Reference Manual: This book is the reference for the p–System implementation of BASIC.

Optional Products Reference Manual: This book is actually a collection of several independent manuals. These manuals describe tools and program building blocks that are not necessarily part of the standard p–System. Currently, the following optional products are covered:

- EDVANCE
- KSAM
- SofTeach
- XenoFile

9.2 p–SYSTEM CATALOGS

The first catalog described in this section is published by SofTech Microsystems on a periodic schedule (approximately every six months). The second catalog is part of the UCSD p–System User's Society (USUS) periodic newsletter.

p—System Applications Catalog: This book describes hundreds of software packages that are compatible with the p—System and offered by independent software distributors. For each program, the distributor, price range, and brief functional description are provided. Names and addresses of distributors are also included.

USUS Software Source Directory: This catalog is part of the USUS newsletter and lists vendors of p—System applications and other p—System—related products.

9.3 OTHER BOOKS

There are dozens of books on Pascal in general and UCSD Pascal in particular. Since the choice among those books depends so much on your background and areas of interest, we don't try to enumerate them here. After you've learned the basics of UCSD Pascal using one of those other books, you may wish to go further by exploring one or both of the following volumes:

UCSD Pascal Handbook, Randy Clark and Stephen Koehler (Prentice—Hall, Englewood Cliffs, New Jersey, 1982): Indispensable if you're programming in UCSD Pascal. Includes a full reference description of the UCSD Pascal language, along with a series of tested example programs that illustrate many useful UCSD Pascal programming techniques.

Advanced UCSD Pascal Programming Techniques, Eliakim Willner and Barry Demchak (Prentice—Hall, Englewood Cliffs, New Jersey, 1985): Reveals the "tricks of the trade" of the experienced UCSD Pascal programmer. Full of useful examples. Depends on a separate reference description of the language (such as that in the *Handbook*, above).

A

ERROR MESSAGES FOR MAJOR ACTIVITIES

This appendix summarizes the error messages produced by the activities of the Operating System, the Filer, and the Editor. Each error is discussed, and potential diagnoses and recovery actions are listed.

In many cases, only the meaningful part of the error message is listed here. Often, when displayed on the screen, this is preceded by the word "ERROR:" or perhaps followed by a phrase like one of these:

```
Type <spacebar> to continue, <esc> to abort.
Do you wish to continue (Y/N) ?
```

When you understand the nature of the particular error, the remaining part of the message should be clear.

A.1 OPERATING SYSTEM ERRORS

A(ssemble

Cannot find SYSTEM.ASSMBLER: That file (which should contain an assembler) is not present on any on–line volume. If it is present, the file is corrupted.

xxxx.OPCODES not on any volume: The "xxxx" is a processor name (such as Z80 or 8086). This opcodes file is necessary in order to run the assembler. The file was not found on any on–line volume.

Can't find VOL:WORKFILE.TEXT: The text file that you indicated is not present. Or, if you didn't indicate a text file, at some point you had a workfile which is no longer on—line. You may have R(emoved the workfile without doing a N(ew. Or, the disk containing the workfile may not be in the proper drive.

Can't open VOL:FILE.CODE: The code file that you indicated can't be opened because the volume is not on—line, or the file name that you gave is incorrectly specified, or there is no room on the disk. If you are using a workfile, there is no room for SYSTEM.WRK.CODE on the system disk.

Syntax errors: The assembler, itself, displays errors if your text does not conform to the correct syntax of the assembly language. These errors are not covered in this book.

C(ompile

Cannot find SYSTEM.COMPILER: That file (which should contain a compiler) is not present on any on—line volume. If it is present, the file is corrupted.

Can't find VOL:FILE.TEXT: The text file that you indicated is not present. Or, if you didn't indicate a text file, at some point you had a workfile which is no longer on—line. You may have R(emoved the workfile without doing a N(ew. Or, the disk containing the workfile may not be in the proper drive.

Can't open VOL:FILE.CODE: The code file that you indicated can't be opened because the volume is not on—line, or the file name that you gave is incorrectly specified, or there is no room on the disk. If you are using a workfile, there is no room for SYSTEM.WRK.CODE on the system disk.

Syntax errors: The compilers display errors if your text does not conform to the correct syntax of the language being compiled. These errors are covered in Appendix C.

D(ebug

No debugger in system: The Debugger segments have not been placed in SYSTEM.PASCAL. (This must be done by using the Library utility.)

E(dit

Cannot find SYSTEM.EDITOR: That file (which should contain an editor) is not present on any on—line volume. If it is present, the file is corrupted.

Workfile lost: At some point you had a workfile which is no longer available. You may have R(emoved the workfile without doing a N(ew.

(You can simply enter the Filer and select N(ew if this is the case.) Or, the disk containing the workfile may not be in the proper drive.

Buffer overflow: The file you are trying to load is too large to fit into your workspace in main memory. You can edit it, but only the first part of the file is available. You should *not* save the workspace under its old name; if you do, you lose the portion of the file that did not fit into memory.

Error reading file (or) Disk error: The file can't be read into the workspace. There may be a bad block or the disk may have been removed in the middle of the reading process.

Unable to allocate buffer: If your computer has a very limited amount of main memory, this error indicates that you can't use the Screen–oriented Editor because there is not enough room to hold a workspace.

Editor activity errors: There are errors that can occur while you use the Editor. These are covered later in this appendix.

Screen problems: If the Editor doesn't display material on the screen properly, or if the cursor movement keys don't work, the file SYSTEM.MISCINFO has not been properly configured using the SETUP utility, or the GOTOXY unit within the operating system is not correct for your console. You should run the Screentest utility to verify that screen handling is functioning properly on your terminal.

F(ile

Cannot find SYSTEM.FILER: That file is not present on any on–line volume. If it is present, the file is corrupted.

Filer activity errors: There are errors that can occur while you use the Filer. These are covered later in this appendix.

L(ink

Cannot find SYSTEM.LINKER: That file is not present on any on–line volume. If it is present, the file is corrupted.

No file FILENAME.CODE: The file that you indicated as a host file or lib file doesn't exist on the expected volume.

All segs linked: Your host file does not have any references to external assembly language routines. Or, if it does contain such references, those routines have already been linked into it.

Code open error: The file that you indicated as an output file can't be opened. The name may be incorrect (e.g., too long), the volume that you specified may not be on–line, or there may not be enough room on the volume for the file.

Code write error: The output file could not be created. There may not be enough contiguous disk space on the volume to hold the resulting file. Or, a bad block may exist where the file was being created.

M(onitor

No monitor open: When you leave the monitor using R(esume, this warning says that you have not designated a disk file to hold your keystrokes and therefore monitoring is not being done.

Can't open file: The script file that you indicated with B(egin can't be opened because you used an illegal file name, or the volume you specified is not on–line, or there is no room on the volume.

File already open: You attempted to use B(egin to open a new script file, but you had already used B(egin and a file is already open. You must use E(nd or A(bort on the current script file before you can use B(egin again.

Can't close file: You selected E(nd to save your script file, but that file can't be closed. You may have removed the disk that contains the file.

U(ser–restart

U not allowed: You can't restart the last program for one of several reasons: you just reinitialized (perhaps after an execution error); the last program failed to start (e.g., because it wasn't found); the last program was the C(ompiler or A(ssembler, which can't be restarted.*

X(ecute

Illegal file name: The file name you entered is not a valid name. Check the actual name of the program you want to invoke, and try again.

No file FILENAME.CODE: The file that you indicated wasn't located on the indicated disk, or that disk isn't on–line. (If you didn't specify a disk, then this applies to the prefix disk even though its volume name isn't included in the message.)

No program in FILENAME.CODE: The file that you indicated doesn't contain an executable program. It may be a unit (which can't be run by itself). Or, it may not be a code file at all. If it does contain a program, the file is probably corrupted.

---

* *IV.2 users, note:* The limitation mentioned here does not exist for you.

Redirection error: You made a mistake while using execution option strings. This may be a mistake in the syntax of the execution option string, itself. Or, an input (or output) file that doesn't exist or can't be opened may be the problem.

FILENAME.CODE is not a code file: The file you indicated is not of the CODE type, and therefore can't be executed.

Error reading (or rereading) segment dictionary (or program code file): The program file you indicated could not be read successfully. The file may contain a bad block.

Error reading library code file (or library LIB.NAME.CODE): A library file referenced by the program you invoked was not readable.

I/O Error reading library list file FILE.NAME.TEXT: The file containing the current list of libraries could not be read. Perhaps you made a mistake in specifying the file with the "L=" execution option. Try using the Editor or the Filer to check that the library text file you intend to use is valid; then use "L=" again to designate it.

Library list file FILE.NAME is not a text file: Try designating the library text file again, after confirming with E(xtended list directory that it is indeed a text file.

Warning: Library LIB.NAME.CODE not found: The named file occurs in the current library text file, but cannot be found. Processing continues, since the program being invoked may not need anything in the missing file.

Unit UNITNAME not found: The named unit is required for execution of the program you indicated. Unfortunately, this unit cannot be found by the p—System. Perhaps you didn't set up the library text file properly, or perhaps you made some other error in preparing the program for execution.

Duplicate unit UNITNAME: There is more than one instance of the named unit in the program being invoked, or perhaps there is a clash between the names of a unit in the program (or a library file) and a unit in the operating system.

Program must be linked via L(ink: The program being invoked contains unsatisfied references to assembly language routines. You must use L(ink before this program can be executed.

Segment SEGNAME is an obsolete code segment: The named segment was produced in an earlier and incompatible version of the p—System. The program that contains it must be recompiled with the current p—System version.

Too many library code files (or system units) referenced: The limits on the number of library code files (or the number of operating system units referenced) have been exceeded.

Program environment too complicated: The number of units used by the program and the complexity of their relationships mean that this program can only be executed after being processed by the Quickstart utility.

Environment construction error: An unknown error occurred while the program was being prepared for execution. The cause may be a flaw in the p–System's program invocation mechanism.

Insufficient memory to construct environment: You may be able to improve this situation by coalescing or removing libraries from the library text file list.

Insufficient memory for environment: The program is too complicated to run in the main memory available.

Insufficient memory to allocate data segment: The data storage needed for the program or one of its units is too large. This program cannot be run in the current memory configuration.

Insufficient memory to load fixed–position segment: The program contains or references an assembly language segment that must be loaded throughout execution of the program. There is not enough room to load it; therefore, this program cannot be executed in the current memory configuration.

A.2 EDITOR ERRORS

A(djust

Bell beeps when [esc] is typed: You can't exit A(djust with [esc]; you must use [etx].

Bell beeps when other keys are typed: You can't use any alpha–numeric keys or cursor movement keys except the ones which are indicated on the A(djust prompt.

C(opy

Buffer overflow: There is not enough room in your workspace to hold what you are attempting to copy into it (either from the copy buffer, or from a file).

File not present: The file from which you wanted to copy text is not on the indicated disk.

Marker not there: You are attempting to copy text from a disk file using markers. But, one of the markers that you indicated doesn't exist in that file.

Improper marker specification: You did not correctly indicate two markers, separated by a comma, between square brackets.

Disk error (or) Bad disk transfer: Text in the disk file can't be correctly read. There may be a bad block or the disk may have been removed.

Marker exceeds file bounds: Something is wrong with the marker in the disk file. It indicates a position that is outside of that file. The disk file is probably corrupted.

D(elete

Bell beeps when characters are typed: You can only use the cursor movement keys in D(elete.

There is no room to copy the deletion: The amount of text that you are trying to delete can't be placed in the copy buffer. You may go ahead and delete it, but if you do, you can't copy it back into your workspace later.

F(ind

Invalid delimiter: You did not use a correct delimiter (which must be a special character such as "," or "/") before starting to enter your target string.

Pattern not in the file: The sequence of characters that you entered, or the n'th occurrence of it (if you used a repeat factor) does not exist in your workspace.

No old pattern: You attempted to use the "same" option by entering "S" instead of a delimited sequence of characters. But, you have not yet used F(ind or R(eplace since starting the current editing session so there isn't an existing pattern.

I(nsert

You are about to discard more than 80 characters: You have inserted more than 80 characters and then pressed ⟦esc⟧. This warning informs you that your insertion is going to be discarded if you go ahead and exit I(nsert with ⟦esc⟧. You may, instead, return to I(nsert.

No insertion to back over: You have attempted to erase characters that you did not insert since starting the current I(nsert activity. Either you used ⟦bs⟧ one time too many, or you used ⟦delete line⟧ on the first line of the insertion.

Please finish up the insertion: There are less than 1000 characters of available space in your workspace and every time you start an insertion this is displayed. You should consider breaking up the file if there is very much material that you still need to add. S(et E(nvironment informs you exactly how much space is left.

No room to insert: There is no remaining space (or almost none) within your workspace and the Editor will not allow any more text to be added. *You should never push the Editor this far!*

Buffer Overflow!!!!: You added more text to your workspace than it can hold. You have now lost something off the end of your workspace.

J(ump

Not there: The marker that you indicated is not present within the workspace.

K(ol

Bell beeps when [esc] is typed: You can't exit K(olumn with [esc]; you must use [etx].

Bell beeps when other keys are typed: You can't use any alpha–numeric keys or cursor movement keys except the ones which are indicated on the K(olumn prompt.

M(argin

Inappropriate environment: M(argin can't be used because A(uto indent is not false or F(illing is not true within S(et E(nvironment.

Q(uit

ERROR writing out the file: You used Q(uit U(pdate or Q(uit W(rite but the workspace can't be saved on disk for one of several reasons: there is not enough room on the disk; the volume where the file is to be saved isn't on–line; you indicated a syntactically incorrect file name. (This topic is discussed in detail in Chapter 5 in the section "Leaving the Editor.")*

---

* *IV.2 users, note:* Instead of getting the general message described above, you'll see a specific I/O error message. Check Appendix B in the section, "p–System I/O Errors," for advice on those messages.

R(eplace

Pattern not in the file: The target doesn't exist in your workspace, or the n'th occurrence of that target doesn't exist when repeat factors are used. If the target does exist, it may be that the direction indicator is not set as you thought.

No old pattern: You attempted to use the "same" option with either the target or the substitution string (by typing "S" instead of delimited strings). But, you have not used R(eplace since starting the current editing session and there isn't any "same" pattern.

Buffer full. Aborting Replace: There are less than 200 characters remaining in your workspace and R(eplace won't allow you to make any more substitutions (since they may add to the size of the workspace).

S(et E(nvironment

T or F: If you do not respond with a "T" or "F" to a true/false option you receive this prompt. You should then enter either "T" or "F."

#: If you don't respond to a numeric S(et E(nvironment option with a number, you receive this prompt. You should then enter a numeric value.

S(et M(arker

Marker ovflw. Which one to replace?: You have already set 20 markers in your workspace. You must throw one away if you want to set another.

X(change

Buffer is filling up... watch it!: The workspace is nearly full (less than 128 characters remaining). Be very careful since X(change can add characters to your workspace. You should probably break up the workspace into two or more files before you continue editing.

Z(ap

You are about to zap more than 80 chars: This warns you that more than 80 characters are about to be deleted if you follow through with the Z(ap activity. (It is easy to accidentally type "Z" and that is why the warning is given. If you do accidentally Z(ap something, you can usually copy it back using C(opy B(uffer.)

There is no room to copy the deletion: The amount of text that you are trying to Z(ap can't be placed in the copy buffer. You may go ahead and Z(ap that text, but if you do, you can't use C(opy B(uffer to get it back into your workspace later.

Invalid ZAP: You can't do Z(ap twice in a row or this error occurs. Also, you may not have done a F(ind, R(eplace, or I(nsert in the current editing session.

A.3 FILER ERRORS

In this section, the Filer error conditions are listed and explained. In the errors that apply to files or volumes, you will often see <source> or <dest>, for example:

```
List what vol ? PRINTER: [ret]
PRINTER: Unblkd vol, File/(blkd vol) expected <source>
```

```
Transfer what file ? #4: [ret]
To where ? #100: [ret]
Transfer 320 blocks ? (Y/N) Y
Put in #100:
Type <space> to continue
#100:[320] - No such vol on-line <dest>
```

"<Source>" refers to the file or volume that the activity uses as its input. (In the first example, the volume to be listed, the source, was incorrect.) "<Dest>" refers to the file or volume where the activity sends its output. (In the second example, the destination for the T(ransfer operation was incorrect.)

There are many errors which can occur in almost any Filer activity. Rather than cover them repeatedly under each activity, we summarize them here.

Bad file name: The file name that you used was not syntactically correct.

Bad form (Wild <to> Non–Wild) card: With a Filer activity that requires an input and output file, you attempted to use a wild card on only one side.

Bad I/O operation: You attempted to do an I/O transaction which can't be done. For example, it is not possible to T(ransfer something **from** the printer.

Bad unit number: You used an incorrect device number.

FILENAME..too long <file name 15–char. max>: The file name you entered contains more than the 15 character maximum that is allowed.

File not found: The file that you indicated does not exist. Perhaps you gave the wrong volume name. Or, you may have forgotten to use the file name suffix (such as .TEXT or .CODE) in a situation where it is required.

Ill file/vol name: You used a file or volume name which is syntactically incorrect. This message can occur in several error messages.

No directory on vol: The storage volume that you are trying to access does not contain a p–System directory. Perhaps it has not been Z(eroed.

No room on vol: This error indicates that you are attempting to add a file to a storage volume, but there is not enough contiguous disk space to hold it.

No such vol on–line: The volume that you indicated is not present. Perhaps you removed the disk from its drive, or used the wrong name. If you receive this error while using the Z(ero activity, you may need to format the disk before you Z(ero it.

Parity (CRC) error: This indicates that an I/O error occurred during a disk read or write or a communication volume transaction. The disk may have bad blocks or you may have removed it in the middle of the operation. The communication volume may not be functioning correctly.

Unblkd vol, File/(blkd vol) expected: This sort of error can occur in various combinations and permutations. "Unblkd vol" refers to unblocked volume (or communication volume). "Blkd vol" refers to blocked volume (or storage volume). The message indicates that you incorrectly specified a communication volume when a file or a storage volume was required. If, for example, you attempt to L(ist PRINTER: you receive this message (since communication volumes don't have directories).

VOLNAME..too long <vol name 7–char. max>: The volume name you entered contains more than the 7 character maximum that is allowed.

Vol went off–line: A volume which was on–line when the activity began is no longer present. Perhaps you removed a disk from its drive.

Wildcard not allowed: You attempted to use a wild card in a situation where the Filer does not allow it. For example, you can't designate more than one workfile, so wild cards are not allowed with G(et.

B(ad blocks

Invalid #: When responding to the "Scan for how many blocks" prompt, you entered an incorrect number (such as 0).

C(hange

Ill change (Vol <to> file) name: You attempted to change a volume name to a file name (or a file name to a volume name). You may have forgotten to include the colon after a volume name.

Vol already on–line: You attempted to change the name of a volume to the name of another volume which is currently on–line. The p–System doesn't allow this because confusion can result when two volumes with the same name are on–line at the same time. (You should always try to avoid this situation!)

Flip swap/lock

Not enough memory: Your computer does not have enough main memory to contain the entire Filer. You are unable to use this activity.

G(et

No file loaded: You incorrectly indicated the file you want to designate as the workfile. You probably specified a file that doesn't exist.

K(runch

Invalid #: You indicated an inappropriate block number (such as a negative number) in response to the "Starting at block #" prompt.

Please re–boot: The K(runch activity moved SYSTEM.PASCAL and/or SYSTEM.FILER on the system disk. The p–System can't gracefully recover from this situation and requests that you bootstrap again.

M(ake

Nested subsidiary volumes are not permitted: You attempted to create a .SVOL file within a subsidiary volume. Subsidiary volumes can't be created within other subsidiary volumes.

O(n/off–line

FILE ––> NOT mounted: The file that you indicated can't be mounted. Perhaps it is not a correct .SVOL file. Or, if it is correct, you may have already mounted as many subsidiary volumes as you can on your configuration. (If this is the case, you can dismount one of the subsidiary volumes that is already mounted. Or, you may be able to use Setup to increase the maximum number of subsidiary volumes that are allowed to be mounted at one time.)

S(ave

No workfile to save: You don't presently have any workfile and so S(ave doesn't do anything.

Workfile is saved: You already have a permanent workfile and no temporary version of it exists. Therefore, S(ave does nothing.

Text file lost or **Code file lost:** Your text or code workfile can't be saved because it can't be found. You may have R(emoved SYSTEM.WRK.TEXT or SYSTEM.WRK.CODE without doing a N(ew or S(aving them first. Alternatively, the system disk may be out of its drive.

T(ransfer

Output file full: There is not enough contiguous disk space to complete the T(ransfer. This error is similar to the "No room on vol" message which can also be issued by T(ransfer.

X(amine

No room on vol: If this error occurs within X(amine, it indicates that there is not enough disk space (or there are already too many files) to create the BAD.xxxxx.BAD file.

Z(ero

Invalid #: You indicated an incorrect number of blocks for the size of the new volume.

B

EXECUTION ERRORS

This appendix describes errors that can be detected and reported by the p–System while a program is running. Two categories of errors are addressed: 1) errors that can occur in any p–System program, and 2) errors that can only occur in a program written in FORTRAN. A section of the appendix is devoted to each of these categories.

Most of these errors are reported in the manner described in Sections 1.7 and 3.7, with the error message at the bottom of your screen. For the p–System errors, a textual error message, such as "Program interrupted by user," is provided if possible. If the system disk is not available, or if there is insufficient main memory available when the error occurs, an error number replaces the textual message. Both the number and the message are given for the errors listed in this appendix.

Your direct response to any of these errors will probably be to press ⟦space⟧ (once you have absorbed the error message, and possibly written down the details for later reference). The program that was executing will then be cancelled, and the p–System will reinitialize itself (to correct any damage that might have been done as a result of the error).

Some of these errors may be detected by an application program and handled by it (possibly with your assistance). For instance, if an application program asks you to specify a disk file for it to process, it may determine that the file you specify does not exist. After informing you of the problem, the program usually gives you a chance to specify a file that does exist. This approach is used by the major p–System components. Many of the error messages listed in Appendix A result from the detection of an error described in this appendix.

For each of the p–System errors, we provide some diagnosis and recovery advice. Your response to an error will probably depend on whether it occurs in a program that you are developing yourself, or in an application program that you have acquired. In the latter case, you should make a note of the error coordinates that occur in the execution error message, and contact the supplier of the application for assistance. In some cases, however, there may be simple things you can do differently when you next use the program to avoid an execution error. If so, we have tried to anticipate and describe them. Since there are so many different circumstances in which execution errors can occur, our diagnosis and recovery advice in this appendix is not comprehensive. We believe it will be useful to you, nevertheless.

B.1 p–SYSTEM EXECUTION ERRORS

The first subsection describes the general execution errors that can occur. One of these (#10) is used whenever a program has a problem that involves input/output (I/O) activities (writing information onto a disk, for instance). Since there are so many kinds of I/O errors, these are treated separately in a second subsection.

General Execution Errors

#0––System error: The operating system has detected an internal inconsistency. There is no effective recovery action you can take. You must simply reboot the p–System.

#1––Value range error: A program attempted to use a number that is either larger or smaller than it should be. You may have made a request of the program that it isn't prepared to handle.

#2––No proc in seg table: A program attempted to call a procedure that does not exist. One possibility is that the program references external routines, but the necessary link editing step was not done to install those routines.

#3––Exit from uncalled proc: An invalid attempt was made to use the EXIT procedure in UCSD Pascal. An EXIT call names a procedure which is to be "exited." During this EXIT attempt, the named procedure could not be found, so the EXIT was impossible to perform. This is probably an error in the program.

#4––Stack overflow: The p–System has run out of main memory. Possibly this program is fundamentally too large to run in your configuration. Alternatively, you may have asked it to perform a task that requires more memory than you have. In this latter case, you may still be able to use this program, as long as you are more modest in your demands of it. You might consider changing the configuration of your p–System to make more memory available. For instance, if you have the Print Spooler installed, memory is occupied even if you aren't using the Spooler.

#5––Integer overflow: An arithmetic calculation has been attempted that would have resulted in a number larger than the p–System can handle. This is probably an error in the program.

#6––Divide by zero: An attempt has been made to divide by zero, which is an invalid operation. This is probably an error in the program.

#7––NIL pointer reference: A program has made an invalid reference to main memory. Specifically, it may have attempted to use a Pascal pointer variable that contained a value of NIL. This is illegal, and is probably a program error.

#8––Program interrupted by user: You pressed the ⟦break⟧ key (perhaps by accident). If you didn't intend to press ⟦break⟧, make sure you know what the ⟦break⟧ key is on your computer, and try to avoid this mistake in the future. If you don't know what ⟦break⟧ is (even after looking at the front inside cover of this book) check your p–System documentation or use the Setup utility.

#9––System I/O error: An I/O error has been detected during a critical operation of the operating system. No recovery from this error is possible. You should simply reboot the p–System.

#10––I/O error: This error is usually coupled with a further description indicating what type of I/O error occurred. Check the "p–System I/O Errors" subsection (which is next).

#11––Unimplemented instruction: An attempt has been made to execute an invalid p–code instruction in a program. The most likely cause is that the program code file is corrupted in some way. Try getting another copy of the program. Another possibility is that a program got out of control and inadvertently corrupted a program segment stored in main memory.

#12––Floating point error: During a computation involving real (or "floating point") numbers, an error has been detected. This is probably an error in the program.

#13––String overflow: A program attempted to use an overly long character string. This is probably an error in the program. Possibly you provided a response to a data entry prompt that had more characters than the program was intended to handle.

#14––Programmed HALT: The program has executed the UCSD Pascal procedure, HALT. This usually means the program has detected an error from which it cannot recover.

#15——Illegal heap operation: The heap is a dynamically managed storage area available to UCSD Pascal programs. Some illegal operation was attempted involving the heap. This is probably an error in the program.

#16——Breakpoint: This execution error is intended to be intercepted by the p–System Debugger. It is used as a signal to the Debugger to stop execution of the program and give you a chance to decide what to do next. If you see this error, there is probably an internal p–System problem.

#17——Incompatible real number size: The program that is running is configured for a size of real numbers that does not match the size for which the p–System has been configured. Section 1.18 provides some background on this topic. Agreement about the real number size must exist among the operating system, the p–machine emulator, and the program being executed.

#18——Set too large: An operation has been attempted involving the Pascal data type, "Set." The set was too large to be correctly handled. This is probably a program error.

#19——Segment too large: A program attempted to load a program segment that was too large to be handled on this p–System implementation. Check your computer–specific documentation to find out what this limit is.

p–System I/O Errors

The items listed in this subsection are also known as **I/O Results.** Whenever a p–System I/O operation is done, a report on its success or failure is made to the requesting program. This I/O Result is in the form of a number. If the number is zero, the operation was successful. If the number is not zero, some difficulty occurred, and the value of the number indicates the problem. If the program receives a non–zero I/O Result, it may simply pass on the number to you in a simple error message. If this happens, you need to look in this subsection to find out the details of the error.

Programs may also choose not to handle the checking of the I/O Result themselves, leaving that responsibility to the p–System, instead. In this case, when a non–zero I/O Result is detected, a standard p–System execution error is reported (with the message on the bottom line of the screen giving the error coordinate, and so on).

This list includes errors that are defined in Version IV.2 p–Systems, but not in earlier versions. Some of these occur only in the variant of IV.2 that includes the "Advanced File System" (or "AFS"). Since AFS is not available at the time of this writing, AFS–specific errors are simply listed without explanatory comments.

#1——Parity error (CRC): A read or write operation has resulted in invalid data. "Parity" and "CRC" refer to two ways in which such an error can be detected. Both involve adding extra information to the data which can be used to check the correctness of data, itself. The most likely cause of this error is a damaged area (also known as a "bad block") on a storage medium (such as a diskette). It is also possible that a diskette was not properly inserted when the I/O operation was attempted. For instance, you may have forgotten to close a drive door, or removed a diskette prematurely.

This error can also be reported in connection with I/O operations on communication devices (such as the printer).

#2––Illegal unit #: An I/O operation has been attempted using an illegal device number. (Recall that "unit" is sometimes used as a synonym for "device.") For instance, you may have referred to storage device #9: when you only have storage devices #4: and #5: on your computer.

#3––Illegal I/O request: An I/O operation has been attempted that is inappropriate for the device involved. For instance, there may have been an attempt to read data from a printer (which is ordinarily an output–only device).

#4––Data–com timeout: "Data–com" refers to "data communi–cations." This seldom seen error can indicate that some difficulty has occurred in a communication channel (through the REMIN: and REMOUT: devices, for instance) between your computer and another computer or peripheral device.

#5––Volume went off–line: A storage or communication volume that had been on–line is no longer on–line. Perhaps you inadvertently turned off a device that was still in use, or removed a diskette prematurely.

#6––File lost in dir: A file that used to be in the directory of a storage volume is no longer there. That file has been in use, and the system now needs to confirm its status.

#7––Bad file name: The specification of a file is invalid. It may be too long, for instance. If you have just entered a file specification in response to a data entry prompt, that specification may be wrong. See the inside back cover of this book for a summary of the requirements on file specifications.

#8––No room on vol: There is insufficient room on the designated volume for the operation requested. There may have been an attempt to create a file on the volume. If so, there is insufficient space on the volume to hold the file, or the directory capacity of 77 files is exhausted.

#9––No such volume on–line: The designated volume cannot be located by the p–System. If it is a storage volume, you may have removed a diskette prematurely. If it is a communication volume, such as a printer, the device may not be turned on, or not ready for operation.

#10––No such file on volume: A file specification has designated a file on a particular volume. However, no such file exists on that volume. You may have forgotten that you need to explicitly provide a Volume ID when you designate a file that's not on the prefix, or default, volume.

#11——Dup dir entry: Somehow there are two files with the same name in the directory of a volume. This may have happened because a program was interrupted, and didn't complete execution normally. Try rebooting the p–System with the affected volume on–line; that may clean out the extra directory entry.

#12——File already open: A program has attempted to open a file variable that is already open. This is a program error.

#13——File not open: A program has attempted to access a file variable that is not open. This is a program error.

#14——Bad input format: You probably just responded incorrectly to a data entry prompt requesting that you enter a number. For instance, you may have entered letters rather than digits. Or, you may have entered a real number (such as "4.356"), when the program expected an integer number (with no fractional part).

#15——Ring buffer overflow: On some p–Systems this error is reported when you have tried to type too many characters before the p–System has a chance to process them. On other p–Systems, such an attempt to enter too many "type ahead" characters is signaled by the sounding of the bell. If you continue typing after the bell, characters are discarded.

#16——Write–protect: An attempt has been made to write data on a volume that is **write–protected**. Diskettes distributed by p–System suppliers or application suppliers are often write–protected so you can't destroy them by mistake. You may have write–protected a volume, yourself, and forgotten about it.

#17——Illegal block: A program has attempted to access a block number that doesn't exist on the storage device involved.

#18——Illegal buffer: The main memory address involved in a program's low–level ("device I/O") operation is inappropriate.

#19——Illegal size: A program has attempted to access or set a file attribute improperly.

#20——Past end of file: A program has attempted to read past the end of a file.

#21——Data size error: AFS only.

#22——Corrupt tree: AFS only.

#23——Duplicate key: AFS only.

#24——No current record: AFS only.

#25——Key size error: AFS only.

#26——Illegal operation: A program has attempted to access an illegal attribute or made another AFS–specific error.

#27——Not available: A program has attempted an operation on a file that is inappropriate because of uses being made of the file by another program (perhaps sharing access to the file over a network). Such a clash can also occur between concurrent processes within a single program. Refer to the *Operating System Reference Manual* for more details on possible error situations.

#28——Illegal file type: AFS only.

#29——No directory: A program has attempted to access a disk volume that has no valid directory.

#30——Network transmission error: A program running in Liaison has attempted a network I/O operation and it failed.

#31——Network timeout: A program running in Liaison has attempted a network I/O operation and that operation was aborted because no response was received in the alloted time.

B.2 FORTRAN EXECUTION ERRORS

600: Format missing final ')'
601: Sign not expected in input
602: Sign not followed by digit in input
603: Digit expected in input
604: Missing N or Z after B in format
605: Unexpected character in format
606: Zero repetition factor in format not allowed
607: Integer expected for w field in format
608: Positive integer required for w field in format
609: '.' expected in format
610: Integer expected for d field in format
611: Integer expected for e field in format
612: Positive integer required for e field in format
613: Positive integer required for w field in A format
614: Hollerith field in format must not appear for reading
615: Hollerith field in format requires repetition factor
616: X field in format requires repetition factor
617: P field in format requires repetition factor
618: Integer appears before '+' or '–' in format
619: Integer expected after '+' or '–' in format
620: P format expected after signed repetition factor in format
621: Maximum nesting level for formats exceeded
622: ')' has repetition factor in format
623: Integer followed by ',' illegal in format
624: '.' is illegal format control character
625: Character constant must not appear in format for reading
626: Character constant in format must not be repeated
627: '/' in format must not be repeated
628: '\' in format must not be repeated
629: BN or BZ format control must not be repeated
630: Attempt to perform I/O on unknown unit number

631: Formatted I/O attempted on file opened as unformatted
632: Format fails to begin with '('
633: I format expected for integer read
634: F or E format expected for real read
635: Two '.' characters in formatted real read
636: Digit expected in formatted real read
637: L format expected for logical read
639: T or F expected in logical read
640: A format expected for character read
641: I format expected for integer write
642: w field in F format not greater than d field + 1
643: Scale factor out of range of d field in E format
644: E or F format expected for real write
645: L format expected for logical write
646: A format expected for character write
647: Attempt to do unformatted I/O to a unit opened as formatted
648: Unable to write blocked output, possibly no room on device for file
649: Unable to read blocked input
650: Error in formatted textfile, no <cr> in last 512 bytes
651: Integer overflow on input
652: Too many bytes read out of direct access unit record
653: Incorrect number of bytes read from a direct access unit record
654: Attempt to open direct access unit on unblocked device
655: Attempt to do external I/O on a unit beyond end of file record
656: Attempt to position a unit for direct access on a nonpositive record number
657: Attempt to do direct access to a unit opened as sequential
658: Attempt to position direct access unit on unblocked device
659: Attempt to position direct access unit beyond end of file for reading
660: Attempt to backspace unit connected to unblocked device
661: Attempt to backspace sequential, unformatted unit
662: Argument to ASIN or ACOS out of bounds (ABS(X) .GT. 1.0)
663: Argument to SIN or COS too large (ABS(X) .GT. 10E6)
664: Attempt to do unformatted I/O to internal unit
665: Attempt to put more than one record into internal unit
666: Attempt to write more characters to internal unit than its length
667: EOF called on unknown unit
697: Integer variable not currently assigned a format label
698: End of file encountered on read with no END= option
699: Integer variable not ASSIGNed a label used in assigned goto
1000+ Compiler debug error messages – should never appear in correct programs

C

SYNTAX ERRORS

C.1 UCSD PASCAL SYNTAX ERRORS

1: Error in simple type
2: Identifier expected
3: Unimplemented error
4: ')' expected
5: ':' expected
6: Illegal symbol (terminator expected)
7: Error in parameter list
8: 'OF' expected
9: '(' expected
10: Error in type
11: '[' expected
12: ']' expected
13: 'END' expected
14: ';' expected
15: Integer expected
16: '=' expected
17: 'BEGIN' expected
18: Error in declaration part
19: Error in <field–list>
20: '.' expected
21: '*' expected
22: 'INTERFACE' expected
23: 'IMPLEMENTATION' expected

24: 'UNIT' expected
50: Error in constant
51: ':=' expected
52: 'THEN' expected
53: 'UNTIL' expected
54: 'DO' expected
55: 'TO' or 'DOWNTO' expected in for statement
56: 'IF' expected
57: 'FILE' expected
58: Error in <factor> (bad expression)
59: Error in variable
60: Must be of type 'SEMAPHORE'
61: Must be of type 'PROCESSID'
62: Process not allowed at this nesting level
63: Only main task may start processes
101: Identifier declared twice
102: Low bound exceeds high bound
103: Identifier is not of the appropriate class
104: Undeclared identifier
105: Sign not allowed
106: Number expected
107: Incompatible subrange types
108: File not allowed here
109: Type must not be real
110: <tagfield> type must be scalar or subrange
111: Incompatible with <tagfield> part
112: Index type must not be real
113: Index type must be a scalar or a subrange
114: Base type must not be real
115: Base type must be a scalar or a subrange
116: Error in type of standard procedure parameter
117: Unsatisified forward reference
118: Forward reference type identifier in variable declaration
119: Re–specified params not OK for a forward declared procedure
120: Function result type must be scalar, subrange or pointer
121: File value parameter not allowed
122: A forward declared function's result type can't be re–specified
123: Missing result type in function declaration
124: F–format for reals only
125: Error in type of standard procedure parameter
126: Number of parameters does not agree with declaration
127: Illegal parameter substitution
128: Result type does not agree with declaration
129: Type conflict of operands
130: Expression is not of set type
131: Tests on equality allowed only
132: Strict inclusion not allowed
133: File comparison not allowed
134: Illegal type of operand(s)

135: Type of operand must be Boolean
136: Set element type must be scalar or subrange
137: Set element types must be compatible
138: Type of variable is not array
139: Index type is not compatible with the declaration
140: Type of variable is not record
141: Type of variable must be file or pointer
142: Illegal parameter solution
143: Illegal type of loop control variable
144: Illegal type of expression
145: Type conflict
146: Assignment of files not allowed
147: Label type incompatible with selecting expression
148: Subrange bounds must be scalar
149: Index type must be integer
150: Assignment to standard function is not allowed
151: Assignment to formal function is not allowed
152: No such field in this record
153: Type error in read
154: Actual parameter must be a variable
155: Control variable cannot be formal or non–local
156: Multidefined case label
157: Too many cases in case statement
158: No such variant in this record
159: Real or string tagfields not allowed
160: Previous declaration was not forward
161: Again forward declared
162: Parameter size must be constant
163: Missing variant in declaration
164: Substitution of standard proc/func not allowed
165: Multidefined label
166: Multideclared label
167: Undeclared label
168: Undefined label
169: Error in base set
170: Value parameter expected
171: Standard file was re–declared
174: Pascal function or procedure expected
175: Semaphore value parameter not allowed
182: Nested UNITs not allowed
183: External declaration not allowed at this nesting level
184: External declaration not allowed in INTERFACE section
185: Segment declaration not allowed in INTERFACE section
186: Labels not allowed in INTERFACE section
187: Attempt to open library unsuccessful
188: UNIT not declared in previous uses declaration
189: 'USES' not allowed at this nesting level
190: UNIT not in library
191: Forward declaration was not segment

192: Forward declaration was segment
193: Not enough room for this operation
194: Flag must be declared at top of program
195: Unit not importable
201: Error in real number – digit expected
202: String constant must not exceed source line
203: Integer constant exceeds range
250: Too many scopes of nested identifiers
251: Too many nested procedures or functions
252: Too many forward references of procedure entries
253: Procedure too long
254: Too many long constants in this procedure
256: Too many external references
257: Too many externals
258: Too many local files
259: Expression too complicated
300: Division by zero
301: No case provided for this value
302: Index expression out of bounds
303: Value to be assigned is out of bounds
304: Element expression out of range
398: Implementation restriction
399: Implementation restriction
400: Illegal character in text
401: Unexpected end of input
402: Error in writing code file, not enough room
403: Error in reading include file
404: Error in writing list file, not enough room
405: 'PROGRAM' or 'UNIT' expected
406: Include file not legal
407: Include file nesting limit exceeded
408: INTERFACE section not contained in one file
409: Unit name reserved for system
410: Disk error
500: Assembler error

C.2 FORTRAN–77 SYNTAX ERRORS

1: Fatal error reading source block
2: Nonnumeric characters in label field
3: Too many continuation lines
4: Fatal end of file encountered
5: Labeled continuation line
6: Missing field on $ compiler directive line
7: Unable to open listing file specified on $ compiler directive line
8: Unrecognizable $ compiler directive
9: Input source file not valid textfile format

10: Maximum depth of include file nesting exceeded
11: Integer constant overflow
12: Error in real constant
13: Too many digits in constant
14: Identifier too long
15: Character constant extends to end of line
16: Character constant zero length
17: Illegal character in input
18: Integer constant expected
19: Label expected
20: Error in label
21: Type name expected (INTEGER, REAL, LOGICAL, or CHARACTER[*n])
22: Integer constant expected
23: Extra characters at end of statement
24: '(' expected
25: Letter IMPLICIT'ed more than once
26: ')' expected
27: Letter expected
28: Identifier expected
29: Dimension(s) required in DIMENSION statement
30: Array dimensioned more than once
31: Maximum of 3 dimensions in an array
32: Incompatible arguments to EQUIVALENCE
33: Variable appears more than once in a type specification statement
34: This identifier has already been declared
35: This intrinsic function cannot be passed as an argument
36: Identifier must be a variable
37: Identifier must be a variable or the current FUNCTION
38: '/' expected
39: Named COMMON block already saved
40: Variable already appears in a COMMON block
41: Variables in two different COMMON blocks cannot be equivalenced
42: Number of subscripts in EQUIVALENCE statement does not agree with variable declaration
43: EQUIVALENCE subscript out of range
44: Two distinct cells EQUIVALENCE'd to the same location in a COMMON block
45: EQUIVALENCE statement extends a COMMON block in the negative direction
46: EQUIVALENCE statement forces a variable to two distinct locations, not in a COMMON block
47: Statement number expected
48: Mixed CHARACTER and numeric items not allowed in same COMMON block
49: CHARACTER items cannot be EQUIVALENCE'd with non−character items
50: Illegal symbol in expression
51: Can't use SUBROUTINE name in an expression

52: Type of argument must be INTEGER or REAL
53: Type of argument must be INTEGER, REAL, or CHARACTER
54: Types of comparisons must be compatible
55: Type of expression must be LOGICAL
56: Too many subscripts
57: Too few subscripts
58: Variable expected
59: '=' expected
60: Size of EQUIVALENCE'd CHARACTER items must be the same
61: Illegal assignment – types do not match
62: Can only call SUBROUTINES
63: Dummy parameters cannot appear in COMMON statements
64: Dummy parameters cannot appear in EQUIVALENCE statements
65: Assumed–size array declarations can only be used for dummy arrays
66: Adjustable–size array declarations can only be used for dummy arrays
67: Assumed–size array dimension specifier must be last dimension
68: Adjustable bound must be either parameter or in COMMON prior to appearance
69: Adjustable bound must be simple integer variable
70: Cannot have more than 1 main program
71: The size of a named COMMON must be the same in all procedures
72: Dummy arguments cannot appear in DATA statements
73: COMMON variables cannot appear in DATA statements
74: SUBROUTINE names, FUNCTION names, INTRINSIC names, etc. cannot appear in DATA statements
75: Subscript out of range in DATA statement
76: Repeat count must be >= 1
77: Constant expected
78: Type conflict in DATA statement
79: Number of variables does not match number of values in DATA statement list
80: Statement cannot have label
81: No such INTRINSIC function
82: Type declaration for INTRINSIC function does not match actual type of INTRINSIC function
83: Letter expected
84: Type of FUNCTION does not agree with a previous call
85: This procedure has already appeared in this compilation
86: This procedure has already been defined to exist in another unit via a $USES command
87: Error in type of argument to an INTRINSIC FUNCTION
88: SUBROUTINE/FUNCTION was previously used as a FUNCTION/SUBROUTINE
89: Unrecognizable statement
90: Functions cannot be of type CHARACTER
91: Missing END statement
92: A program unit cannot appear in a $SEPARATE compilation
93: Fewer actual arguments than formal arguments in FUNCTION/SUBROUTINE call

94: More actual arguments than formal arguments in FUNCTION/SUBROUTINE call
95: Type of actual argument does not agree with type of format argument
96: The following procedures were called but not defined:
97: This procedure was already defined by a $EXT directive
98: Maximum size of type CHARACTER is 255, minimum is 1
100: Statement out of order
101: Unrecognizable statement
102: Illegal jump into block
103: Label already used for FORMAT
104: Label already defined
105: Jump to format label
106: DO statement forbidden in this context
107: DO label must follow DO statement
108: ENDIF forbidden in this context
109: No matching IF for this ENDIF
110: Improperly nested DO block in IF block
111: ELSEIF forbidden in this context
112: No matching IF for ELSEIF
113: Improperly nested DO or ELSE block
114: '(' expected
115: ')' expected
116: THEN expected
117: Logical expression expected
118: ELSE statement forbidden in this context
119: No matching IF for ELSE
120: Unconditional GOTO forbidden in this context
121: Assigned GOTO forbidden in this context
122: Block IF statement forbidden in this context
123: Logical IF statement forbidden in this context
124: Arithmetic IF statement forbidden in this context
125: ',' expected
126: Expression of wrong type
127: RETURN forbidden in this context
128: STOP forbidden in this context
129: END forbidden in this context
131: Label referenced but not defined
132: DO or IF block not terminated
133: FORMAT statement not permitted in this context
134: FORMAT label already referenced
135: FORMAT must be labeled
136: Identifier expected
137: Integer variable expected
138: 'TO' expected
139: Integer expression expected
140: Assigned GOTO but no ASSIGN statements
141: Unrecognizable character constant as option
142: Character constant expected as option
143: Integer expression expected for unit designation

144: STATUS option expected after ',' in CLOSE statement
145: Character expression as filename in OPEN
146: FILE= option must be present in OPEN statement
147: RECL= option specified twice in OPEN statement
148: Integer expression expected for RECL= option in OPEN statement
149: Unrecognizable option in OPEN statement
150: Direct access files must specify RECL= in OPEN statement
151: Adjustable arrays not allowed as I/O list elements
152: End of statement encountered in implied DO, expressions beginning with '(' not allowed as I/O list elements
153: Variable required as control for implied DO
154: Expressions not allowed as reading I/O list elements
155: REC= option appears twice in statement
156: REC= expects integer expression
157: END= option only allowed in READ statement
158: END= option appears twice in statement
159: Unrecognizable I/O unit
160: Unrecognizable format in I/O statement
161: Options expected after ',' in I/O statement
162: Unrecognizable I/O list element
163: Label used as format but not defined in format statement
164: Integer variable used as assigned format but no ASSIGN statements
165: Label of an executable statement used as a format
166: Integer variable expected for assigned format
167: Label defined more than once as format
200: Error in reading $USES file
201: Syntax error in $USES file
202: SUBROUTINE/FUNCTION name in $USES file has already been declared
203: FUNCTIONS cannot return values of type CHARACTER
204: Unable to open $USES file
205: Too many $USES statements
206: No .TEXT info for this unit in $USES file
207: Illegal segment kind in $USES file
208: There is no such unit in this $USES file
209: Missing UNIT name in $USES statement
210: Extra characters at end of $USES directive
211: Intrinsic units cannot be overlayed
212: Syntax error in $EXT directive
213: A SUBROUTINE cannot have a type
214: SUBROUTINE/FUNCTION name in $EXT directive has already been defined
400: Code file write error
401: Too many entries in JTAB
402: Too many SUBROUTINES/FUNCTIONS in segment
403: Procedure too large (code buffer too small)
404: Insufficient room for scratch file on system disk
405: Read error on scratch file

D

COMPILER DIRECTIVES

You can control the operation of a p–System compiler by embedding compiler directives in your source text. You can, for instance, cause the creation of a compiled listing during compilation. In this appendix, we summarize the compiler directives supported by UCSD Pascal and p–System FORTRAN–77. For additional details on these directives, refer to the appropriate language reference manual.

D.1 UCSD PASCAL DIRECTIVES

These directives appear within **pseudo–comments**, which are like ordinary Pascal comments, except that a dollar sign ("$") is the first character of the comment. Here are some examples:

```
{$I+}
{$R-,I-}
(*$L PRINTER:*)
{$D A_CONDITION}
```

Unlike ordinary comments, which don't affect the behavior of the program or the compiler processing it, these pseudo–comments *do* have an effect on the operation of the compiler. Notice that either style of comment bracket can be used, but (as usual) the style used on the left must match the style used on the right.

There are three kinds of compiler directives, all of which are represented in the examples above.

Switch directives contain a letter designating one of a set of standard "switches" and a "+" or a "−" indicating whether that "switch" (maintained by the compiler) should be turned on ("+") or off ("−"). The first example above shows switch "I" (for "Input/output error checking") being turned on. The second example shows the same switch and another one being turned off.

String directives contain a letter followed by a character string. These directives often control compiler operations involving files. For instance, the last example above shows the "L" string directive which controls the production of compiled listings. In the example, the compiler is directed to produce a compiled listing on the device PRINTER:.

Flag directives are like switch directives, except that the names of the switches are of your own invention, rather than standard switches maintained by the compiler. You can use flag directives to **conditionally compile** a section of source text.

You can only use a particular named flag in your program after it has been "declared" using the "D" flag directive (like that in the example, above). Once a flag has been declared, you can mark the boundaries of an area of source text using directives referencing that flag and arrange, for instance, that the text section be compiled only if the setting of the flag is "+".

A single pseudo−comment may contain any number of switch directives and at most a single string or flag directive (which must be last in the pseudo−comment, if it appears). The string in a string directive consists of the characters between the directive letter and the end of the pseudo−comment (e.g. "PRINTER:" in the example above). If a string directive appears within a pseudo−comment using the "(* *)" style of comment brackets, the string may not contain a "*" character. The flag name in a flag directive consists of the characters after the directive letter and up to the flag setting (such as "+" or "−"), if present. The rules for naming flags are the same as those for naming UCSD Pascal identifiers.

Some directive letters apply to more than one type of directive. For instance, there is the string directive "I" for "Include file" and the switch directive "I" for "I/O error checking".

For some switches and for all flags, the compiler maintains a "stack" of switch settings. When a new setting is introduced, the old one is "pushed" on the stack. In a later reference to the same switch or flag, that old setting can be "popped" off the stack by using "^" to indicate the new state, rather than "+" or "−". Thus, for instance, the I/O Check switch can be turned off and then restored to its previous state by the following sequence of directives:

```
{I-}
 ...Intervening text....
{I^}
```

The stacks in which settings are stored are only 15 levels deep. If more than 15 settings are pushed on a stack, the bottom setting is lost. If a setting is restored from the stack when it is empty, a "+" setting results.

In the first subsection below, the available directives are summarized in alphabetical order. The following subsection presents an extended example showing potential uses of many of the directives.

Summaries

Each directive appears in the context of a pseudo–comment that suggests how you use it. Here are some pseudo–examples:

**{$S string}––p–Seudo–string directive:** An example of this directive might be: {$S MY–STRING}.

**{$S +|–|^}––p–Seudo switch directive:** The vertical bars separate alternatives that can come after the "S". Therefore this directive can take the forms: {$S+}, {$S–}, or {$S^}. {$S^} means "restore the previous setting of the "S" switch."

**{$S flag +|–|_}––p–Seudo flag directive:** The "_" alternative after the flag name indicates that an empty space is valid there. Appropriate examples of this directive include the following: {$S MyFlag}, {$S HisFlag–}, and {$S HerFlag+}.

Many of the switches affected by these directives have default settings that apply until you explicitly set the switches in your program. These settings are noted in the descriptions below.

**{$B flag +|–|_}––Begin conditional section:** Mark the start of a section of conditionally compiled source text. If an explicit flag setting is included in the directive, the section is compiled if the setting of the named flag matches the directive. If no explicit setting appears (the third alternative, above), "+" is assumed. The flag named must have been previously declared via the Declare flag directive. Example: {$B MyFlag–}.

{$C string}––Copyright: Cause the string to be placed in the copyright field of the code file resulting from this compilation. Example:

{$C (C) Copyright 1985, Wizard Software, Inc.}

**{$D flag +|–|^|_}––Declare and/or set flag:** Declare a conditional compilation flag and set it or alter the setting of a flag that has been previously declared. The flag is set according to the character after the flag name. A "+" is assumed if no explicit character appears. If "^" appears, the flag is set to its previous value. A conditional compilation flag must be declared using this directive before you can use the flag to mark a section of your program. Example: {$D MyFlag+}.

{$D +|–}––Debugging information: Determine whether symbolic debugging information is included in the code file resulting from this compilation. See Chapter 8 for a brief discussion of symbolic and non–symbolic debugging. Naturally, "+" means include the information and "–" means omit it. The default is "–".

**{$E flag}––End conditional section:** Mark the end of a conditionally compiled section of your program. Example: {$E MyFlag}.

{$I +|–|^}––Input/output error checking: Control the inclusion in your compiled program of automatic checks on the success of input/output operations. If these checks are included, your program stops with an execution error if an unsuccessful I/O operation (such as an attempt to read a file that doesn't exist) occurs. If the checks are omitted, you have the chance in your program to check for error conditions explicitly and perhaps recover more gracefully from problems of this sort. The default is "+".

**{$I string}––Include file:** Cause the text of the file specified by the string to be "included" in your program (essentially as if your program file contained the lines of that file directly). You can use this directive to break up a large program into more manageable sections, each of which is dealt with as a separate file. If the .TEXT suffix is omitted from the file specification, it is assumed. Nested includes (in which an included file contains another "Include file" directive) are legal up to a depth of three files. Example directives: {$I part_2} or {$I part_2.text}.

{$L +|–|^}––Listing: Control the production of a compiled listing of subsequent text in your program. The compiled listing is produced or not produced for the "+" or "–" alternatives, respectively. The "^" alternative causes the "L" switch to be restored to its previous setting. The default is "–" unless a file is specified in response to the listing prompt that occurs when the compiler begins operation.

**{$L string}––Listing file:** Turn on the listing ("L") switch and determine where the compiled listing for your program goes. The string can specify a disk file (such as "volume:my_list.text") or a communication volume (such as "PRINTER:"). No suffix is automatically appended to the file specification you supply, so include a .TEXT yourself if you want the listing file produced to act like a text file. Example: {$L MYLISTING.TEXT}.

**{$N +|–}––Native code generation:** Determine whether extra information is emitted into the code file that allows the normal p–code representation of your program to be translated to the native code of your computer. (See Chapter 8 for further discussion of native code generation.) By bracketing sections of your program with {$N+} at the beginning and {$N–} at the end, you can cause those sections to be marked for translation to native code.

{$P +|–|_}––Pagination: Determine whether compiled listings are automatically paginated (the "+" alternative) or not (the "–" alternative). If neither "+" nor "–" appear, cause an immediate page break in the compiled listing that is in progress. The default is "+".

{$Q +|–}––Quiet: Control the production of the status information (including dots and line numbers) that is normally written to the console during compilation. The "+" setting suppresses that output, while the "–" setting enables it and is the default.

{$R +|–|^}––Range checking: Control the inclusion of automatic checking code in your compiled program that enforces any value constraints it contains. For instance, if the value of a variable must always be between 0 and 10, this condition is checked every time a new value is about to be placed in the variable. The "–" setting suppresses these checks, while the "+" setting includes them and is the default. The "^" alternative causes the switch setting to be restored to its previous value.

**{$R 2|4}––Real size:** Determine the size of the real numbers manipulated by this program. Possible sizes are two words ("2") and four words ("4"). This rarely used directive is only necessary when you want to compile a program for a different real number size than that supported by your p–System. If you attempt to run a program with an incompatible real size on your p–System, an execution error occurs. If this directive appears in your program, it must precede the first symbol that is not a comment. Example: {$R2}.

**{$T string}––Title:** Specify the string that appears on the title line of subsequent pages in your compiled listing. Example: {$T PROGRAM 1–– Tom Bass}.

**{$U string}––Use library:** Establish the file specified by the string as the current library file, in which units named in subsequent **uses** statements are sought. The .CODE suffix on the library file name is optional. Until an instance of this directive occurs in a program, units are sought in the file SYSTEM.LIBRARY on the system volume. This directive often appears in connection with **uses** statements. Example: {$U MYLIBRARY.CODE}.

{$U +|–}––User program:** Determine whether this compilation is treated as a user program ("+") or as a system program ("–"). The former is the default. The system program setting is rarely used except in the maintenance of the operating system. Its effect is to allow the declaration of units that have the same names as certain important operating system units. It also effectively invokes {$R–,I–}. If present, this directive must occur before the heading of the program (that is, before the first occurrence of the words **program or **unit**).

Extended Example

In the example below, you can see many of the UCSD Pascal compiler directives in the context of a somewhat realistic program. The example is the skeleton of a hypothetical application program. It uses compiler directives (particularly the conditional compilation type) to allow configuring the program in either of two ways. If the flag "FinalBuild" is set to "+", the program is compiled in a form suitable for shipment to customers. If the flag "FinalBuild" is set to "–", the program is compiled in a form suitable for internal development work.

The lines of the example program are numbered. Notes on each line follow the program. Even if you don't follow the details of the operation of the program, it should give you a good context in which to test your understanding of the important UCSD Pascal compiler directives.

```
 1: {$D FinalBuild+}

 2: {$B FinalBuild-}
 3:    {$D+}
 4: {$E FinalBuild}

 5: {$B FinalBuild+}
 6:    {$T Extended Compiler Directive Example}
 7:    {$L PRINTER:}
 8:    {$R-, I-}
 9: {$E FinalBuild}

10: program Example;

11: uses UnitA,
12:    {$U LIBRARY1.CODE} UnitB,
13:    {$U NEXT.LIB} UnitC, UnitD;

14: {$I GlobalData}

15: {$I Procedures}

16: procedure GetFile;
17: begin
18:    {$B FinalBuild-}
19:       writeln ('Entering GetFile.');
20:    {$E FinalBuild}

21:    {$I-}
22:    repeat
23:       write ('Please enter file name: ');
24:       readln (FileName);
25:       reset (InputFile,FileName);
26:    until IOResult = 0;
27:    {$I^}

28:    {$B FinalBuild-}
29:       writeln ('Leaving GetFile.');
30:    {$E FinalBuild}
31: end;

32: begin
33:    {Main Program}
34: end.
```

Line 1: Declare the flag "FinalBuild" and set it to "+". With this setting, the program will be compiled for production shipment. You could change the setting to "–" and recompile to do further development work on the program.

Lines 2–4: A section of text that is compiled when the FinalBuild flag is set to "–".

Line 3: For development work, cause the production of symbolic debugging information. Note that if a compiler directive occurs in a section of text skipped by conditional compilation, the directive is not processed.

Lines 5–9: A section of text that is compiled when FinalBuild is set to "+" (implying the final production configuration).

Line 6: Establish a heading line for the compiled listing.

Line 7: Cause the listing to be produced on the PRINTER: device.

Line 8: Disable range–checking and Input/output error checking. Omission of these checks will make the resulting program somewhat smaller and faster, but is only reasonable after the program has been thoroughly shaken down.

Line 9: End the conditionally compiled section.

Lines 10–34: The program Example.

Line 11: Make the facilities provided by UnitA (in *SYSTEM.LIBRARY) available to this program.

Line 12: Make UnitB (found in LIBRARY1.CODE) available to this program.

Line 13: Make UnitC and UnitD (found in NEXT.LIB) available to this program.

Lines 14–15: Include the files containing the global data and procedure declarations.

Lines 16–31: A procedure that asks the application user to provide a file name and then associates an internal input file with that name.

Lines 17–31: The body of procedure GetFile.

Lines 18–20:A section of text that is compiled when FinalBuild is "–".

Line 19: A debugging message announcing entry into the procedure.

Line 20: Omit automatic I/O error checking, so that user gets several chances to specify a valid file name.

Line 21–26: Repeat this section of program until the user specifies a valid file. This is signalled by a value zero returned by the built–in function IOResult.

Lines 22–25: Prompt the user for a file name, accept it and attempt to open the specified file.

Line 27: Restore the "I" switch to its previous value. (That depends on the setting of FinalBuild. See the conditionally compiled I– directive on Line 8.)

Lines 28–30: Conditionally include a statement that produces a "Exit GetFile" message in the development configuration.

D.2 FORTRAN–77 DIRECTIVES

In p–System FORTRAN–77, a compiler directive is distinguished by a "$" in column one of a line. A word identifying the directive immediately follows the "$". A directive line can contain only one directive.

Directives can generally occur anywhere a comment can, but there are some restrictions for certain directives. Blanks are significant within directives and serve to separate information items.

The FORTRAN–77 directives are summarized below:

$INCLUDE filename: Textually include the specified file at this point in the source program. Nested includes (in which an included file contains another INCLUDE directive) are supported to a depth of five files. Example:

```
$INCLUDE MY–FILE
```

$EXT SUBROUTINE name parameter–count: The named sub–routine is an assembly language routine with parameter–count parameters. That routine can be called subsequently in your program. The routine must be separately assembled and then linked to this host before your program can be run. The parameter–count must be an integer constant. Example:

```
$EXT SUBROUTINE getdata 3
```

$EXT type FUNCTION name parameter–count: The named func–tion is an assembly language routine with parameter–count parameters. The type of the function can be specified as INTEGER, LOGICAL, or REAL. If the type is omitted, FORTRAN's normal first letter conventions determine the type. After this directive, the named function can be called in your program. The routine must be separately assembled and then linked to your program before you can run it. The parameter–count must be an integer constant. Example:

```
$EXT LOGICAL okport 1
```

$USES identifier IN filename: This directive is similar in effect to the **uses** statement in UCSD Pascal. The identifier specifies a "unit" (either a UCSD Pascal unit or a collection of FORTRAN–77 routines that have been separately compiled). The routines in the referenced unit become available for calling in your program. The optional "IN filename" clause specifies the library file in which the unit "identifier" is sought. If the clause is absent, the file *SYSTEM.LIBRARY is searched. This directive must precede the first non–comment line in your compilation. Examples:

```
$USES services IN SERVICE.LIB
$USES math IN VOLUME:MATH.LIB
$USES special
```

The unit named in the last example is sought in *SYSTEM.LIBRARY and the others in the specified files.

Separate compilation in FORTRAN is somewhat complicated (particularly when both FORTRAN and Pascal are involved). Consult your language reference manual for more detail.

$XREF: Produce a cross–reference listing after each routine compiled showing where in the routine identifiers were defined or referenced.

E

THE p–SYSTEM ON THE IBM PC

This appendix is a summary of those aspects of the p–System that are specific to the IBM Personal Computer (IBM PC, for short) and other members of the IBM PC family. At the time of this writing, the other members include the IBM PC/XT, the Portable PC, the PCjr, and the PC/AT. Since the IBM PC architecture has become a de facto industry standard, this appendix also applies to many close compatibles of the IBM PC, as well. Unless specifically noted otherwise, references to the IBM PC refer to any of the family members or compatibles.

E.1 p–SYSTEM SOURCES AND HARDWARE REQUIREMENTS

The p–System is available for the IBM PC from several sources. The first source is IBM itself (through its dealers and Product Centers). The second source is Network Consulting, Inc. (NCI), in Vancouver, British Columbia, Canada. The third source is SofTech Microsystems, Inc. (SMS). There is considerable variation among the p–Systems offered by these suppliers. Some of this variation arises in the parts of the p–System that are specific to the host computer, but there is also variation in the overall p–System version offered. Our goal is to make it easy for you to use any of these p–System variations with this book. When distinctions are necessary, we refer to a particular variation by specifying the p–System version and the vendor.

The minimum hardware requirements for running the p–System on the IBM PC are:

- 64k bytes of memory,
- one disk drive, and
- a display.

A second drive and 128k bytes or more of memory are highly recommended.

We assume that your IBM PC hardware meets these minimums and is installed and configured correctly. If you need to, follow the configuration instructions in IBM's *Guide to Operations* or comparable document for your computer.

If you wish to use PC–DOS or MS–DOS on your computer as well as the p–System, you may benefit from the facilities offered by both SofTech Microsystems and Network Consulting that allow you to go back and forth easily between DOS and the p–System. These facilities are summarized in the last section of this appendix.

E.2 STARTING THE p–SYSTEM THE FIRST TIME

This section is coordinated with the Section 1.3. It contains two subsections. The first subsection helps you to fill out the inside front cover of this book. The second subsection describes how to start the p–System running on the IBM PC.

Recording Your p–System Details

The first task in this appendix is to fill in the blanks inside the front cover of this book. Much of this information is not yet relevant to you, but we ask you to fill it in, nevertheless. As you progress through the hands–on exercises of Part 1, you will need this information.

First, enter the brand and model of your personal computer (e.g. IBM PC/XT) in the space provided.

Next, enter the name of the overall p–System version you're using. This information should be prominently noted on your p–System documentation or on the labels of your p–System disks. At the time of this writing, here are the versions offered by the various vendors:

- **IBM**: Version IV.0. When IBM offers a later version, it is likely to follow the conventions of the corresponding SMS version, so if you acquired Version IV.1 or later from IBM, follow the directions in this section for the corresponding SMS version.
- **NCI**: Version IV.1. The directions in this appendix will probably not be affected by a decision at NCI to distribute Version IV.2.

- **SMS**: Version IV.2. The material in this appendix should be applicable even if you have Version IV.1 from SMS.

If you can't easily determine which version you have, wait until you start up the p–System in the next subsection. Then it will be easy to tell.

Next, you need to fill in the storage volume descriptions. There has been a steady advance in the capabilities of IBM PC disk hardware since the introduction of the family in 1981. One change was from the use of single–sided disks to double–sided disks (with double the storage capacity). Another change was an increase in the amount of information stored in each of the concentric **tracks** that make up the storage area on a disk. Finally, the number of tracks has been increased (along with the density of information in each) in the high–capacity flexible disk drives first introduced with the IBM PC/AT.

In addition, of course, there has been the advent of hard disk technology (as in the IBM PC/XT), but we don't deal with that in this book.

If you have Version IV.0 from IBM, most of these advances are irrelevant to you because your p–System can't take advantage of them; simply enter the relevant information from this table (where capacities are given in blocks):

Size	:	Device Description
320	:	**single–sided diskette**
640	:	**dual–sided diskette**

If you have a more recent p–System than Version IV.0, more variation is possible (as shown in the following table). Since single–sided drives are now relatively rare, the table omits them; divide the given capacities by two if necessary. The principal variation is in the number of **sectors** stored in each track on the disk. Here are the capacities (in blocks) for the various possibilities (including the high–capacity PC/AT–compatible drive, which contains 160 tracks with 15 sectors per track):

Size	:	Device Description
640	:	**dual–sided, 8–sector/track**
720	:	**dual–sided, 9–sector/track**
800	:	**dual–sided, 10–sector/track**
2400	:	**high–capacity (160 15–sector tracks)**

Except for the high–capacity drive, p–Systems are usually configured initially to use the 8–sector/track density. The standard disk configurations from NCI, however, typically use the 10–sector/track density. Using a configuration utility, however, you can change your p–System to any density your hardware can support.

These potential differences in density can be a source of confusion in your use of the p–System unless you standardize on a single choice. When you have diskettes of different capacities swapped in and out of a single disk drive, the p–System can get confused and you may lose information on the disks. You can sometimes configure a drive to automatically handle either of two densities (say, 8– or 9–sector/track), but that may cause disk operations to go more slowly.

If you're new to the p–System, we recommend you use it as configured by the vendor and save any optimizations until later.

The remainder of the items in your front cover table are relatively independent of the vendor of your p–System. Where there are differences, we indicate them. The information to be written in the blanks is usually **emphasized** in the text below. It isn't emphasized when a description of a key's symbol is given (as opposed to a word or letter on the key). You can simply draw the special symbol that appears on the key in the appropriate blank.

When the Ctrl key and another key should be typed together to produce a p–System special key, we put "Ctrl–" in front of the name of the other key (and similarly for other keys used like Ctrl). Example: "Ctrl–C".

#4: storage device: **left** or **top drive**
#5: storage device: **right** or **bottom drive**
RAM disk volume name: **RAMDISK:** (IBM or SMS) or **RAM:** (NCI)
Utility to format diskettes: **DISKFORMAT.CODE** (IBM or SMS)
CONFIG.CODE (standard p–System from NCI)
SCONFIG.CODE (Practical Pascal from NCI)
Need to Z(ero after formatting? **Yes** (IV.0 IBM) **No** (others)

[ret]	Enter; may be marked with left bent arrow
[bs]	Large left arrow; Backspace on PCjr
[delete line]	**Ctrl–[bs]**; **Ftn–[bs]** on PCjr
[break]	**Ctrl–Break**; **Ftn–B** on PCjr
[stop/start]	**Ctrl–S**
[flush]	**Ctrl–F**
[esc]	**Esc**
[eof]	**Ctrl–C**
[tab]	Left and right arrows; **Tab** on PCjr
[up]	Up arrow
[down]	Down arrow
[right]	Right arrow
[left]	Left arrow
[exch–ins]	**Ins**
[exch–del]	**Del**
[etx]	**Ctrl–C**

You can summarize the information below in the space provided under "Other Notes."

Pressing a Shift key (marked with an open upward pointing arrow) together with the PrtSc key causes the contents of the screen to be printed.

If you use the PCjr, the remainder of this subsection is not relevant to you; skip to the next subsection. If you use another member of the IBM PC family, read on.

Special p–System keys on the numeric pad are only correctly produced when the numeric pad is in "cursor movement" mode (which is its initial condition). In the numeric mode, digits are produced (instead of cursor movement signals) when these keys are pressed. Repeated pressing of the Num Lock key causes the p–System to go back and forth between cursor movement mode and numeric mode.

Sometimes you may press the NumLock key by accident (when you intend to press ⟦bs⟧, for instance). If you're using the Editor when that happens, your attempts to move the cursor with the arrow keys will be unsuccessful. Digits will be produced by your keypresses instead. In a cursor movement setting, digits are interpreted by the Editor as a repeat factor. If you type more than four digits without typing a cursor movement key, the Editor complains:

```
ERROR: Repeatfactor > 10,000  Please press <spacebar> to continue.
```

To recover, type ⟦space⟧, followed by NumLock, to return the numeric keypad to cursor movement mode.

Bootstrapping the p–System

Your next task is to start the p–System running on the personal computer. This process is often called bootstrapping. Locate your system disk. It may have a volume name such as SYSTEM:, or SYSTEM4:, or PSYSTEM:. If you have a choice of either SYSTEM2: or SYSTEM4:, choose the latter.

Open the drive cover of the left hand (or top) drive, insert your system disk, and close the drive cover. The disk should be inserted with the label facing up, under your thumb. The remainder of the start–up process depends on whether your PC is already turned on.

If your computer is turned off, turn on your printer (if you have one), and your television display or video monitor (if you use one); then switch on your computer. There should be several seconds of silence as your computer checks itself. (If you have expansion memory installed, this period could be 20 or 30 seconds.) If the check up finds no problems, a "beep" sounds; then the left (or top) drive light comes on and you hear whirring as the p–System is read into the main memory of your computer.

If your PC is already turned on, press and hold down the two keys marked "Ctrl" and "Alt" on the left side of your keyboard. While holding those keys down, press the key marked "Del". Release all three keys together. An immediate "beep" occurs, the left (or top) drive light comes on and you hear whirring as the p–System is read into main memory.

On an NCI p–System, you may be prompted to enter the date. Simply enter [ret] for now. We deal with dates later.

Eventually a line like the following appears on the top of your screen. There may be a company logo displayed, as well. The version number in square brackets on the right may be different from that shown below. That number tells you which of Versions IV.0, IV.1 or IV.2 you have. If you didn't fill in your version field on the inside front cover, do so now.

```
Command: E(dit, R(un, F(ile, C(omp, L(ink, X(ecute, A(ssem, ? [IV.03]
```

If you can see this entire line on your screen, the start–up operation is complete. If you just did it for the first time, resume your reading of Chapter 1 at Section 1.3.

If your display is only capable of showing 40 characters per line (which is usually the case with an ordinary television), the appearance of your screen is quite different. The top line looks something like this:

```
k, X(ecute, Assem, ? [IV.0]
```

These are the last forty characters of the 80–character line. If your screen looks like this, read the section "Dealing With a 40–Character Screen" later in this appendix. Then return to Chapter 1 at Section 1.3.

E.3 MAKING BACK UPS

This section describes operations that you need to do in Section 1.7. The task in this section is to make a back up copy of your system diskette and begin using the back up. You need a blank diskette to go on from here.

Before you can use a new diskette with the Personal Computer, it must be formatted. (If one of your old disks goes bad, you may also be able to recover and continue using it if you format it again.) Formatting a disk completely erases any information you had previously stored on it. Don't apply this process to a used disk unless you're positive you don't need the information it contains.

Your next steps depend on which variation of PC p–System you're using. Read the appropriate subsection and then resume your reading in Chapter 1.

Back Ups with Version IV.0 from IBM

Disk formatting is done by a utility program called DISKFORMAT. Invoke that utility now with the X(ecute activity in the Command menu. The following series of prompts and responses show how to format the disk in drive #4. (DISKFORMAT can also be applied to diskettes in other drives.) You will be prompted to put the disk to be formatted in drive #4. When that happens, remove your system disk and insert the new disk. Before you press [ret] to indicate you've done that, *always check that the disk in that drive is the one you intend to format.*

```
Execute what file? DISKFORMAT [ret]
Enter unit number of diskette to be formatted (4..5): 4 [ret]
Insert disk in unit 4 and press <enter>... [ret]
```

DISKFORMAT takes a while to run. When it successfully finishes, one of the following reports is made (depending on whether you used a single–sided drive or a dual–sided drive):

```
320 block disk formatted
```

```
640 block disk formatted
```

If DISKFORMAT gives you an error message instead of one of these reports, there is probably something wrong with the diskette you used. You should try another diskette.

When the formatting is done, return the system disk to drive #4; then invoke F(ile and its T(ransfer activity.

If you have two drives, insert the newly formatted disk in drive #5 and follow the sequence of prompts and responses shown below:

```
Transfer what file? #4: [ret]
To where? #5: [ret]
Transfer 320 blocks? (Y/N) Y
SYSTEM4:                  --> #5:
```

This completes the two–drive copy operation. Skip to the subsection, "Completing the Back Ups."

If you have only one drive, respond to the first three Filer prompts as follows:

```
Transfer what file? #4: [ret]
To where? #4: [ret]
Transfer 320 blocks?(Y/N) Y
```

The Filer then copies into main memory the first chunk of disk information to be copied. After that, you are prompted as follows:

```
Insert destination disk
Type <space> to continue
```

Now put the blank formatted disk in drive #4 and press [space]. The Filer writes the stored chunk of disk information onto the new disk. This process continues (with disk swaps each time) for as many chunks as necessary to copy your system disk. In each cycle you see one of the following prompts:

```
Put SYSTEM4: in unit #4
Type <space> to continue
```

```
Put destination disk in unit #4
Type <space> to continue
```

Continue this process until the p–System no longer prompts you. Then skip to the subsection, "Completing the Back Ups."

Back Ups with Version IV.1 or IV.2 from SMS

Disk formatting is done with a utility program called DISKFORMAT. You must first locate that utility, which should either be on your system disk or your utility disk. With your system disk in drive #4, enter the Filer, select the L(ist activity, and respond #4: [ret] to its prompt. Check the directory listing for DISKFORMAT.CODE. If you don't see the file, place your utility disk in #4 and do the same thing again.

After you know where DISKFORMAT.CODE is located, leave its disk in drive #4 and Q(uit the Filer.* Then invoke the program by entering X #4:DISKFORMAT [ret] from the Command menu. The following series of prompts and responses show how to format the disk in drive #4. (DISKFORMAT can also be applied to diskettes in other drives.) You will be prompted to put the disk to be formatted in drive #4. When that prompt appears, remove the disk in #4 and insert the blank disk. Before you press [ret] to indicate you've done that, *always check that the disk in that drive is the one you intend to format.*

```
Enter diskette device number to format: 4 [ret]
Parameters of Disk Device 4:
    Bytes per Sector      = 512
    Sectors per Track     = 8
    Tracks per Side       = 40
    Number of Sides       = 2
Are these the correct parameters (Y/N)? Y
Insert diskette in drive.  Press any key.   [space]
Formatting side 0
........................................
Formatting side 1
........................................
640 block disk formatted
Enter volume name for formatted disk: BLANK [ret]
Format another disk ? N
```

Some of the disk parameters you see may be different from those shown above and your final report may indicate a different sized disk. You rarely need to reply N to the "Are these the correct parameters?" question.

If DISKFORMAT gives you an error message instead of this display, there is probably something wrong with the diskette you used. You should try another diskette.

When the formatting is done, return the system disk to drive #4; then invoke F(ile and its T(ransfer activity.

If you have two drives, insert the newly formatted disk in drive #5 and follow the sequence of prompts and responses shown below:

---

* *IV.2 users, note:* If you get a missing segment message when you Q(uit the Filer, you need to return the system disk to drive #4 temporarily to accomplish the Q(uit and subsequent X(ecute.

```
Transfer what file? #4: [ret]
To where? #5: [ret]
Transfer 640 blocks? (Y/N) Y
Destroy BLANK:? Y
SYSTEM4:                 -->  #5:
```

This completes the two–drive copy operation. Skip to the next subsection, "Completing the Back Ups."

If you have only one drive, respond to the first four Filer prompts as follows:

```
Transfer what file? #4: [ret]
To where? #4: [ret]
Transfer 640 blocks?(Y/N) Y
Destroy BLANK:? Y
```

The Filer then copies into main memory the first chunk of disk information to be copied. After that, you are prompted as follows:

```
Insert destination disk
Type <space> to continue
```

Now put the blank formatted disk in drive #4 and press [space]. The Filer writes the stored chunk of disk information onto the new disk. This process continues (with disk swaps each time) for as many chunks as necessary to copy your system disk. In each cycle you see one of the following prompts (in which your system disk is named):

```
Put SYSTEM4: in unit #4
Type <space> to continue
```

```
Put BLANK: in unit #4
Type <space> to continue
```

Continue this process until the p–System no longer prompts you. Then skip to the subsection, "Completing the Back Ups."

Back Ups with an NCI p–System

Disk formatting is done with a utility program called CONFIG in the standard NCI p–System or a simplified version called SCONFIG in Practical Pascal. Invoke one of these by typing X #4:CONFIG [ret]. (Use SCONFIG instead of CONFIG if appropriate.) The following series of prompts and responses show how to format the disk in drive #4. CONFIG can also be applied to disks in other drives.

```
Get Bootstrap from: unit 4, 5, 9..12 [<sp> is 4] [space]
```

```
Get miscinfo: unit 4, 5, 9..12 [<sp> is 4] [space]
```

The CONFIG utility is used to configure the p–System as well as format disks. The prompts above have to do with the configuration function. The next screen you see summarizes the current configuration of your p–System. Choose the F(ormat activity from the menu at the top of that screen:

```
Config: F(ormat disk, P(rinter, S(erial, R(am disk, C(ode pool, ? [] F
```

Next you are requested to designate the drive in which you'll format the disk. Choose drive A:

```
Format: drive A, B, C, D, Q(uit [] A
```

You are warned in the following screen that formatting destroys the information on a diskette and asked to type "ok" to continue. Do so. Then select the ten–sector–per–track density by entering T.

```
WARNING:  The format command will erase any data on the diskette
          It is for initializing new diskettes

          To proceed type ok.  Any thing else will exit! ok
```

```
Format [A]: T(en, N(ine Drive A, B, C, D, Q(uit [] T
```

Now remove your system disk from drive A, insert the new disk and close the drive door. Type ⟦space⟧ when you've done that, as directed by the following screen:

```
Put disk to format in drive A type <space> to continue <Esc> to quit
```

If the disk to be formatted already contains a p–System volume, you are asked to confirm that you wish to destroy the information on that disk by a message like the following. After that confirmation (if it's necessary), formatting of the disk proceeds. If an error is reported during that process, there is probably something wrong with your diskette. You should try another one.

```
Do you want to format 'VOLUME:'? (yes/no) Y
```

```
Formatting ........................................
```

Now remove the newly formatted disk, restore your system disk to drive A and type Q twice to return to the Command menu. Then invoke F(ile and its T(ransfer activity to copy your system disk onto the newly formatted disk.

If you have two drives, insert the newly formatted disk in drive #5 and follow the sequence of prompts and responses shown below:

```
Transfer what file? #4: [ret]
To where? #5: [ret]
Transfer 800 blocks? (Y/N) Y
Destroy FMT800:? Y
SYSTEM4:                  -->  #5:
```

This completes the two–drive copy operation. Skip to the next subsection, "Completing the Back Ups."

If you have only one drive, respond to the first four Filer prompts as follows:

```
Transfer what file? #4: [ret]
To where? #4: [ret]
Transfer 800 blocks?(Y/N) Y
Destroy FMT800:? Y
```

The Filer then copies into main memory the first chunk of disk information to be copied. After that, you are prompted as follows:

```
Insert destination disk
Type <space> to continue
```

Now put the blank formatted disk in drive #4 and press [space]. The Filer writes the stored chunk of disk information onto the new disk. This process continues (with disk swaps each time) for as many chunks as necessary to copy your system disk. In each cycle you see one of the following prompts (in which your system disk is named):

```
Put SYSTEM4: in unit #4
Type <space> to continue
```

```
Put FMT800: in unit #4
Type <space> to continue
```

Continue this process until the p–System no longer prompts you.

Completing the Back Ups

Remove the new system diskette and label it. (If you write on the label after it's on the diskette, be sure to use a felt tip pen.) Your back up task is now complete.

The last thing to do is start up the p–System again using your newly made system disk. Remove the original system diskette and store it in a safe place. Using your new system diskette, follow the procedure in "Bootstrapping the p–System," above. Be sure to take advantage of the shorter process that applies when your system power is already on. If you're not using an NCI p–System, return to Section 1.9.

If you're using an NCI p–System, one more step may be needed in order for the step–by–step directions of the rest of Chapter 1 to be accurate. If your PC has 256k bytes of memory or more, the NCI p–System automatically uses part of that memory as a RAM disk and copies several important parts of the p–System to that RAM disk. It then sets the RAM disk as your system volume. This setup is very convenient for routine use of the p–System, but it conflicts with the assumptions made in the step–by–step instructions in the remainder of Chapter 1. In fact, some of the parts of Chapter 1 that you've already read are also affected by this setup, as you may have noticed.

So, if your PC has 256k bytes of memory or more, we ask that you temporarily reconfigure your NCI p–System. After you've finished the step–by–step exercises of Part 1, you will probably want to change the configuration back, since the performance of your p–System may be improved substantially by doing so.

With your newly made system disk booted, execute #4:CONFIG (or #4:SCONFIG for Practical Pascal users) from the Command menu. Respond to the first two familiar prompts by entering [space]. Then select the R(am disk activity from the menu that appears next.

```
Get Bootstrap from: unit 4, 5, 9..12 [<sp> is 4] [space]
```

```
Get miscinfo: unit 4, 5, 9..12 [<sp> is 4] [space]
```

```
Config: F(ormat disk, P(rinter, S(erial, R(am disk, C(ode pool, ? [] R
```

Respond as shown below to the three prompts that follow:

```
Ram disk volume: unit 4, 5, 9..12 [<sp> is 12] [space]
```

```
Ram disk copy from volume: unit 3, 5, 9..12 [<sp> is 4] [space]
```

```
Root volume: unit 4, 5, 9..12 [<sp> is 12] 4
```

As you can see, the only one of these choices that is not the default choice is the root volume. You have chosen to designate #4 as the root volume rather than the RAM volume. This setup will avoid surprises as you follow the instructions in the remainder of Chapter 1. You should eventually return to this utility and type [space] for all these choices. This will reinstate the RAM volume as your system disk and improve the performance of your p–System. Now reboot your p–System to cause this change to take affect; then return to Section 1.9.

E.4 DEALING WITH A 40–CHARACTER SCREEN

The p–System is most convenient to use when the display can show a full 80–character line at one time, but 40–character displays can also be productively used, because the Personal Computer stores the entire 80–character line in memory, and allows you to choose which of three 40–character portions you want to see.

The choices are the left half (columns 1–40), the middle half (columns 21–60) and the right half (columns 41–80). When the p–System is started, the portion that you see first is the right half.

The rest of this book assumes an 80–character screen. Sample displays shown in the book are full width. You can use the control sequences described below to see any part of the screen you wish.

Press the "Ctrl" key and hold it while pressing the left arrow key. You should see the following characters on the top line:

```
, F(ile, C(omp, L(ink, X(ecute, A(ssem,
```

This is the middle 40–character portion of the line. Do the same thing again. Now you see the left half of the line:

```
Command: E(dit, R(un, F(ile, C(omp, L(in
```

Press the same pair of keys one more time, and you are back to the right half of the line, where you started.

Now move the "window" in the other direction by holding down "Ctrl" and pressing the right arrow key several times.

There is one other potential difficulty that you may have with your display. With some television sets, there is a tendency to "lose" the first one to three characters on a line. If this is the case for you, the 40–character chunks you just saw on your screen have been missing the first few characters (as compared to the printed versions in this book). Check your p–System documentation for details on how to recover from this situation.

When you are ready, return to your reading of Chapter 1, Section 1.3.

E.5 USING BOTH DOS AND THE p–SYSTEM

Since DOS is so widely used on the IBM PC and its compatibles, you may wish to move easily back and forth between the two systems. Both SofTech Microsystems (SMS) and Network Consulting provide p–System facilities to help you do that.

SMS offers two products: 1) Xenofile for DOS and 2) the MS–DOS–hosted p–System. The first of these is like the *Xenofile for CP/M* product that we described briefly in Chapter 8. It allows you to access DOS disks from a p–System environment (either from a running program or directly from the console). One disadvantage of this product is that existing programs cannot use DOS files without being changed, since a special UCSD Pascal unit must be used to read data from and write data into a DOS file. An advantage of this product is that you don't need a copy of DOS for your computer to use it, since it runs entirely on the p–System.

In the DOS–hosted p–System, on the other hand, the p–System runs *under* DOS as if it were a DOS application. The storage volumes accessed by a DOS–hosted p–System can be either standard p–System diskettes or *files* on a DOS disk. Furthermore, p–System applications can access DOS files just as if they were p–System files. So p–System applications can read, for instance, text files produced by DOS applications, and vice versa. (Naturally the communicating applications need to agree on the form of the data.)

Another aspect of the DOS–hosted p–System is that you don't have to reboot DOS in order to move from the p–System back to DOS. In fact, since DOS is always present when the p–System is running, the p–System can access the peripherals, such as hard disks, that are set up for DOS. This means you can use the available space on the hard disk very flexibly for either DOS–related information or p–System–related information without having to make a decision beforehand on how much space to assign to each environment.

If you are considering developing p–System applications for distribution to DOS users, the DOS–hosted p–System can offer you the best of both worlds. You get the convenience and programmer productivity that come with the integrated p–System development tools, plus the easy marketability that comes with the use of DOS. And the users of your application may not even be aware that they have a p–System application!

Network Consulting's approach to DOS compatibility emphasizes file access from the p–System to DOS volumes. Just as with the DOS–hosted p–System, a p–System application can read and write DOS files just as if they were p–System files. Even though they don't cater to running the full p–System under DOS as in the DOS–hosted p–System, Network Consulting does provide a utility that allows a p–System application to be executed directly from DOS without rebooting of either DOS or the p–System.

F

THE p–SYSTEM ON OTHER COMPUTERS

This appendix summarizes the computer–specific information that is needed in order to use this book. There is not enough room in the book to have an appendix for each of the computers that run the UCSD p–System. This appendix provides general guidance for those using computers that we haven't covered specifically in the previous appendix.

Your p–System supplier may have anticipated your use of this book and provided a section in your p–System documentation that follows the format of this appendix. If so, use that section instead of this appendix. Otherwise, use this appendix to help you find the information that you need in the documentation provided by the p–System supplier. If your documentation package contains a supplement that is specific to your computer, that is an excellent place to look.

F.1 SOFTWARE AND HARDWARE REQUIREMENTS

We assume here that your computer's hardware is installed and configured correctly. We also assume that the p–System is adapted to your particular computer. If it is not, you should read Section 1.2.

There are two major configurations of the p–System offered on many computers. One is called the *runtime system* and the other is called the *development system.*

The runtime system is an inexpensive way to get the capability of running p–System application programs that others have developed. This package does not necessarily include all of the major p–System components. If this is the case with the p–System package that you have, the parts of this book that deal with those components will not apply directly to you. You may want to look through those sections anyway to help decide whether you want to acquire the full p–System.

If you want to develop your own programs, you'll need to acquire the development system. This package usually includes the major p–System components described in this book (although some of these components may be optional products).

There are certain minimum hardware facilities that are required in order for the p–System to run on a particular personal computer. These requirements are:

- At least 64k bytes of main memory. (Each "k" of memory is 1,024 bytes.)
- At least 160k bytes of disk storage for simple applications and 320k bytes of disk storage for larger applications and program development work.
- A display and keyboard.

F.2 STARTING THE p–SYSTEM THE FIRST TIME

This section is coordinated with the Section 1.3 in Part 1. It has two subsections. The first subsection should help you to fill in the blanks on the inside front cover of this book. The second subsection is intended to help you start the p–System running on your computer.

Recording Your p–System Details

The "p–System Details for Your Computer" form inside the front cover is a handy place to record computer–specific details about your p–System. You may want to look at the corresponding sections in the three previous appendices to see the type of information you'll be entering.

In the first two blank lines, you should enter the type of your computer (such as DEC Rainbow) and your major p–System version (such as IV.0 or IV.1). If you are uncertain about the latter item, wait until the next section, when you will start up the p–System. The p–System version number will be displayed in square brackets at the upper right–hand corner of the screen.

In the next four lines, you can record the type and capacity of the various disk types that can be used with your computer. It is likely that you'll only need one of these lines because you have only one type of disk on your computer, but we provided four lines just to be safe.

For each type of disk on your computer, enter its capacity in blocks, followed (after the colon) by the disk type. For instance, you might enter

"320" and "single–sided diskette". If you have trouble finding out this disk capacity information, skip it for now.

In the next two lines, you should identify your first and second disk drives. These drives are called #4 and #5, respectively, in the p–System. On your computer, for example, #4 may be the left drive, drive A, or drive 0.

If a RAM disk is available on your computer, you should next record the name used to refer to that "disk" in your p–System. You can go through all of Part 1 of this book without knowing this name, so don't worry if you can't determine it easily. Enter "none" if you don't have RAM disk.

The next line refers to a program you may be using in the next subsection to format your two blank diskettes. You should record the name of the program used for this purpose on your computer. Possible names include DISKFORMAT, FORMAT, TURNKEY, and CONFIG. (All these names would have the .CODE suffix.)

The next line also deals with the preparation of diskettes for use. On some computers, you need to do a "Z(ero" operation after formatting a disk. On other computers, the "Z(ero" is done automatically as part of the format operation. You'll find out in the next subsection which of these alternatives applies on your computer (and what a "Z(ero" operation is!).

The remaining items of the form describe the special keys used in the p–System. Somewhere in your documentation there should be a table of these keys. This table should show you what you need to type in order to produce them. Some of these keys may be obvious. For example, ⟦ret⟧ is often marked "RETURN". For some of these keys, you may have to type two physical keys, together. For example, ⟦eof⟧ is often produced by holding down the Control key and typing "C". The special keys you'll need to use first in Chapter 1 are ⟦ret⟧, ⟦bs⟧ and ⟦break⟧.

You can use the "Other Notes" section of this form for any miscellaneous information that you find pertinent.

Bootstrapping the p–System

The next step is to start the p–System running on your computer. You should consult your documentation to see how to bootstrap the p–System.

This process usually involves placing a bootable system disk into the appropriate drive, so make sure you have the correct disk. Depending upon the computer, the bootstrapping process may take from several seconds to a minute to complete. When it's done, a welcome message is displayed. At that point, you should return to Section 1.9.

F.3 MAKING BACK UPS

This section describes operations that you need to do in Section 1.7. The task in this section is to make a back up copy of your system diskette and begin using the back up copy. This task requires a blank diskette, so you need one to go on from here.

On many computers, you must format a new diskette before you can use it. Sometimes a used disk may be reformatted in an attempt to eliminate diskette surface problems. However, formatting a disk completely erases any information you had previously stored on it. Don't apply this process to a used disk unless you're positive you don't need the information it contains.

If you need to format disks with your computer, you will find a disk formatting utility in your p–System package. You may have already determined (in the previous subsection) what this utility is called. You should now consult your documentation to find out how to use your disk formatting program (if your computer requires one). Then format the new diskette.

The next step is to copy a system disk onto the newly formatted disk. If your p–System has a utility that does this job, use it.

Otherwise, if you have two drives, place one of the newly formatted disks in #5, and the system disk in #4 (where it probably is already). Invoke F(ile and its T(ransfer activity. Then follow the sequence of prompts and responses shown below. (The fourth line may not appear.)

```
Transfer what file? #4: [ret]
To where? #5: [ret]
Transfer ### blocks? (Y/N) Y
Destroy BLANK: ? Y
VOLNAME:                  -->  #5:
```

You should see the capacity of your system disk (in blocks) instead of the "###" shown above. The "Destroy BLANK:" prompt only appears if your disk formatting utility places a p–System directory on a newly formatted diskette. This prompt may contain some other volume name than "BLANK". Skip now to the subsection, "Completing the Back Up."

If you have only one drive, make sure your system disk is mounted, then invoke F(ile and its T(ransfer activity. Then respond to the first four Filer prompts as follows:

```
Transfer what file? #4: [ret]
To where? #4: [ret]
Tranfer ### blocks? (Y/N) Y
Destroy BLANK:? Y
```

The capacity of your system disk appears instead of the "###" shown above and the fourth prompt may not appear. After these responses, the Filer copies into main memory the first chunk of disk information to be copied. After that, you are prompted as follows:

```
Insert destination disk
Type <space> to continue
```

Now put the blank, newly formatted disk in drive #4 and press [space]. The Filer writes the stored chunk of disk information onto the new disk. This process continues (with disk swaps each time) for as many chunks as necessary to copy your system disk. In each cycle you see one of the following prompts (in which your system disk is named):

```
Put SYSTEM: in unit #4
Type <space> to continue
```

```
Put BLANK: in unit #4
Type <space> to continue
```

Continue this process until the p—System no longer prompts you.

Completing the Back Up

There may be one more step you need to take to complete your new system disk. During the bootstrap process, most computers load a small program from a fixed place on the disk (often at the beginning). This "bootstrap code" proceeds to load the rest of the p—System and start it. A system disk is only bootable if it has this code. If you're lucky, the volume—to—volume transfer operation above moved the bootstrap code from your current system volume to the new one. Alternatively, your disk formatter may automatically install this bootstrap code on new disks it creates.

If neither of the possibilities above applies on your computer, you probably need to do an explicit operation to copy the bootstrap code from your current system disk to the new one you're creating; therefore, you should have a utility program (or an activity within a utility program) to do the job. This utility is often called "Booter." Your documentation should give details on using this bootstrap copy facility if you need it. Follow those directions to complete the creation of your new system diskette. If no such directions are provided, you don't need them (probably because your bootstrap code was automatically copied by one of the methods described in the previous paragraph).

Now, remove the new system diskette and label it. (If you write on the label after it's on the diskette, be sure to use a felt tip pen.) The back up task is now complete.

The last thing to do is start up the p—System again using your newly made system disk. Remove the original system diskette and store it in a safe place. Using your new system diskette, follow the bootstrapping procedure that you used earlier in this appendix. If there is a short cut procedure for booting when the computer is already turned on, you may want to use it. When your new p—System diskette has successfully boostrapped, return to Part 1 at Section 1.9.

G

SPECIAL EDUCATIONAL p–SYSTEMS

This appendix describes the special educational configurations of the p–System that have been developed by SofTech Microsystems. These configurations are intended to be used by students learning UCSD Pascal or FORTRAN–77. They have most of the facilities of the standard p–System, but cost substantially less to acquire. This appendix summarizes the differences between the standard p–System and these special configurations.

Two special educational versions of the p–System are available: 1) the Learning Environment, which is available for the IBM PC family and the Digital Equipment Rainbow and 2) four IBM PC Apprentice products that are jointly marketed by IBM and Prentice–Hall, Inc. For both products, UCSD Pascal and FORTRAN–77 variants are available.

G.1 THE LEARNING ENVIRONMENT

The Learning Environment supports either UCSD Pascal or FORTRAN–77. It is offered either on an individually packaged basis (singly or in quantity) or on a "site license" basis for use throughout an educational institution. Here are the main differences between the Learning Environment and the standard p–System as offered by SofTech Microsystems at the time of this writing:

- The Learning Environment is based on Version IV.1 of the p–System while the latest p–System release is Version IV.2. The newest version contains both functional and performance improvements over its predecessor.

- The Learning Environment comes complete on a single diskette rather than the several diskettes that make up the standard p–System. A number of the standard utilities are omitted, including Markdupdir and Copydupdir. The system is permanently configured for two–word real numbers and cannot support four–word real numbers. Several of the programmatic utilities are included, such as Screen_Control, Turtlegraphics and a special unit that allows access to many of the special hardware facilities of IBM PC or DEC Rainbow. However, the other more sophisticated programmatic utilities, such as Kernel and Command_IO, are omitted.
- Learning Environment student disks are copy protected while the standard release disks are not. Also, many of the programs on a Learning Environment disk will not operate on standard p–Systems.
- The minimum hardware configuration for the Learning Environment includes 128k bytes of main memory, an 80–column display and at least one dual–sided disk drive. The minimums for the standard system are smaller, but those smaller configurations probably aren't very usable, anyway.

Most of these differences are not relevant to the intended users: novice programmers learning UCSD Pascal or FORTRAN–77. Both languages are supported in full by the respective variants of the Learning Environment. Users of the Learning Environment should have no difficulties using this book as a tutorial and/or as a reference.

G.2 IBM PC APPRENTICE PRODUCTS

Four p–System–based IBM PC Apprentice products are offered. They include a beginning and advanced version for both the UCSD Pascal and FORTRAN–77 languages.

These products are offered under a unique licensing approach. Teachers are provided with a master disk containing the special p–System version. Students buy a workbook and exchange a registration card bound into the workbook for a copy of the software made from the teacher's master disk. Since this distribution arrangement avoids the necessity to pack disks with the student work books, they are very inexpensive.

The software used in the beginning and advanced levels is the same—– only the workbook is different. The following limitations have been applied to the Apprentice versions of the p–System, compared to the standard releases:

- UCSD Pascal units (and their analogue in p–System FORTRAN–77) cannot be created. Units can be "used", however, by Apprentice p–System programs.
- Include files, which are useful in building large programs that cannot fit entirely in the editor workspace, cannot be used.
- Hard disks are not supported.
- The Assembler, Linker and Debugger components of the standard p–System are not included and cannot be used, even if they are acquired by some other means.

As with the Learning Environment, a minimum of utilities is provided. Even though limited, these systems are fully capable of handling the programs of beginning and even intermediate programmers.

H

UCSD p–SYSTEM USER'S SOCIETY

USUS is the society devoted to the users of the UCSD p–System, UCSD Pascal and Apple Pascal. Its goal is to promote and influence the development of the UCSD p–System and to help users learn more about their systems.

As a member of USUS, you can get access to:

- The latest p–System information.
- An extensive software exchange library.
- Activist special interest groups.
- Electronic mail communication with other users and with vendors.
- Informative national meetings.
- Useful quarterly newsletters.
- UCSD Pascal expertise.

An application for USUS membership is reproduced on the next page. USUS can be contacted at the following address:

P.O. Box 1148
La Jolla, California 92038

USUS MEMBERSHIP APPLICATION

I am applying for: ☐ $25 individual membership for North American residents.
☐ $40 individual membership for those residing outside North America (includes $15 airmail service surcharge).
☐ $500 organizational membership.

Name ______________________________

Address ______________________________

____

City__________ State__________ Zip__________ Country__________

Phone ( ) __________ TWX/Telex/EMail__________

Title/Affiliation ______________________________

Option: ☐ Do not print my phone number in **USUS** rosters.
Option: ☐ Print only my name and country in **USUS** rosters.
Option: ☐ Do not release my name on mailing lists.

Computer System:
☐ Z-80 ☐ 8080 ☐ PDP/LSI-11 ☐ 6502/Apple ☐ 6800 ☐ 6809 ☐ Other__________
☐ 9900 ☐ 8086/8088 ☐ Z8000 ☐ 68000 ☐ MicroEngine ☐ IBM PC

I am interested in the following Committees/Special Interest Groups (SIGs):

☐ Advanced System Editor SIG
☐ Apple SIG
☐ Application Developer's SIG
☐ Communications SIG
☐ DEC SIG
☐ File Access SIG
☐ Graphics SIG
☐ IBM Display Writer SIG
☐ IBM PC SIG
☐ Meetings Committee
☐ Modula-2 SIG
☐ Publications Committee
☐ Sage SIG
☐ Software Exchange Library
☐ Technical Issues Committee
☐ Texas Instruments SIG
☐ UCSD Pascal Compatability SIG
☐ Word Processing SIG

☐ I am willing to volunteer some time and/or talent in the following area(s) __________

____

Mail completed application with check or money order payable to **USUS** and drawn on a U. S. bank or U. S. office, to Secretary, **USUS,** P.O. Box 1148, La Jolla, CA 92038, USA.

GLOSSARY

Activity: An item on the menu of a p–System program. For example, X(ecute is an activity on the Command menu.

Adaptable System: A variation of the p–System that allows you to write the low–level device interface code which handles the peripherals on a specific computer. Once this installation process is done, the p–System can be used on the new computer.

Anchor: In the Screen–oriented Editor, the position of the cursor when D(elete is invoked. When the cursor is moved away from this position, text disappears. When the cursor is moved toward this position, text reappears.

Application Program: A computer program that meets specific needs of a personal computer user. Examples include a payroll program or an oil well supervision program.

Assembler: A program that translates human–readable assembly language into machine code.

Associate Time: The time taken by the Version IV operating system to find and stitch together the units referenced by a program. This stitching together must occur before the program can begin execution.

Back File: A back up file for text files that is identified by the suffix .BACK; for example, FILENAME.BACK.

Back Up: The operation of making an extra copy of important information (usually on a storage volume, in this book). Also, the extra copy that results from this operation.

Bad Block: A 512–byte area on a storage volume that is somehow damaged. The result is that information cannot be stored or retrieved from there.

Bad File: An immobile file used to prevent the use of bad blocks on a disk. A bad file is identified by the suffix .BAD; for example, BAD.00120.BAD.

BASIC: A popular high level programming language that is supported in the p–System.

BIOS: Basic Input/Output Subsystem; that portion of a p–machine emulator that is specific to a particular brand of computer.

Bit: The minimum unit of storage on most computers. A bit is either "on" or "off."

Block: The 512–byte unit of storage and retrieval that is used with p–System storage volumes.

Block–Structured Device: Referred to in this book as "Storage Volume." Earlier p–System documentation, and many p–System prompts and error messages still use "block–structured device," or "blocked device," when referring to storage volumes.

Bootstrap: The action of starting (or that piece of code which starts) the p–System running. You must bootstrap the p–System before you can do anything with it.

Boot Volume: See "System Disk."

Bug: A defect in a program that causes it not to operate as intended.

Byte: A unit of computer storage. Usually has the capacity to store 8 bits of information, or a number in the range 0 through 255.

Chaining: See "Program Chaining."

Client: A program or unit which uses another unit.

Code File: A file that contains the compiled or assembled version of a program or program segment. Usually identified by the suffix .CODE; for example, FILENAME.CODE.

Code Segment: The smallest component of a p–System program that can be moved into (or removed from) main memory during the running of the program.

Communication Volume: A p–System I/O device that doesn't store information on a long–term basis; for example, the console or the printer.

Compilation Unit: A unit (as represented in any of the three p–System languages) or a program. The smallest module that a language allows to be compiled separately.

Compiled Listing: The source lines of a program, annotated by the compiler with details of the results of compilation, including sizes of statements, sizes of data areas, and other information.

Compiler: A program that translates the human–readable source text of a program into p–machine–executable p–code.

Compiler Directive: A command to a compiler that (when embedded in the text of your program) affects the compiler's handling of that program.

Conditional Compilation: Using compiler directives embedded in your source text to selectively compile or not compile portions of that text.

Copy Buffer: In the Editor, a storage area in which text can be temporarily stored after it has been deleted from the workspace or while it is being copied from one place to another in the workspace.

Cursor: An indicator that highlights a particular point on a display screen. In many situations, characters typed at the keyboard appear on the screen at the location of the cursor.

Data Entry Prompt: See "Prompt."

Data File: A file that contains arbitrary user data. No particular internal structure is assumed. No special file name suffix is required, but .DATA is often used.

Declare: To establish the name and type of an identifier used in a computer program. Some languages (Pascal, for instance) require that all identifiers be declared before they are used.

Decode: A utility used to inspect the contents of code files.

Default: A state or action which will take effect unless an explicit action is taken to choose another possibility. For instance, in S(et E(nvironment in the Editor, there are many options that can be set. All of them have default settings which determine the operation of the Editor until they are changed.

Default Disk: The volume where the p–System looks for a file unless the file specification explicitly indicates another volume.

Delimiter: A "fence" that marks the boundaries of a sequence of characters. In the Editor, for instance, delimiters enclose the target string sought by F(ind. These delimiter characters cannot be letters or numbers, but they can be any of the special characters, such as "&" or "/".

Device: Peripheral equipment accessible to the p–System. There are two varieties: storage and communication. Originally, and sometimes still, a device was referred to as a "unit." This usage has been changed to avoid confusion with the UCSD Pascal language construct of the same name.

Device Number: A number used to refer to a particular storage or communications volume. It is always preceded by a number sign (#) and usually followed by a colon (:). Also known as "unit number." Example: #5:.

Direction Indicator: In the Screen–oriented Editor or EDVANCE, the flag at the upper left corner of the screen that indicates the assumed direction for various editor operations.

Directory: An area on a storage volume that contains "house–keeping" information (such as names and locations) about the files on the volume.

Directory Listing: A human–readable list, usually on the console, of the files on a given storage volume, along with miscellaneous information about each file.

Editor: A p–System program that is used to examine, create and modify text files.

EDVANCE: The Advanced Editor. EDVANCE incorporates a wide range of enhancements over the p–System Screen–oriented Editor.

Execute: To give control of the p–System to a program (usually via the X(ecute activity).

Execution Error: An error detected by the p–System during the execution of a program. When such an error is detected, a message is produced on the console. The message includes error coordinates indicating the program section that was executing when the error occurred. Usually the program must be canceled and the p–System reinitialized.

Execution Option String: A sequence of execution option statements, usually entered in response to the X(ecute prompt. Individual execution options can affect a variety of aspects of p–System operation, such as the prefix volume, the source of input, and so on.

Extended Memory: A facility available on some p–Systems that allows programs to use up to 64,000 bytes of main memory for data, plus another 64,000 bytes for program segments. This mechanism has been extended in Version IV.2 to allow much larger amounts of data and code space to be used.

File: A named collection of information on a storage volume. Also (less frequently), a stream of information transmitted through a communication volume.

File Specification: A description of a source for input or a destination for output in the p–System. A file specification has three major components, all of which are optional: the Volume ID, the File Name, and the Size Specification.

File Suffix: One of several special endings for file names. The file suffix usually indicates the file type. The standard file suffixes are .TEXT, .CODE, .SVOL, .BACK, .DATA, .BAD, and .FOTO.

Floating Point Number: See "Real Number."

Format: To prepare a disk for use with the p–System. This involves writing addresses and other control information on the disk. Any user information previously stored on the disk is destroyed by this operation.

FORTRAN–77: A popular high level programming language supported in the p–System.

Foto File: A file that contains graphic images for use by Turtlegraphics. The name of the file has the suffix .FOTO; for example, PICTURE.FOTO.

Fragmented: The condition of a p–System storage volume when the total unused space on it is spread among many small areas. The size of the largest file that can be stored on a fragmented volume is the size of the largest single area.

Hosted p–System: A p–System that runs *under* another operating system, such as MS–DOS. Such a p–System installation may allow p–System applications to be run interchangeably with applications "native" to the host operating system.

Identifier: The name of an object in a programming language such as Pascal.

I/O: Input and output.

I/O Error: An error detected by the p–System during an input or output operation. For example, a disk write will fail if the disk has been inappropriately removed from its drive. An I/O error is one kind of execution error.

I/O Redirection: A feature that allows the p–System's input to come from some place other than the keyboard. Also, output for the p–System can be sent to some place other than the screen.

I/O Result: A number indicating the success or failure of a p–System I/O operation. If this number is zero, the operation was a success; otherwise, the number identifies the problem that occurred during the I/O operation.

Instruction Set: The fundamental operations that a microprocessor is capable of performing. Different kinds of microprocessors usually have different instruction sets.

Integer Number: A whole number (without a fractional part).

Interpreter: See "p–machine emulator."

KSAM: Keyed sequential access method; a file management facility available for the p–System.

Liaison: A variant of Version IV.2 of the p–System that is designed for use in local area networks.

Library: A code file that contains one or more units which can be used by programs or other units.

Library Text File: A text file containing a list of library file names. When a program is invoked, the libraries listed in the current library text file are searched for any units needed by the program.

Library Utility: The p–System library management facility. It is used to inspect, modify, and create libraries and other code files.

Linker: A p–System program that combines assembled code files with each other or with a compiled code file. Also called a "link editor."

Local Area Network: A high speed communication medium that can be used to connect multiple personal computers and allow their users to share data and resources.

Long Integer: A language feature of UCSD Pascal that supports integer arithmetic with up to 36 decimal digits of precision.

Marker: A named, invisible flag on a particular location within a text file.

Menu: A list of available activities that is displayed on the screen by the operating system and many p–System programs. An activity can be selected from a menu with a single keystroke.

Microprocessor: A miniaturized computer. Provides the computational power for most personal computers. Executes the instructions of the software running in the personal computer.

Module: A component of some larger structure with the attribute that it can be handled separately from the rest of the structure in some sense. A UCSD Pascal unit is a module of a program.

Mount: To cause a subsidiary volume to be accessible to the p–System.

Multitasking: The execution of two or more tasks concurrently within a single UCSD Pascal program.

Native Code: Machine level code that is produced by the native code generator as the translation of a section of p–code.

Native Code Generator: A program that translates portions of an executable p–code file into native code. The resulting code file always contains a combination of p–code and n–code.

n–code: See "Native Code."

Nonblock–Structured Device: Referred to in this book as "Communication Volume." Earlier p–System documentation, and many p–System prompts and error messages still use "nonblock–structured device," or "unblocked device," when referring to communication volumes.

Object Code: The machine–readable representation of a computer program.

On–Line: The status of a volume when the p–System can access it. For a storage volume to be on–line, the disk must be in the appropriate drive. For a communications volume to be on–line, the I/O device must be properly connected and turned on.

Pascal: A widely used high level language. UCSD Pascal, an extended version of this language, is the principal programming language in the p–System.

p–code: Pseudo–code: p–machine code generated by the p–System compilers and executed by the p–machine emulators.

p–machine: An idealized pseudo–computer optimized for high level language execution on small host machines; the foundation of the p–

System's portability.

p—machine emulator: The part of the p—System that allows a host microcomputer to imitate the operation of the p—machine. It is implemented in the assembly language of the host computer.

PME: See "p—machine emulator."

Portability: The ability to move executable code between dissimilar microcomputers without recompilation or other change. This is possible in the p—System because programs are compiled into p—code that can be executed on any computer on which the UCSD p—System has been installed.

Prefix Disk: See "Default Disk."

Print Spooler: A facility for printing text files concurrently with other activities in the p—System (particularly text editing).

Procedure: A named subprogram that handles part of the job of a larger program or unit.

Program: A set of detailed instructions that direct a computer in the performance of a specific task. Also, the process of creating such a set of instructions.

Program Chaining: Causing the automatic execution of one program from another program.

Prompt: A request (by a p—System program) for information from the p—System user; the user is expected to enter the information at the keyboard, followed by ⟦ret⟧.

Pseudo—comment: In UCSD Pascal, a comment that is actually a compiler directive. The first character inside such a comment is "$".

p—System: See "UCSD p—System."

RAM: Random Access Memory. See "Main Memory."

RAM Disk: A logical storage volume maintained in main memory. It can generally be used for the same purposes as a conventional disk volume (including storage of files), but the information it contains is usually lost when the computer is turned off.

Real Number: A number that can have a fractional part, such as "5.67982".

Reboot: To start up the p—System again. To "rebootstrap."

Redirect: See "I/O Redirection."

Root Volume: See "System Disk."

Runtime Software: p—System software that is needed to run programs.

Screen—oriented Editor: The principal text editing tool of the p—System. It is optimized for use with display consoles, rather than printing consoles.

Script File: A file containing characters representing the keystrokes that you would type during a session with the p–System. When p–System input is redirected to this script file, those keystrokes are read as if they were coming from the keyboard, and the session is recreated.

Sector: A unit of storage on a disk. The size of a sector varies across models and brands of computers and disks. Normally each concentric **track** on the disk holds several sectors.

Segment: See "Code Segment."

Source text: The human–readable form of a computer program. (Also referred to as "source code.")

Special Character: A visible character that is not a number (0 through 9) and not a letter (A through Z). Examples of special characters include "*", "/", "(", and "@".

Special Key: A keyboard key that has a particular meaning to the p–System other than representing an ordinary visible character. Example: the ⟦ret⟧ key.

Storage Volume: An input/output device that can store information written to it, for retrieval at a later time. Usually some sort of a disk, but can be an area of main memory, as well. (See "RAM disk".)

Subsidiary Volume: A file on a storage volume that contains its own volume structure with a directory and files. This subsidiary volume becomes accessible to the p–System when it is "mounted." The subsidiary volume facility of p–System Version IV.1 supports a two–level file hierarchy.

Substitute String: The character pattern that is to take the place of instances of the target string which are found by the R(eplace activity in the Screen–oriented Editor.

.SVOL File: A file identified by the suffix .SVOL that contains a subsidiary volume; for example, NAME.SVOL.

Syntax: The rules governing the structure of a program written in a computer programming language.

Syntax Error: A place in a computer program where the rules of the programming language are violated.

System Disk: The disk from which the p–System was bootstrapped. It contains the operating system software. Also known as "root" or "boot" disk. All three of these adjectives also occur with "volume" instead of "disk."

System Files: The disk files which contain the main components of the UCSD p–System.

Target String: The character pattern sought by the F(ind and R(eplace activities in the Screen–oriented Editor.

Text File: A file that contains user–readable information (as opposed to machine code); usually identified by one of the suffixes .TEXT or .BACK.

Track: One of the concentric circles that normally make up the storage area on a disk. Each track ordinarily contains several **sectors** of information.

Turtlegraphics: A package of routines that creates and manipulates images on a graphic display.

Type Ahead: A capability of a p–System implementation to store keystrokes that are typed before the p–System is ready to process them.

UCSD: University of California at San Diego. Site of the original development work on the p–System.

UCSD Pascal: A programming language, an extended version of the language Pascal.

UCSD Pascal System: The original name of the p–System.

UCSD p–System: A portable microcomputer software environment for execution and development of applications programs.

Unblocked Volume: See "Nonblock–structured Volume."

Unit: A package of routines and associated data structures written in a p–System programming language (usually UCSD Pascal). The facilities implemented by the unit (or a subset of them) can be used by programs or by other units.

Universal Medium: A 5–1/4 inch diskette format that is accessible to many types of small computers. It facilitates the distribution of p–System–based personal computer application programs. This proposed standard has not received wide use.

Utilities: Programs that assist in various areas of p–System use such as developing programs, maintaining files, printing files, and so forth.

Volume: A logical entity representing a p–System peripheral device. There are two categories of volumes: storage volumes (such as a disk) and communication volumes (such as the console or the printer).

Volume ID: Short for "Volume Identifier." The designation of a particular volume; for instance, its name or device number.

Wild Cards: Special symbols in file names that allow a group of files to be represented by a single file name.

Window: In the Screen–oriented Editor, the portion of the display screen that is used to show a section of the workspace being edited.

Workfile: Special file(s) that are automatically processed by major p–System components, including the editors and compilers. This automatic handling is particularly convenient during the development of small programs.

Workspace: Text kept in main memory by a p–System Editor during the editing process. Also called the "buffer."

Write–Protect: Mark a storage volume in some way so that an error is reported if the p–System attempts to write information onto the volume. (Reading is allowed, but writing is not.) Used to protect valuable data from accidental erasure. The physical mechanism used to signal write–protection of a volume varies with the storage medium used. For instance, 5–1/4 inch diskettes have a different convention than 8 inch diskettes. Check the documentation for your computer to find out how to write–protect the media that you use.

XenoFile: A utility package that allows you to access disks that contain data formatted for other operating systems. Both CP/M and DOS are supported with separate packages.

YALOE: Yet Another Line–Oriented Editor; the p–System editor used with printing terminals rather than with display terminals. This editor is no longer available.

INDEX

V

W

X

Z

QUICK INDEX TO MAJOR p–SYSTEM ACTIVITIES

General Filer errors (p. 247) can occur in any Filer activity.